Vandals
in the Stacks?

Recent Titles in
Contributions in Librarianship and Information Science

Innovation and the Library: The Adoption of New Ideas in Public Libraries
Verna L. Pungitore

The Impact of Emerging Technologies on Reference Service and Bibliographic Instruction
Gary M. Pitkin, editor

Brief Tests of Collection Strength: A Methodology for All Types of Libraries
Howard D. White

Censorship and the American Library: The American Library Association's Response to Threats to Intellectual Freedom, 1939–1969
Louise S. Robbins

Librarianship and Legitimacy: The Ideology of the Public Library Inquiry
Douglas Raber

Scholarly Book Reviewing in the Social Sciences and Humanities: The Flow of Ideas Within and Among Disciplines
Ylva Lindholm-Romantschuk

Libraries, Immigrants, and the American Experience
Plummer Alston Jones, Jr.

Preparing the Information Professional: An Agenda for the Future
Sajjad ur Rehman

The Role and Impact of the Internet on Library and Information Services
Lewis-Guodo Liu, editor

Development of Digital Libraries: An American Perspective
Deanna B. Marcum, editor

Diversity in Libraries: Academic Residency Programs
Raquel V. Cogell and Cindy A. Gruwell, editors

Immigrant Politics and the Public Library
Susan Luévano-Molina, editor

VANDALS IN THE STACKS?

A Response to Nicholson Baker's Assault on Libraries

RICHARD J. COX

Contributions in Librarianship and Information Science,
Number 98

GREENWOOD PRESS
Westport, Connecticut • London

Library of Congress Cataloging-in-Publication Data

Cox, Richard J.
     Vandals in the stacks? : a response to Nicholson Baker's assault on libraries / Richard J.
Cox.
        p.   cm.—(Contributions in librarianship and information science, ISSN 0084–9243 ;
     no. 98)
     Includes bibliographical references and index.
     ISBN 0–313–32344–5 (alk.   paper)
        1. Baker, Nicholson. Double fold.   2. Baker, Nicholson—Views on libraries.   3.
     Collection management (Libraries)   4. Library materials—Reproduction.   5. Library
     materials—Conservation and restoration.   6. Newspapers—Conservation and restoration.
     I. Title.   II. Series.
     Z687.C75   2002
     025.2'1—dc21   2002016087

British Library Cataloguing in Publication Data is available.

Library of Congress Catalog Card Number: 2002016087
ISBN: 0–313–32344–5
ISSN: 0084–9243

First published in 2002

Greenwood Press, 88 Post Road West, Westport, CT 06881
An imprint of Greenwood Publishing Group, Inc.
www.greenwood.com

Printed in the United States of America

The paper used in this book complies with the
Permanent Paper Standard issued by the National
Information Standards Organization (Z39.48–1984).

10 9 8 7 6 5 4 3 2

Copyright Acknowledgments

The author and publisher gratefully acknowledge permission for use of the following
material:

Excerpts from David Stoker. "Should Newspaper Preservation be a Lottery?" *Journal of
Librarianship and Information Science* (September 1999): 131–134. Reproduced with the
kind permission of CSA, part of Cambridge Information Group.

From *Double Fold* by Nicholson Baker, copyright © 2001 by Nicholson Baker. Used by
permission of Random House, Inc.

From *Double Fold.* Copyright © 2001 by Nicholson Baker. Reprinted by permission of
Melanie Jackson Agency, L.L.C.

Extracts from *Double Fold: Libraries and the Assault on Paper* by Nicholson Baker
published by Vintage. Used by permission of the Random House Group Limited.

Contents

Introduction

What is *Double Fold* about? The book is an investigation into what the author perceives to be the misdirection, indeed what Baker terms as a deception, of research libraries and their maintenance of books and newspapers, their paper collections. Baker's journalistic account (that is, based on interviews, some visits, and an impressionistic analysis of the professional literature) surveys the microfilming (mostly) and digitizing (somewhat) reformatting of books and newspapers determined to be in dangerous condition. Nicholson Baker, in a highly idiosyncratic fashion, finds both newspapers and books assigned brittle value to have life left in them. He parodies library and preservation administrators' decision making, arguing that originals can be warehoused and that this is, in fact, the mission libraries hold on behalf of society. Baker also argues that the costs of reformatting are far more than what it would be to store the originals, and that the replacement of originals with surrogates undermines scholarly use of the books and newspapers. In *Double Fold*, Baker also chronicles his personal establishment of a repository for original newspapers, mainly deaccessioned (that is, formally removed from a repository's holdings) and sold from other institutions such as the British Library. The book spins a powerful story with an assortment of odd characters, and it is an engaging (and frustrating) reading because of the author's caustic and sometimes vindictive style. The combination of Baker's stature as a writer and his compelling exposé (what else can we call it?) has given *Double Fold* considerable media play.

Some librarians or archivists may wonder why they should worry about

Nicholson Baker, a novelist and essayist, *not* a library or archives professional. Librarians need to be careful to not disregard Baker's book whatever
its origins, intent, or veracity, because it is a book aimed at libraries and
librarians and receiving considerable public exposure. Many librarians will
find it necessary to answer questions and justify activities based on questions framed from *Double Fold*, Baker's public appearances about the book
and its topic, and reviews and public perceptions of the book. Archivists
might wonder especially why they should devote any attention to *Double
Fold*, a book primarily focusing on books, newspapers, and libraries rather
than archives. I think there are important reasons why archivists need to
pay attention to this book and its author, and I have endeavored to try to
explain these in this review turned into a book in its own right.

Much of what follows in this extended essay is based on my perspective
as an archivist, and I have written it mainly for that segment of our modern
information professions, while hoping that librarians, preservation administrators, and others concerned about American libraries also will gain a
better understanding of the limitations and distortions of Nicholson Baker's
Double Fold. Again, why should archivists be concerned about this book?
First, the media does not distinguish between libraries and archives, but it
emphasizes in reviewing the book and Baker's arguments the threats to
documentary materials (often not distinguishing between print and manuscript, library and archival material). Archives and archivists are implicated
in the book even if they are not the main targets. Second, some libraries
and librarians have already reacted to Nicholson Baker and the public attention on his book by announcing plans no longer to discard anything
that has been microfilmed or digitized. Archivists working in research and
other libraries may find themselves needing to justify their appraisal process
and other functions to their administrators and funders. Third, a major
theme of *Double Fold* is that *everything* should be saved, an argument that
has found resonance with the media and public. The selection process of
archivists, an activity that is not understood by the media and public, may
come under intense scrutiny. Fourth, Baker, despite his repeated efforts to
deny this, has depicted a conspiracy in which librarians and libraries are
seen as misguided, evil, and/or stupid in their preservation activities. Again,
because archivists are not distinguishable by the public and media, they
may be viewed in a similar or worse manner (since archival appraisal is a
much more intensive selection process than anything employed by librarians) because of the response to this book. Fifth, as the title suggests, Nicholson Baker is arguing that paper is the superior means of preserving
information and that the book and newspaper must be saved as both artifact and information source. Archivists, contending with a much larger
documentary universe than that represented by print and a universe that is
becoming much more complex because of electronic record-keeping systems, may find it far more difficult to explain their mandate to deal with

the range of records' media and reasons for maintaining records that cut across evidence, accountability, and public and organizational memory. Finally, Baker's *Double Fold*, replete with statistics, numerous quotations from professional literature and professional leaders, and interviews builds a strong case, even in its most exaggerated forms, that casts a shadow on professionals like librarians and archivists. Archivists need to be aware that they may be likewise criticized in the wake of the book's media frenzy.

This is a book I never intended to write. It just happened. I had written a few essay responses to Nicholson Baker's earlier essays, using his article on the destruction of library card catalogs as a springboard for a coauthored piece on librarians and their view of their history and then responding to Baker's writing about the destruction of newspapers.[1] These sound like dry academic exercises, and I suppose they might be, especially in comparison to the light, evocative prose employed by Nicholson Baker. These essays reflect, however, my own changing perspectives of mulling over Baker's writings. My coauthored essay on the card catalogs used Baker to make the point that librarians had to be much more serious about the documents of their own past. My response to Baker's lament about newspaper destruction was very different. His essay made me angry because it so blatantly overstated the case about what was occurring with newspapers and, as well, the nature of the value of the old newspapers. While there is a decided similarity in the arguments in these two essays written between 1994 and 2000, I nevertheless sense a growing stridency about Baker's arguments and tone (perhaps explaining why in *Double Fold* Baker makes references to his earlier arguments about the card catalogs but does not fully incorporate it in the text).

There is value to Baker's writings, an important point to make near the outset of this book since so much of what follows is a critique of his arguments. I had used Nicholson Baker's essay on the destruction of library card catalogs as an exercise in my graduate course on archival appraisal— asking the students to debate the merits of saving these old catalogs and the process of making such a decision—and the essay worked very well as a stimulus for discussion because the author made such an eloquent case for the value and beauty of the old catalogs. Students generally divided down the middle in their theoretical discussion, and many were not so happy when I indicated that the decisions that they would be making in real life would be this hard and sometimes even more difficult. It is difficult to argue for the destruction of objects that at one time were so functional and may now even, with the patina of age and lens of nostalgia, seem quaint and beautiful. Nicholson Baker's obvious skills as a writer make for even more compelling arguments why not to destroy books or newspapers. But this is where Baker can provide a service to librarians and archivists, because behind the persuasive arguments and lilting prose, there are weaknesses that make us stop and reflect. The *real-life* criterion is important, since Nicholson Baker makes little effort to understand the nature and responsibilities of libraries and, especially, archives.

When I discovered that Nicholson Baker was expanding his writings as a library activist into a book, I became more interested in what I perceived to be Baker's increasing stridency about what was going on in libraries. Even so, it is important to note that my own school is using *Double Fold* as a required reading for library students, and I will certainly make my own archival studies students read the book as well. Despite its many faults, the book makes many compelling arguments that librarians and archivists will need to respond to and ones that they have had to deal with before, although not so much in the public glare induced by *Double Fold*. The real moral of the story here may be the failure of archivists and librarians to *explain* to the public and policymakers *what* it is they do, must do, and should do in terms of managing our nation's documentary heritage. If we had done a better job, then Nicholson Baker's writings would not have attracted so much attention, although some of the aspects of Baker's arguments are almost impossible to deal rationally with as they appeal to romantic notions of old and common objects.

In January 2001, while having dinner with one of my former doctoral students, Jeanette Bastian, a faculty member at Simmons library school, I learned that Baker would be a guest speaker at Simmons Alumni Day in mid-May 2001. I expressed interest in an opportunity to debate the writer, and Dr. Bastian, with her customary diplomatic skills, managed to engineer the debate. Just prior to the debate Baker's *Double Fold* appeared, along with an avalanche of positive reviews, and I settled into the more serious business of reading one of the most frustrating, stimulating, and outrageous books about libraries ever written. The appearance and substance of the book provided a new impetus for my one personal encounter with Nicholson Baker, who is charming and polite and who seems somewhat puzzled by the public attention of his book (although it is difficult for me to accept that a writer of Baker's stature, with the support of a major trade publisher like Random House, can be all that surprised or disappointed with the attention). As an academic, I certainly expect little public attention to be given to this book; indeed, it was written to be used by librarians, preservation administrators, and archivists.

As I finished reading Baker's book, the Society of American Archivists sensed that they needed to craft a response to this new example of library muckraking with all its archival implications. The Society's Executive Director, Susan Fox, contacted me and asked that I write a review of the book for the Society's newsletter, and I spent Easter weekend writing a seven-thousand-word essay, never anticipating writing something quite this long and yet feeling that I had barely scratched the surface. Susan and the Society approached me because of the longer response I had written to Baker's *New Yorker* essay about the destruction of original newspapers and because they knew of my impending debate. The Society mounted my review on its Web site, and I began to receive both laudatory and highly critical letters and e-mails about my views. Just as Baker's early essays had done, his book sparked lengthy and contentious chatter on all sorts of professional listservs, and I began to sense that I needed to craft a fuller response.

Other opportunities for speaking about Nicholson Baker developed in this period. Asked to talk to the Preservation class at the University of Michigan's School of Information by my friend and colleague Elizabeth Yakel, I decided to discuss "Nicholson Baker's Assault on Libraries and Archives." Then an opportunity came to speak to the Coalition of Research Libraries because of its work on reformatting and preserving newspapers, a group obviously feeling pressure from and frustration with the views of Nicholson Baker and the mounting media hype about the book, its author, and his crusade. I realized that I had a pile of notes, essays, partial articles, and other materials related to Baker's book and his perspectives. Whenever I turned my attention to one of my other, higher priority writing projects, something else about the Baker affair jumped up to grab my attention. The editors of *Archival Science*, a new journal, asked me to expand my Society of American Archivists (SAA) review, and I tried to craft an essay implying the meaning of *Double Fold* for the international archival community; armed with this assignment, I wrote an essay twice the length that I had for the Society. All of these earlier efforts in commentary on *Double Fold* have been incorporated into this book.

I am not ashamed about my obsession with Baker's book because, despite its many flaws, it is an important book about libraries and the preservation-archival mission of libraries. Who can remember the last time a book about libraries or the preservation of documentary materials made the national news? Earl Daschlager, writing for the *Houston Chronicle*, states, "*Double Fold* is an important and timely book, a sort of *Silent Spring* calling for a stop to the annihilation of our printed heritage. It should be required reading for all librarians, for all those who are responsible for keeping and maintaining books and newspapers, and for anyone who believes that books and newspapers are the lifeblood of a healthy civilization."[2] And here the problems begin. The result of Rachel Carson's environmentalist alarm was long overdue and addressed serious problems confronting the future of our world. Nicholson Baker's book, however, was full of exaggerated and inaccurate information, and it came as a surprise to many in the public. Roger Bishop writes, "The author's remarkable skill with language, linked with his obvious concern for the many aspects of his subject, enables him to share his curiosity and insight in a compelling way. *Double Fold* should appeal to anyone interested in our shared cultural heritage. It might also provoke some well-informed person who disagrees with Baker to write a book in response."[3] Well, I was provoked, but I will leave it to others to determine just how well informed I am in my response.

Honestly, I am expecting my book will draw as much criticism, if not more, than Nicholson Baker's writings. It may be that libraries are simply overdue to be the focus of controversy. Perhaps libraries are becoming like museums. Steven Dubin writes, "Museums and their exhibitions have become controversial sites. . . . They no longer merely provide a pleasant refuge from ordinary life, nor are they simply repositories of received wisdom. Museums have moved to the forefront in struggles over representations and over the chronicling, revising, and displaying of the past."[4] Libraries have been the sites of controversies, too—in the kinds of books they acquire and provide access to, their commitment to providing access to the World Wide Web with all its fears of pornography being viewed by children, and so forth. As Dubin says about museums: "Today museum staffs cannot focus exclusively upon their subjects; they must pay closer attention to the social ecology in which they are embedded."[5] Libraries and librarians must also take cognizance of their social ecologies. The uproar of Nicholson Baker's book is as much because it portrays important, seemingly benign, institutions as misguided and even devious.

Whatever controversy my small book will generate will probably be very different from that accorded Baker and his. I expect my critics will come from *within* the library and archives community since I have little name recognition outside of it. Nicholson Baker drew much wider publicity because he is a well-known writer. Columnist Howard Kurtz wrote that "serious news" is generally made through a "hook—preferably one with a famous name—before jumping on important societal issues."[6] This is what I think happened with *Double Fold*. Certainly a claim that American libraries were destroying their valuable holdings is important news, but it attracted attention initially because this charge emanated from someone of Nicholson Baker's stature. That Baker, a non-librarian and non-archivist displaying a remarkable lack of understanding about what these institutions and their professionals do, should get so much credibility may relate to another problem these kinds of programs have faced. Art dealer Richard Feigen wrote a sober and disturbing critique of art museums with some applicability to the situation of libraries. He lamented: "In this new era of museology, a director's success has come to be measured by the crowds he attracts, the funds he raises, the buildings he builds, and how effectively he can dodge political cross fire." Feigen sees "box office" as the critical factor, even threatening a "museum's scholarly projects." Trustees have taken over and professionals have lost their influence: "The thinking seems rooted in our Calvinist heritage: everything is black or white, never gray." Feigen makes an astute comment about art museum boards that may say something profound about Nicholson Baker and his book on libraries. Feigen thinks one of the difficulties with these boards is that "art is a field in which almost everyone thinks he knows enough," even when "expert practitioners on the staff have Ph.D's and decades of scholarship behind them."[7] This is even more the case with libraries. Anyone who *likes* books thinks they can be a librarian. One who writes books, like Baker, thinks he knows even more. This is why individuals, again like Baker, will make snide comments about the education and knowledge of librarians. This is why the references to spectacles, bow ties, and other physical features of librarians in Baker's *Double Fold* are as much cheap appeals to the popular stereotypes of librarians.

Most of this book is original to my debate with Baker, drawing upon a few essays commenting on Baker's writings previously published elsewhere. The initial two chapters provide an orientation to Nicholson Baker. The first chapter introduces Nicholson Baker and *Double Fold* and the presumptions of its author. This chapter plays with the fact that Baker is a novelist and it is difficult to see how the story Baker tells is more than a good story, not very different from some of his other fiction. This chapter also discusses the early reception of *Double Fold*, with reviews written by professional reviewers who obviously like books and print and who, even when criticizing Baker's methodology and style, get easily caught up in getting convinced by his story. The second chapter is a characterization of how Baker views libraries and archives, arguing that he does not really understand these institutions or the nature of the work of the professionals who staff and run them. This chapter considers how Baker considers the misguided intentions of libraries and archives, perhaps because he is worried about the future of his own publications. Chapter 2 compares the simplistic notion of Baker versus the realities and complexities of real libraries and archives.

The next two chapters consider Baker's notion of saving everything, a perspective I believe is absolutely fatal to the arguments the author presents. Despite claims after the publication of *Double Fold* to the contrary, Baker suggests that everything must be saved, an impossible task as described in Chapter 3. Both librarians and archivists make selection decisions for a variety of reasons, but primarily because it is both impossible to keep everything and because much of what is published or created has marginal or no value. A focus of Baker's *Double Fold* is his fascination with preserving the originals of newspapers, the topic of Chapter 4. While Baker stresses the examples of a few major urban dailies, his arguments suggest that *all* newspapers have to be kept in original format and that libraries and archives are really little more than warehousing operations. Baker also exaggerates the importance of newspapers as documentary sources—romanticizing their nature and use, while failing to understand the magnitude of administering this aspect of information.

The next two chapters concern the idea that libraries and librarians are self-deceived in their own priorities. Nicholson Baker makes a lot about his view that our libraries and archives are working under the wrong priorities. Focusing on his arguments about newspapers, Chapter 5 considers the ways librarians and archivists are and can be selective in how they deal with the magnitude of material represented by documentary sources like newspapers. Assessing priorities requires considering all that librarians and archivists are responsible for, providing a more accurate (and complex) notion of how priorities are formed. What all this leads up to is the need to use the same standards for evaluating Baker's book, writings, and other critiques that he himself employs to evaluate library and archives preservation efforts (and other library and archival functions he decides to become a critic of) of the past half-century. Nicholson Baker also makes an impassioned plea for the preservation of original objects, but he does not consider the nuances of the nature and value of print versus reformatted copies, or print versus digital information. Chapter 6 considers how this is a complicated, ongoing debate, one typical to all previous generations involved in the transition from one information technology to another.

Baker's career as a library activist started with his writing about the discarding of card catalogs. Chapter 7 puts his arguments in a broader context, demonstrating that complaints such as made by Baker have been made before with shifts in library cataloguing. There is concern, however, because of the often nonhistorical approach to matters by librarians and other information professionals, but this is very different than the kinds of arguments made by Baker, in which he becomes obsessed with the physical artifact of card catalogs, most notably their weakest contribution to libraries and society.

It is easy to characterize Baker as a Luddite, dismissing technology and its applications in libraries and archives. This is a mistaken assumption, but the alternative is not any prettier. Chapter 8 reviews Baker's notions of the convenience of technology, but in it I also argue that the manner in which he examines technology is really part of a diatribe against the loss of the artifact and his playful storytelling in which he pokes fun at the conspiratorial and misguided (in his view) ways in which librarians have adopted technological solutions such as microfilming and digitization.

The final two chapters wrap up my arguments with Nicholson Baker. Nicholson Baker provides lots of information on financial matters and on the nature of the technical aspects of preservation/conservation. His figures and his views are highly flawed as they are embedded within a framework of conspiracies, poor priorities, and misguided (and evil?) administrators of librarians and archivists. Chapter 9 considers some of the problems with Baker's approach, suggesting that it is not just about money and that the lineage of conservation/preservation approaches presented by Baker as problematic can also be seen as the changing notions and experimentation with preserving our printed heritage. Nicholson Baker also loves the dramatic image. In his earlier card catalog article, he compared the tossing of card catalogs to the burning of the ancient library at Alexandria. In his recent writings, Baker compares the use of microfilming and technologies for reformatting as equaling book destruction not seen since the destruction of monastic libraries in sixteenth-century England. In this concluding chapter, I try to address the problem of dealing with a highly visible public critic and the irony of having been an internal critic for years now trying to defend librarians and archivists. Much of the blame for the public reception for *Double Fold* rests at the feet of librarians and archivists who have not been as skillful in describing the nature of their work and mandate as they should have been. However, such internal problems pale in comparison with the weaknesses of Baker's library jeremiad, no matter how well intentioned Baker says he was in offering his book to us.

My book is my sole responsibility. I have learned from many through the years about library, preservation, and archival issues. While I was working on this response, I had continuing dialogue with Jim O'Toole, Christinger Tomer, and Tom Dubis. Drs. O'Toole and Tomer always told me when I needed to be a bit more restrained. Tom Dubis continually supplied me with citations to reviews of or references to Baker's *Double Fold*. I am indebted to others as well. Jane Greenberg, when she was a doctoral student at my school, wrote a fascinating paper on librarians' responses to Baker's notions of the paper card catalog; as always with Jane, I learned a lot from her. I also learned much about preservation issues from Sally Buchanan and Elizabeth Yakel, both former faculty colleagues of mine, as well as the writings of Paul Conway (an individual who actually receives positive comments by Baker). I am indebted to all those individuals who invited me to speak about Baker or who sent me messages (both critical and laudatory) through the months that I was thinking about Nicholson Baker and his book (and crusade).

Finally, I am indebted to Nicholson Baker who was not afraid to speak his mind about the present state of library preservation and libraries' archival functions, and who moved the discussion into a more public forum. I hope he learns from this book as well, although I am reasonably sure he will simply agree to disagree. I can hear him telling others that he never wrote about a conspiracy and that he only reported what others told him. Well, he never asked me, so here are my comments at last.

There is a need to tell one final part of the story of this book, and one that will put Nicholson Baker in the best light. As this book was completed with its final copy editing and about to go into production, I received a letter from Random House, the publisher of *Double Fold*, that I had been denied permission to quote from that book. In a telephone call to Random House, I learned that the reasons for this decision was that they believed that my book was not in the best interests of their author. This is, of course, a commentary on the problems with modern publishing and the specter of "fair use" facing every author and publisher. Through a series of efforts, I reached Mr. Baker directly and he was surprised to hear about this decision by his publisher. As I suspected, he preferred to be quoted rather than paraphrased, and he welcomed the continuation of our debate. Readers will note that Nicholson Baker is generously quoted in this book, and I thank him for this.

In a conversation with him about the quotations, Nicholson Baker did ask if I clarified that the title of this book, *Vandals in the Stacks*, comes from a review of *Double Fold* and not *Double Fold* itself. As I describe in the first chapter, the "vandals" allusion graced the pages of the April 15, 2001, *New York Times Book Review*. I wanted to title my book *Him and Me*, a parody on Nicholson Baker's *U and I* about his obsession with John Updike and mocking my own seeming obsession with Baker, but the publisher thought that the allusion would not be clear. If anything, using this title does comment on the reception of the *Double Fold* book. As for Nicholson Baker and myself, it appears that we will continue to debate about the issues he raises and, hopefully, the mission of libraries and archives alike will be strengthened through improved public understanding and empathy.

NOTES

1. Richard J. Cox, Jane Greenberg, and Cynthia Porter, "Access Denied: The Discarding of Library History." *American Libraries* 29 (April 1998): 57–61 and "The Great Newspaper Caper: Backlash in the Digital Age." *First Monday* 5 (December 4, 2000), available at *http://firstmonday.org/issues/issue5_12/cox/*.

2. Earl Daschlager, "Fahrenheit 98.6: Scholar Says Librarians Are Destroying Our Printed Heritage," *Houston Chronicle* April 27, 2001, available at *http://www.chron.com/cs/CDA/story.hts/ae/books/reviews/890602*, accessed June 4, 2001.

3. Roger Bishop review, *Bookpage*, April 2001, available at *http://www.bookpage.com/0104bp/nonfiction/doublefold.html*, accessed June 4, 2001.

4. Steven C. Dubin, *Displays of Power: Controversy in the American Museum from the Enola Gay to Sensation* (New York: New York University Press, 1999), p. 5.

5. Dubin, *Displays of Power*, p. 63.

6. Howard Kurtz, "Stumbling to a Story," *Pittsburgh Post-Gazette*, June 20, 2001. This column was published originally in the *Washington Post*.

7. Richard Feigen, *Tales from the Art Crypt: The Painters, the Museums, the Curators, the Collectors, the Auctions, the Art* (New York: Alfred A. Knopf, 2000), pp. 109, 111, 152.

Chapter One

Life Imitates Art?

At one far distant point (the year ten million) in Kurt Vonnegut's *Sirens of Titan* (1959), museums and archives are emptied because they are "crowding the living right off the earth" and a million-year period is summed up in a single sentence in the history books. Guy Montag, a "fireman" in Ray Bradbury's *Fahrenheit 451* (1953), suffers a crisis when he discovers the content of the books he is burning and flees to join with a group who memorizes books in order to protect them from the authorities. Long after a nuclear holocaust, a group of monks discovers a sacred text (a shopping list) from the prewar years in *A Canticle for Leibowitz* (1959) by Walter M. Miller, Jr., a revelation because of the mass destruction of books and archives. In George Orwell's *1984* (1949), Winston Smith contends with a society in which everyone is always monitored and all information is controlled by the government. Smith works in the government's archives, altering records, and, as he develops his own critical notions purchases a book in order to start keeping a diary (an unlawful act).[1]

These are all classic, fictional accounts commenting on post–World War Two society's concern with government control of information, the role of books and records in society, and the nature of personal knowledge. They are also good stories, replete with conspiracies, interesting characters, secret societies, humorous asides, and chilling similarities to present events. Now we have another good story, revolving around misguided government policies, well meaning but often hapless characters, humorous anecdotes about simplistic procedures and tests, and, most of all, a vast conspiracy involving CIA operatives and those other powerful government agents—librarians.

However, in this case, the story is *true*, or so we are told. I am referring to, of course, Nicholson Baker's book, *Double Fold*.[2] Instead of television screens in every room repeatedly showing government propaganda films, we have the creation of a widely shown film, *Slow Fires*, as being part of "incessant" propaganda by librarians and preservation administrators who have deceived the public into believing that paper becomes brittle and turns to dust. Instead of government book burners, such as in *Fahrenheit 451*, we have professional librarians destroying books to microfilm or digitize them. Rereading a novel like Bradbury's makes one think that Baker may have also read the novel recently, as the tone and commentaries about books and culture in *Double Fold* are eerily reminiscent of those in *Fahrenheit 451* (the people memorizing books are also suspicious of the utility of microfilm).

Perhaps someone may have wondered whether Mr. Baker is playing with us, creating a work (just like his *U and I* describing a supposed obsession with John Updike[3]) in which we must scratch our heads and wonder whether we should take *Double Fold* as fiction or nonfiction. One reviewer of *Double Fold* called the book "resolutely absorbing" and indicated that it "reads like a spy novel."[4] I prefer to see *Double Fold* as a gift to educators training the next generation of archivists, librarians, and preservation administrators, even though this might annoy Mr. Baker given his harsh attitudes about such education. Unlike most academics, myself included, Nicholson Baker is a witty and charming writer and a superb storyteller. While, for librarians and archivists, at least, he may anger us, we should channel this anger into rethinking our assumptions and, most certainly, our approaches to how we explain ourselves to the public. I have used his essay, "Discards," in my course on archival appraisal and his more recent essay, "Deadlines," in a course on understanding information.[5] I have not used them because I agree with them but because they challenge us, and especially students, to determine what and how we function as librarians and archivists.

Yet, there are stories, and then there are stories. Writer Ron Hansen argues: "We fiction readers are questioners. We find ourselves wondering if the facts are right, if a scene truly occurred, what will happen next in the story, and how and where we are being taken."[6] If fiction readers are questioners, than the readers of nonfiction are even more critical. Is *Double Fold* fiction or nonfiction? Hansen continues:

[I]t's far easier to say what a story is not than to say what a story is. True stories are not anecdotes, sketches, character studies, or moral pieces. They are not psychology or sociology or history or biography, though they may adapt elements of all these forms to create their effects. Stories are not about theories or themes, though our high school practice of talking about books in this way often gives people the false impression that serious writers first of all have a point they're trying to prove. What stories try to present is generally sensory, to pursue a white whale across the Atlantic, to float in and out of consciousness within view of the snows of Kilimanjaro.[7]

Perhaps Baker's *Double Fold* is a confused tale because it mixes the genres of storytelling (Baker's expertise) with history or journalism (*not* Baker's specialty).

If I consider *Double Fold* a gift for educators like myself, then I also believe that librarians and archivists likewise should use it as an opportunity to explain themselves, especially as he operates in influential public opinion forums most librarians and archivists do not have access to, as they lack the profile and literary agents if not the time and motivation. That he takes his case to the public forum, a practice that annoys many inside the library and archives disciplines, is useful because he elevates public discourse and provides a forum for the professionals to participate in, although it has proved to be difficult for library and archival scholars and practitioners to break into print in the same forum.[8] Nicholson Baker is wrong (mostly), but you need to twist a bit, scratch about in your strongest opinions, and indulge in self-scrutiny to determine just why he is wrong. That his writing captivates students or forces professionals to rethink what they are doing are added bonuses to having *Double Fold*. Whether having this work from a purported lover of books and libraries is useful to librarians and archivists depends more on how they respond to it, since if left unanswered it makes them look evil, deceiving, and stupid. If the public buys Baker's depiction of libraries and archives, it will be more difficult to meet any mission (his or ours) because it will be difficult to gather support for what archivists and librarians do.

The public can find better sources than *Double Fold* or any of Nicholson Baker's other writings to gain an appreciation of the nature and function of libraries. Shortly before the appearance of Baker's *Double Fold*, Lionel Casson's brief, excellent history of ancient libraries was published, written for public consumption. While Baker evokes the destruction of the library of Alexandria or the looting of the monasteries in medieval England as symbols of the nature of the modern destruction of libraries being perpetuated today, Casson's book provides a more balanced portrait of what such entities represented. The dumping of card catalogs is related to the destruction of the ancient library, admittedly in a quotation from one of Baker's sources, but it provides, nonetheless, a powerful allusion.[9] Baker's use of this imagery is interesting. The Alexandrian library was comprehensive, acquiring everything "from exalted epic poetry to humdrum cookbooks." But the scale was very different in contrast to its modern counterparts; at its peak, the rolls in this ancient library numbered about half a million, what would today be a small research library. Moving a few hundred years ahead, looking at the libraries at the height of the Roman Empire, we find that libraries were "ruthlessly selective" in what they acquired. And the space issues were not peculiar to the libraries in modern America. Ancient Roman libraries became heavily specialized in scope as they confronted space shortages.[10] Baker's preoccupation with matters such as book selection, space issues, copying, and other issues are not issues unique to the modern American library, but counter to Baker's view, they are common to the historical evolution of libraries. Baker's *Double Fold* is not a historical analysis, but it provides instead a truncated view of the development of libraries and also archives.

This does not mean we should not take seriously the popular reactions to book and newspaper destruction or deaccessioning that Baker's writings have created. In this business of deaccessioning and destruction, librarians and archivists are faced with immense problems, perhaps because we have simply fumbled about in explaining what we do or in having to take positions that seem to be against the most basic human nature. H. R. Woudhuysen, an English professor at University College, London, gives us a view into the challenge we face:

Nicholson Baker has pleaded eloquently that libraries should take the long view of their curatorial duties—that is what is wrong with demand-led policies. For once libraries start getting rid of material of one kind or another, then it is hard to judge where that policy will or should end. Compared to the huge buildings and amounts of land for which, say the National Trust, is responsible, newspapers and books are small and, one would have thought, easily managed. Organizations like the National Trust rely on the good will of their friends and supporters. Deaccessioning from national, copyright libraries opens up fissures in the complicated relationship between librarians and users. But there is another problem about deaccessioning that needs to be raised: getting rid of material, for whatever reason, is liable to alarm and put potential donors and benefactors off. The National Art Collections Fund is clear about its policy, that it will not give its support to institutions which sell off items it has helped to pay for. I do not know what the Friends of the National Libraries think about the BL's decision to get rid of the newspapers. Museums and art galleries are sometimes urged to get rid of items which are not often put on show. One defense for them against this demand is that they should be thought of as being like libraries: not everything in them is going to be exhibited, but it can be made available. Yet if libraries, if the national library, do not want to keep what they own, then the way is open for getting rid of anything and everything that is disliked by curators.[11]

This seems like good advice, except that it does not acknowledge that past acquisitions may have been faulty, that present needs dictate difficult deaccessioning decisions be made, or that librarians and archivists usually have the expertise to make careful decisions of this nature. The fault lies when librarians and archivists undertake such actions without trying to educate the public, as the case may have been with the San Francisco Public

Library move into a new facility and the tossing of perhaps two hundred thousand books.[12]

Archivists and librarians obviously need to be careful about how self-reflective they become when reading and responding to *Double Fold*. As a result of Mr. Baker's book, archives, historical manuscripts, rare books, and newspaper collections have become the subject of journalists, book reviewers, and radio and talk show hosts around the country, and many of them may have wondered whether they were the focus of a fictional essay à la Orwell, Vonnegut, Miller, or Bradbury. Archivists and librarians are not just *in* the news, they are *the* news, thanks in part to Baker's stature as a writer, his celebrity, and his access to publication outlets like the *New Yorker*. Unlike academic and professional books about libraries and archives, we can find *Double Fold* prominently displayed in the bookstore chains rather than in the specialized scholarly or professional association shops librarians and archivists must frequent to find studies in their fields.

Librarians (and archivists more by implication) are being discussed in publications like the *New York Times, Newsweek,* the *Christian Science Monitor,* and the *New York Review of Books.* And something is amiss, since normally in the media's coverage of libraries and archives the staffs of these repositories are invisible.[13] Librarians and archivists are being attacked in the very area they thought they had gained substantial public support, the preservation of our documentary heritage. Little more than two or three decades ago, librarians and even archivists barely allocated funds for preservation or conservation, except to bring the books or records into their facilities. And they are not just being sniped at, they are under a major siege—perhaps one that is just getting started. Robert Darnton, in his review, notes that *Double Fold* is a *"J'accuse* pointed at the library profession."[14] The David Gates review of the book in the April 15, 2001, *New York Times Book Review* was the cover story with the headline shouting "Vandals in the Stacks!" and featuring a less than flattering illustration depicting librarians (and archivists?) climbing up a stack of newspapers to destroy them before the public gets access to them. These are mostly reviews by professional book reviewers and other writers, rather than individuals who are immersed in working with books, libraries, special collections, and archives.[15] The early *Double Fold* reviews also not only spread worldwide but they declared a victory (perhaps even before the war had begun and only one battle fought). Ed Vulliamny wrote for the April 21, 2001 *Manchester Guardian*: "Signs within America's bibliophile establishment indicate Baker's book has not only sounded the alarm but won the debate. The Washington-based Council of Library and Information Resources issued a draft report this month rescinding decades of received wisdom by recommending a nationwide effort to save original copies of books and newspapers."[16]

As time goes on, and more detailed reviews by librarians and archivists appear, we will see much more balanced assessments of *Double Fold*.[17] Yet, Robert Darnton, the important historian of books and publishing, is of a different type.[18] I was dumbfounded that although Robert Darnton notes that Baker "overstates his case" and that his book suffers at times from the confusion of "investigative journalism" with history, that Darnton still agrees with the premise of *Double Fold*: "Hyperrealism as a morality tale: it is a tour de force and a great read. But is it true? On the whole, I think it is, although it is less innocent than it seems. It should be read as a journalistic jeremiad rather than as a balanced account of library history over the last fifty years."[19] Darnton even takes seriously Baker's policy recommendations, which take up one (final) page of the text and look like a hasty add-on. That Darnton believes that Baker's "policy" recommendations "coincide" with a draft report issued by the Council on Library and Information Resources (CLIR) on preserving artifacts is also surprising since the CLIR report recognizes the complexities and challenges associated with defining, identifying, and selecting artifacts while Baker adheres (seems to anyway) to a romantic notion that *all* originals ought to and must be saved.[20] It is obvious that Baker's book is striking at the heart of something many feel passionately about, the maintenance of artifacts. David Lowenthal, in his sweeping *The Past Is A Foreign Country*, captured it well when he wrote: "To see and touch palpably aged documents heightens the appeal of the past." But it goes even beyond this. Lowenthal again: "We respond to relics as objects of interest or beauty, as evidence of past events, and as talismans of continuity."[21] In the same vein, a book collector once wrote: "Always before me is the lure of the chase. Every little stall, every dusty window with a few books in the corner sets my heart beating." Why collect? "He collects because he wants to, and the acquisitive instinct is inherent in all humans."[22] As one reads *Double Fold*, this instinctive urge seems rampant, as Baker literally drools over the beautiful and sometimes antiquated objects threatened with destruction by librarians and archivists. A journalism professor responded positively to Baker's book and his defense of saving original newspapers by noting:

Newspapers are living originals. They have a unique tactile intimacy, an exotic scent, a singular drawing-power keyed as much to their shape and feel as to their content. They are tangible artifacts, with innate historical and literary value. Neither microfilm nor digitization, for all their archival benefits, can re-create the bond of touch to text. . . . The house where I grew up sat a couple of lots away from the local weekly. From my bedroom, I would watch as newspapers rumbled off the monstrous old flatbed press. I could see, hear and even smell them. They blazed with a special sensuous appeal. . . . For one who loves print, reading a newspaper online is about as satisfying as viewing digital images of your children and grandchildren sent via the Internet. They are lovely to look at, and a deeply appreciated gift from technology. But virtual viewing simply cannot approach the experience of cradling the little beauties in your own arms.[23]

These are powerful impulses to overcome, even with other pressing challenges or competing mandates to meet for information access.

Librarians and archivists might want to pay more attention to how the public responds to the book. Perhaps the reviews posted to Amazon.com will provide a clue to the kind of response *Double Fold* is getting. One reviewer writes: "I started reading this book as part of the Librarian's Book Club and found that it is a book that contains many important points. The conversion of original documents to microfiche without keeping the source material may have been a grave error by libraries around the country." Another reviewer argues: "I was afraid this book was going to be rather dry and brittle, being about old paper and all, but I gave it a chance because I like Nicholson Baker's writing so much, and know from experience he can write about anything—and does—and make it fascinating. But I defy you to read this book 'just' for Baker's writing, as I did, and not get involved in this subject." Another reviewer states:

Baker has done the world a great service by pointing out the inherent hypocrisy in the library profession. . . . I applaud Baker for his courage to enter such a closed world. Too many within the profession are going to write scathing reviews here, but I'd encourage them to note the positive comments in the book. . . . Baker is NOT the liar, misinterpreting the facts of preservation; librarians sometimes are, hiding the truth of their misguided activities.

And, as just one more example:

"Double Fold," however, makes a compelling case that has left me convinced. Baker is now arguing that a vast treasure trove of cultural information is being lost as libraries destroy old newspapers in the process of "preserving" them by placing them on microfilm. Not only, he suggests, is information contained in the newspapers-as-physical-object being lost, but he suggests that microform preservation is dubious and may not last as long as the original newspapers would have. He dashes pretty convincingly all the arguments in favor of this method of preservation (space, longevity, etc.), and even suggests that the trend toward microfilm is a relic of cold war ideology that now trudges along for its own sake rather than because it is the best way to keep information around forever. Anyone who has read Baker's fiction knows what a wonderful writer he is, and this book is engaging, engrossing, at times hilarious, and at times powerful enough to make the reader furious.[24]

People, including the initial wave of professional reviewers, responded to the book's solid story line, its sensationalism, the conspiratorial tone, and the potential personal implications posed by the loss of original newspapers and books.

The intensity of response to this book may stem from many common, sometimes knee-jerk, reactions the public has to professionals or to old artifacts, as one of the above quotations suggest. One is sentimental nostalgia and the other is the general antipathy in America toward anything smacking of elitism. Baker's fascination with the preservation of original newspapers, for example, may be the result more of a kind of nostalgia. J. B. Jackson notes that we often "admire and try to collect things not so much for their beauty or value as for their association with a phase of our past, a kind of private vernacular past—what we cherish are mementos of a bygone daily existence without a definite date."[25] While this may be a portion of how archivists and librarians approach their responsibilities, it is a minor concern in comparison to matters like accountability, evidence, information, and other roles that libraries and archives must serve. Old books and newspapers might be neat artifacts in their own right, but they are so in addition to being many other things. Both of these attitudes play off each other, and they are compounded by the fact that there is a perception that any one who likes books can become a librarian while few understand what an archivist is or does (an important distinction since we are really considering the *archival* function of libraries here).

The real appeal may be that the book, *Double Fold*, criticizes and mocks what the professionals are telling us is important. The public attack on professionalism is as old and as natural as the oldest professions, but it certainly has been a feature of American life since the late nineteenth century. Morris Berman, a social critic, considering how the finer aspects of American culture might be preserved, argues that one of the problems is that "we regard elitism as a dirty word" and, thus, doom our civilization to mediocrity. While Berman calls for a new class of monks "to preserve the treasures of the dying civilization and use them, like seeds, to impregnate a new one,"[26] Baker sees librarians and archivists, the modern equivalents of these monks who maintained the documentary heritage, as those who are against this tradition. Is Baker's assessment accurate, or is it simply a cheap ploy to gain sympathy for his attack on librarians and archivists by denigrating their decision making, knowledge, education, and honesty.

From these reviews it is obvious that people will be attracted to *Double Fold* because they are already fans of Mr. Baker's writings or because they are simply curious about why an essayist and novelist like him would turn his attention to a subject like book and newspaper preservation. From my vantage we need to understand that the preservation of objects such as books and newspapers is merely an extension of Nicholson Baker's writing. A critic, Arthur Saltzman, of Baker's literary output notes that one of the keys to Baker's success is his "extraordinary attention to ordinary objects" and the everyday. Baker's writing style includes a "jeweler's intensity of focus, a forensic scientist's ferocity of detail, a monk's humble delight in private discipline, and a satirist's sensitivity to oddities and errors." Saltzman, reflecting on Baker's collection of essays published as *The Size of Thoughts*, notes that some think Baker is an "essayist masquerading as a novelist," wanting to "lecture on the luster and necessity that live in or-

dinary things or to rail against the casualties one allows them to become."
It is not difficult to surmise that Baker's *Double Fold*, focusing on what is
happening with books, newspapers, and card catalogs—all certainly everyday objects—is part of his general orientation to life and not an aberration
from his previous literary pursuits. Saltzman argues that Baker is fighting
with the "plight of obsolescence"; "Baker trails behind the changing times,
raking the fossil remains, picking up the sloughs." For Saltzman, Baker is
battling with "cultural amnesia" and he is a "conservationist of the highest
order."[27] As another writer reviewing *Double Fold* suggests, Baker's interests in library preservation is a natural. Jeet Heer writes:

Following in the tradition of Vladimir Nabokov and John Updike, Baker has ex-
celled at writing tingling sensual prose which is fully responsive to the passionate
urges of the human body. . . . At first glance, Baker's new book, a critique of the
public library policy of throwing away old newspapers and brittle books, might
seem a sharp departure from his sex-obsessed novels. Yet, as with Nabokov and
Updike, Baker's interest in sex is linked with a larger concern for memory. Like
the hero of an old movie, a memory-writer always sees the past as a lover who
recedes into the distance while the train of time chugs forward. . . . Always aching
for yesterday, these writers use their powerful prose to conjure up seemingly inef-
fable moments of time: the flutter of butterflies, for example, which recur so often
in Nabokov. Sex—an event both memorable and hard to describe—is merely a
special test of how to revive what the clock always destroys.[28]

One can also sense that Baker has found a new source of inspiration in
his writing, since sex may be overdone in our modern age. In an article
about the "overexposure of sex," we find this reaction by Baker:

So what about the guy who kind of started all the dirty talk, Nicholson Baker,
whose literate phone-sex novel, *Vox*, was one of Monica Lewinsky's early, pro-
phetic gifts to the President? Mr. Baker is now in rural Maine where, he told *The
Observer*, "I'm writing about libraries—ha, ha, ha." "Sex is always exciting intrinsically," said Mr. Baker, "but, putting that aside, in order for it to be exciting to
write about, there has to be a little tropical foliage of forbiddenness. And that's
gone away, temporarily. It will inevitably come back. We just need a little mini-
Victorian episode to kind of help things along. It's just that there's a fatigue with
the subject. It's not even distaste, it's, "Let's give it a rest for a bit, it could be more
interesting in a decade." Certainly, I think, with the whole Clinton stuff, whatever
reserves of enthusiasm we had for talking about sex—they're gone."[29]

Some might believe that Baker would make a good archivist, focused as he
is on details, societal memory, and preservation. (I am not sure what to
state about the sexual aspects of any of this.)

Perhaps we need only to accept, as Baker states in his preface, that he is
a lover of libraries, and that anyone reading *Double Fold* will be convinced

of this. For a major literary figure to take the time to write such a book, possibly with far less potential financial gain and the distractions from other writing, suggests that Baker has made a commitment to take on this challenge because he is concerned about the fate of the books and newspapers he is writing about. In a cynical moment, however, especially given the intensive publicity about the book, Baker's numerous interviews and book signings, and the regular appearances he has made about the book, we might conclude that this promotional tour is part of a strategy to market and sell a book containing some *juicy* gossip about the library world and defending against the destruction of *old* objects (books and newspapers) that the public loves. It is also not difficult to believe in his passion for his cause, since *Double Fold* reveals that he is *not* a fan of those who run libraries and who make decisions about preservation and reformatting. Just as librarians long ago discovered that they can convince the public to love books and even libraries but not necessarily understand the professionals who manage them, so Baker has driven a wedge between the objects (books) and the places (libraries) where they are stored and the people (librarians and preservation administrators) who administer them. A greater wedge may be evident for archivists since they are all but invisible in Baker's book.

If this is what we must do, then we may need to accept the fact that Nicholson Baker does not fully understand the objects of his affection. At the heart of Mr. Baker's *Double Fold* are assumptions about the mission(s) of libraries and archives. Archivists and librarians have been debating their mission(s) for a long time, with librarians wrestling with the roles of their institutions in the information or knowledge or digital age and archivists struggling with the symbolic or cultural aspects of this mission in relation to the value of records for evidence and accountability. Some of the aspects of these debates are mirrored in *Double Fold*, but not in a manner suggesting that its author comprehends the debate. Indeed, it is not his responsibility to understand the intricacies of such debates. Librarians and archivists need to shoulder the blame for not explaining what they do, in all of its complexities, to the public. They have tended to adopt simplistic messages, and some of this simplicity is evident in Nicholson Baker's work, something most of us would not have worried about until he started writing about librarians and archivists and their repositories. The public has, in fact, *many* perceptions of libraries and archives, seeing them as repositories of interesting stuff, documents and artifacts, all of human history, all of human memory and knowledge, and simply as one more source of entertainment (although in this latter one they may be losing out to the super bookstores with their coffee shops, easy chairs, and other diversions).[30]

Nicholson Baker's view of libraries, with his emphasis on warehousing, preserving, and doing scholarship, does not capture the diversity of responsibilities librarians face. Redmond Kathleen Molz and Phyllis Dain, in their important book on American public libraries, give us a glimpse into the more complex world of these kinds of libraries. They note that "public librarians all speak the same language: there is a more or less common understanding of what their libraries are—agencies offering to the public the means of acquiring information, knowledge, education, aesthetic experience, and entertainment." Molz and Dain write of these libraries providing a "civic space," "educational agencies," and an archival function. These authors also chronicle a century of debates about the mission of the public library, noting that in the nineteenth century the "mission was relatively simple: by housing a collection of books the library was intended to educate and nourish the intellectual and civic life of the community."[31] Notice how this older, simpler mission seems to correspond to Baker's conception of the modern library.

Double Fold is a book by an individual who loves libraries but who perhaps does not understand them (I love my wife and daughter but that does not always mean I understand them, and they would be the first to admit this). Another weakness is the lack of distinction about types of libraries and the scope of other responsibilities and mandates made by Baker when considering the plight of the preservation of the book, the newspaper, and the artifacts housed in libraries. Archives are barely figured in Baker's book. One does not sense that Baker understands the differences between archives and libraries, and in fairness not many outside these disciplines perceive the differences, certainly not how difficult it would be to scale up the preservation and access challenges posed by the countless unique materials housed in archives and the growing challenges of electronic record-keeping systems. Indeed, one must acknowledge that Baker confuses things because when he focuses on libraries he stresses their *archival* role, arguing that librarians' "primary task" is to be "paper-keepers."[32]

This mission might be true for large libraries like the Library of Congress, the New York Public Library, and the major academic research libraries around the country, but they represent only a fraction of all the libraries in existence and only a portion of even these libraries are mentioned; in a discussion about the book, Mr. Baker suggests that he really is only focused on the major research libraries and the need for them to keep what they already have on the shelf (ignoring the fact that there are *many* kinds of research libraries and that *many* notable research collections are in smaller libraries and archival repositories). In one of his many interviews, Nicholson Baker states: "A lot of my book is concerned with the decisions that research libraries have made about the things that are already on the shelf. And here I believe (and I'm talking not about little suburban public libraries that cycle their collections all the time, but big research libraries whose collections have become, in effect, public landmarks) that libraries do have a responsibility to keep what they have on the shelf."[33] In a debate I had with the author at Simmons on May 16, 2001, Nicholson Baker suggested that he was sorry about the confusion about the nature of the libraries he described, although this is additional evidence about his lack of understanding of the nature of libraries, since it is not just large research libraries holding important research collections or, most certainly, significant collections of local newspapers. All of this may not matter much anyway, since the reviews made little distinction between the kinds of libraries or the professionals employed by them.

And these libraries serve many other and often competing functions ranging from community literacy programs to community social centers; for most libraries, the kinds of issues Baker discusses are way out of scope for them *except* for hoping they have the funds to purchase the microfilm copies or to sustain programs where they can provide access to the online digital versions of the newspapers, books, and journals—so that they can provide access to information their patrons need and want. When Baker does mention access, it is limited to the kind of scholarship carried out in the academic or major research libraries.[34] However, libraries and archives have a much broader scope of concerns than the very *simple* view of the world presented by Nicholson Baker. Archivists are concerned with the constantly evolving notions of records and their supporting technologies,[35] the impact of these technologies on the reliability of records,[36] whether a society immersed in nostalgia and memory will remember to value archival records,[37] whether records will be used in effective ways or even at all,[38] and the ethical challenges to managing increasingly complex and sensitive records.[39] Librarians are concerned with how to provide access to the information in a wide diversity of print, digital, and other resources,[40] censorship,[41] threats to free speech and access to information,[42] and the changing sensitivities to how information sources are seen and used.[43]

And these are just broad categories of contentious and complex issues. Libraries and archives are not just about shelves and warehouses, but they are living and often endangered organizations. Publishers, for example, as represented by the Association of American Publishers, seem to be locking horns with libraries. Seth Shulman writes: "As we plunge into the digital realm, the nation's 16,000 public libraries are striving to uphold their tradition as protectors of public access to new books and articles. But publishers, in an increasingly bold, frontal assault on the library's mission, have something very different in mind: a pay-per-use model for information content that will largely shut libraries out."[44] Here I should note that *access* is a matter Nicholson Baker largely ignores in his evaluation of library and archival preservation, including even his own newspaper archives (and it is an issue that most of the positive early reviewers of *Double Fold* also sidestepped).

For Nicholson Baker, libraries and archives should be *static* places, not institutions dealing with or accepting any change in purpose. Canadian archivist Terry Cook suggested that archivists have an important place in the modern information age if they realize that "they are in the understanding business, not the information business."[45] We can add, as well, that archivists must realize that they are not in the curatorial, warehousing, or the history business, and they are not somehow beyond problems with objectivity or subjectivity with what resides in the archives. In meditating on the nature of evidence and the value of oral history, Paul Thompson reminded historians that archives are not "innocent deposits," and that "it is always necessary to consider how a piece of evidence was put together in the first place."[46] The need is even greater for such caution in the age of still-not-tamper-proof electronic records and the tendency of companies, governments, and organizations (including even archivists) to rush to embrace the new digital technologies.[47]

There are other matters, far more fundamental and important, that archivists and librarians need to keep in their sight. The institutions creating the record-keeping systems and producing books and other information sources are changing rapidly, in a pull-and-tug fashion with the rapidly changing information technologies. Some institutions will prosper, some will be transformed, and some will disappear. This is happening to the venerable university. Economics professor Eli Noam has predicted a transformation or end of the modern university. Why? Because there is a "reversal in the historic direction of information flow. In the past, people came to the information, which was stored at the university. In the future, the information will come to the people, wherever they are."[48] This may be happening to both the library and the archives, providing additional problems for Nicholson Baker's warehouse imagery. Even distinctions between certain kinds of information sources, such as between the book and the homepage or between the record and the artifact, are blurring. As long as librarians and archivists keep in mind the contributions their principles and knowledge have for a range of Information Age concerns, such as classification and retrieval, there will be enhanced opportunities for them to have a vital role.

Nicholson Baker is highly suspicious and critical of the new Information Age emphases of librarians and other information professionals like archivists. In his public outcry about the discarding of books at the San Francisco Public Library, Baker made his case in a very pointed and sarcastic fashion:

From one point of view, destruction on such a scale makes perfect sense. To a manager who has no personal interest in old books, no conception of why anyone would want to spend his or her life reading and thinking about them—to a manager who believes in the pipeline model of information, and who expects databases and Internet access to replace large numbers of monographs in the library of the future, no easy first step to take, even before you buy a database or a CD-ROM jukebox, even before you have digitized one paragraph of text, or designed one Web page, or had lunch with one multiplexer salesman, is simply to reduce the number of old books you own.[49]

It is one thing to take on Ken Dowlin, then the head of the San Francisco Public Library and an unabashed library futurist, but it is quite another to understand how many of these new information technologies are demanded by library users or that we are merely seeing the same tensions in evidence when society made a transition from orality to literacy, from manuscript to print.[50] If it was the twelfth century, would Baker be reminiscing about the loss of oral tradition, or if the sixteenth century the loss of fine calligraphic script used in the production of books? Probably.

There are some hard issues to work on. Archivists and librarians, when they reflect on their own institutions and the transforming nature of information technology in our modern society, must not take it for granted that their institutions will always exist in their current form, as Baker assumes they must. As one recent sociological study of professionalism has suggested, the past three decades have supported a transformation of professions from public welfare to expert knowledge-based disciplines—a seeming fit with the modern Information Age that the Internet symbolizes; however, a persistent weakness of many of the modern professions has been the tendency to fail to understand their own social and historical context.[51] The Internet is a harbinger—warts and all (and there are many)—of a continuing change in expectations by society for information access that they as information professionals must be responsive to in their continuing work on practice and standards. While archivists and librarians might argue about whether they should be user-centered or materials-centered in their basic work, a more essential concern might be whether they are relevant in today's Information Age organization or environment. Even though there is a certain serendipity in collecting, analyzing, and using information by humanists and social scientists, this really requires archivists and librarians to design retrieval systems that mimic such behavior.[52] As information scientist Donald Case has suggested: "while we cannot easily re-order our archives and library collections, we may be able to *bridge* them through special services and tools for the scholar."[53]

There is little question that we are living in a transition period from paper and print to paperless and electronic-based information sources and records, although we also know that none of us alive now will likely see an entirely electronic Information Age (despite what the pundits and advertisers seem to suggest about the present). This is a crazy time. We also know that many of our traditional views about books and records, libraries and archives rest on complex assumptions about society, technology, information, and information use that are, in fact, quite prone to change, and these are prone to be challenged.[54] Then again, we know that many scholars and many forms of research require the maintenance of the artifact, requiring us to work with legacy systems whether we wish to or not.[55] Ivan Illich, writing from a historical perspective, identified a shift from the book and reading as a quest for wisdom and knowledge to the computer and net surfing as a search for information.[56] If the power of the personal computer has become such that we identify ourselves and our world by as far as we can move from the computer and still rely on it, just what is this going to do to traditional repositories of information, evidence, and knowledge represented by libraries and archives? In other words, librarians and archivists need to understand what one author has recently termed the "revenge of unintended consequences" of an acceptance of and blindness to technology,[57] but this is a very different perspective than the kind of harsh response Baker has given us in *Double Fold*.

NOTES

1. Ray Bradbury, *Fahrenheit 451* (New York: Ballantine Books, 1996 reprint; org. pub. 1950); Walter Miller, Jr., *A Canticle for Leibowitz* (New York: Bantam Books, 1997 reprint; org. pub. 1959); George Orwell, *1984* (New York: New American Library, 1983 reprint; org. pub. 1949); and Kurt Vonnegut, Jr., *Sirens of Titan* (New York: Delta, 1998 reprint; org. pub. 1959).

2. Nicholson Baker's book is *Double Fold: Libraries and the Assault on Paper* (New York: Random House, 2001).

3. *U & I* (New York: Vintage Books, 1995; org. pub. 1991). In this novel, labeled a true story, Nicholson Baker describes being obsessed with John Updike and Updike's literary fame although he admits to not having read most of his writings.

4. Review by Stephanie Zacharek in *Salon.com*, available at *http:// www.salon.com/books/review/2001/04/27/baker/index.html*.

5. The earlier article was published as "Discards," *New Yorker*, April 4, 1994, pp. 64–70, reprinted in his *The Size of Thoughts: Essays and Other Lumber* (New York: Vintage Books, 1997), pp. 125–174. It prompted me to coauthor an essay on one particular card catalog still in existence, published as Richard J. Cox, Jane Greenberg, and Cynthia Porter, "Access Denied: The Discarding of Library History," *American Libraries* 29 (April 1998): 57–61.

6. Ron Hansen, *A Stay Against Confusion: Essays on Faith and Fiction* (New York: HarperCollins, 2001), p. 31.

7. Hansen, *A Stay Against Confusion*, p. 33.

8. I discussed this in my "Accountability, Public Scholarship, and Library, Information, and Archival Science Educators," *Journal of Education for Library and Information Science* 41 (Spring 2000): 94–105. A particular example of this can be seen in the debate a few years ago about documentary editions and their funding. In a great debate about the priorities for documentary editing as established by the National Historical Publications and Records Commission, archivists lost the arguments because the documentary editors could muster support from well-known public figures like Arthur Schlesinger, Jr. who could publish articles in major news-

papers and other outlets and who had better access to political figures on Capitol Hill. For a description of this case, see my "Messrs. Washington, Jefferson, and Gates: Quarrelling about the Preservation of the Documentary Heritage of the United States," *First Monday* 2, no. 8 (August 1997), available at *http://firstmonday.org/issues/issue28/cox/*.

9. Nicholson Baker, *The Size of Thoughts* (New York: Vintage, 1997), p. 128.

10. Lionel Casson, *Libraries in the Ancient World* (New Haven, Conn.: Yale University Press, 2001), pp. 35, 36, 98, 100.

11. H. R. Woudhuysen, "Begging Other Questions," paper presented at the University of London conference, March 2001, available at *http://www.sas.ac.uk/Ies/RCHB/News%20Woudhuysen.htm*.

12. Baker gave a spirited discourse in 1996 on the deaccessioning of some two hundred thousand books by the San Francisco Public Library between 1989 and 1996, contending that this action was the result of poor planning for a new facility, the futuristic visions of its director, and the lack of regard for the value of books by the director; see Baker, "Weeds: A Talk at the Library," in James Brooks, Chris Carlsson, and Nancy J. Peters, eds., *Reclaiming San Francisco: History, Politics, Culture* (San Francisco: City Lights Books, 1998), pp. 35–50. However, it seems that the problems of the SFPL had at least as much to do with political issues, funding problems, diverse and often conflicting community interests, and other matters; see Norman Oder, "SFPL Faces a Host of Challenges: There's money for the branches but not the New Main, and the library must do more to build public confidence," *Library Journal*, June 1, 2001, p. 60.

13. See, for example, my "International Perspectives on the Image of Archivists and Archives: Coverage by *The New York Times*, 1992–93," *International Information & Library Review* 25 (1993): 195–231. The only times a librarian or an archivist was featured was when the individual was controversial for some reason.

14. Robert Darnton, "The Great Book Massacre," *New York Review of Books* 48 (April 26, 2001), p. 16.

15. It is not unprecedented to have a book like this be celebrated by such reviewers, only to have the specialists and experts later demonstrate that the reviews were too favorable. Robert William Fogel and Stanley L. Engerman's *Time on the Cross*, published in 1974, was hailed as a breakthrough cliometric analysis that would change our perspective on the nature of American slavery. Later, the work was deemed to have been built on faulty data and methods. See Norman R. Yetman, "The Rise and Fall of *Time on the Cross*," *Reviews in American History* 4: 2 (1976): 195–202. Perhaps this may be the fate awaiting *Double Fold*.

16. "History in peril from 'slash and burn' librarians," *Manchester Guardian*, 22 April 2001, available at *http://www.guardian.co.uk/Archive/Article/0,4273,4173746,00.html*, accessed July 10, 2001.

17. See the review by Mark Lambert, the Special Collections and Government Documents Librarian at South Texas College of Law Library in Houston, Texas, in the *H-Law*, June 2001, available at *http://h-net.msu.edu /cgi-bin / logbrowse.pl?trx+x&listŒ-Law&month 106&week†&msg‰2bOC3qO3tRcvD7of/3dsDCA &user=&pw....* James M. O'Toole, a history professor at Boston College and a former archivist and educator of archivists, also has a detailed and negative review of *Double Fold* coming out in the *American Archivist* at the time of my writing this book.

18. See, for example, Robert Darnton, *The Forbidden Best-Sellers of Pre-Revolutionary France* (New York: W. W. Norton and Co., 1995); *The Kiss of Lamourette: Reflections in Cultural History* (New York: W. W. Norton and Co., 1990); and Darnton and Daniel Roche, eds., *Revolution in Print: The Press in France, 1775–1800* (Berkeley: University of California Press, in collaboration with the New York Public Library, 1989). This is especially surprising given Robert Darnton's sensitivity to issues faced by archivists and librarians. In his "An Early Information Society," his Presidential Address to the American Historical Association published in the *American Historical Review* and available on the Web at *http://www.indiana.edu/ahr/darnton/texts/*, Darnton argues that "every age was an age of information, each in its own way, and that communications systems have always shaped events," trying to counterbalance the manner in which we look at computers and the modern variation of *the* Information Age. Darnton looks at France in the mid-eighteenth century, considering how news circulated via "oral, manuscript, and print" means. Darnton suggests that "we imagine the Old Regime as a simple, tranquil, media-free world-we-have-lost, a society with no telephones, no television, no e-mail, Internet, and all the rest. In fact, however, it was not a simple world at all. It was merely different. It had a dense communication network made up of media and genres that have been forgotten." Darnton also explains that we can sort out this world because it was a police state and police kept track of the communications networks and documented it all in its archives.

19. Darnton, "The Great Book Massacre," p. 19.

20. The report is entitled *The Evidence in Hand: The Report of the Task Force on the Artifact in Library Collections* and is available at *http://www.clir.org/*.

21. David Lowenthal, *The Past Is A Foreign Country* (New York: Cambridge University Press, 1985), p. 153.

22. George Tweney, "Collecting Rare Books: Ingenuity and Imagination," *Pacific Northwest Library Association Quarterly* 47 (Summer 1983): 24–34 (quotations, pp. 24–25).

23. Carl Sessions Stepp, "Disintegrating into Dust," *American Journalism Review*, April 2001, p. 61.

24. These reviews are at *http://www.amazon.com/exec/obidos/tg/stores/detail/-/books/0375504443/customer-reviews/qid 88469746/107–2479968–8679702* and they were viewed by the author on April 28, 2001.

25. J. B. Jackson, *The Necessity for Ruins and Other Topics* (Amherst: University of Massachusetts Press, 1980), p. 89.

26. Morris Berman, *The Twilight of American Culture* (New York: W. W. Norton and Co., 2000), pp. 59, 99. For the most spirited critique of this bias against knowledge and expertise, see William A. Henry, III, *In Defense of Elitism* (New York: Anchor Books/Doubleday, 1994).

27. Arthur Saltzman is an English professor at Missouri Southern State College and author of an analysis of Baker's writings, published as *Understanding Nicholson Baker* (Columbia: University of South Carolina Press, 1999); quotations are from pp. 1, 12, 13, 131, 143, 178, 181. In one novel, *The Mezzanine*, there is worry about the demise of the old-style vending machine. In another, *Vox*, telephone sex seems to be treated in much the same manner as modern critics Sven Birkerts and Roland Barthes discuss the pleasures of reading text. In *The Fermata*,

the protagonist can freeze time and motion and extract information from wallets, purses, and other sources.

28. Jeet Heer, "Remembrance of sex, books and memories past," *National Post*, May 12, 2001, available at *http://www.nationalpost.com/search/story.html?f/stories/20010512/561849.html&qs*, accessed July 10, 2001.

29. Alexandra Jacobs, "Enough! The Overexposure of Sex Is Ruining the Mood for Everybody," *New York Observer*, July 17, 2001, available at *http://www.observer.com/pages/story.asp?ID 937*, accessed July 18, 2001.

30. Think about all the views that are out there about books and libraries, records and archives. Paper is a bureaucratic nightmare; Arno Penzias, *Digital Harmony: Business, Technology and Life After Paperwork* (New York: Harper-Business, 1996). Reading has become a lost art in an age overemphasizing information; Sven Bierkerts, *The Gutenberg Elegies: The Fate of Reading in an Electronic Age* (Boston: Faber and Faber, 1995). Everything, books and newspapers included, will become digital; Nicholas Negroponte, *Being Digital* (New York: Alfred A. Knopf, 1995). We need someone, like librarians, to organize all the information that is increasing at unprecedented rates; Clifford Stoll, *Silicon Snake Oil: Second Thoughts on the Information Highway* (New York: Anchor Books, 1995). Information technologies are lessening the quality of writing and, hence, information; Michael Heim, *Electric Language: A Philosophical Study of Word Processing* (New Haven, Conn.: Yale University Press, 1987). The promises of computers for making us more efficient and better informed have never been fulfilled; Thomas K. Landauer, *The Trouble with Computers: Usefulness, Usability, and Productivity* (Cambridge: MIT Press, 1995). And so forth.

31. Redmond Kathleen Molz and Phyllis Dain, *Civic Space/Cyberspace: The American Public Library in the Information Age* (Cambridge: MIT Press, 1999), pp. 2–3, 11.

32. Baker, *Double Fold*, p. 94.

33. This comment is available at *http://slate.msn.com/code/BookClub/BookClub.asp?Sh/2001&idMessage 527&iBio 5*.

34. Baker, *Double Fold*, p. 257.

35. M. T. Clanchy, *From Memory to Written Record: England, 1066–1307* (Cambridge, Mass.: Harvard University Press, 1979), for a historical example.

36. Luciana Duranti, "Reliability and Authenticity: The Concepts and Their Implications," *Archivaria* 39 (Spring 1995): 5–10.

37. Kenneth Foote, "To Remember and Forget: Archives, Memory, and Culture," *American Archivist* 53 (Summer 1990): 378–392; Avra Michelson and Jeff Rothenberg, "Scholarly Communication and Information Technology: Exploring the Impact of Changes in the Research Process on Archives," *American Archivist* 55 (Spring 1992): 236–315; Cynthia J. Durance and Hugh Taylor, "Wisdom, Knowledge, Information and Data: Transformation and Convergence in Archives and Libraries of the Western World," *Alexandria* 4: 1 (1992): 37–61.

38. Martha S. Feldman, *Order Without Design: Information Production and Policy Making* (Stanford, Calif.: Stanford University Press, 1989).

39. Heather MacNeil, *Without Consent: The Ethics of Disclosing Personal Information in Public Archives* (Metuchen, N.J.: Scarecrow Press, 1992); Diane S. Nixon, "Providing Access to Controversial Public Records: The Case of the Robert

F. Kennedy Assassination Investigation Files," *Public Historian* 11 (Summer 1989): 29–44.

40. Clifford Lynch, "The Transformation of Scholarly Communication and the Role of the Library in the Age of Networked Information," *Serials Librarian* 23: 3–4 (1993): 5–20; Gordon B. Neavill, "Electronic Publishing, Libraries, and the Survival of Information," *Library Resources & Technical Services* 28 (January/ March 1984): 76–89; Phyllis Franklin, "Scholars, Librarians, and the Future of Primary Records," *College & Research Libraries* 54 (September 1993): 397–406.

41. Joan DelFattore, *What Johnny Shouldn't Read: Textbook Censorship in America* (New Haven, Conn.: Yale University Press, 1992).

42. Kent Greenawalt, *Fighting Words: Individuals, Communities, and Liberties of Speech* (Princeton, N.J.: Princeton University Press, 1995); Samuel Walker, *Hate Speech: The History of an American Controversy* (Lincoln: University of Nebraska Press, 1994); Herbert Schiller, *Information Inequality: The Deepening Social Crisis in America* (New York: Routledge, 1996).

43. Teresa Grose, "Reading the Bones: Information Content, Value, and Ownership Issues Raised by the Native American Graves Protection and Repatriation Act," *Journal of the American Society for Information Science* 47 (August 1996): 624–631.

44. Seth Shulman, "Looting the Library," *Technology Review* 104 (June 2001): 37.

45. Terry Cook, "Rites of Passage: The Archivist and the Information Age," *Archivaria* 31 (Winter 1990–1991): 176.

46. Paul Thompson, *The Voice of the Past: Oral History* (Oxford: Oxford University Press, 1978), p. 97.

47. Organizations seem to stumble over each other in order to grab onto the latest trend emanating from the high technology industry. The idea of data warehousing is but one recent example, and many organizations rush to use it, naively believing that it will replace the need for records management and archives approaches; see, for example, Piers Cain, "Data Warehouses as Producers of Archival Records," *Journal of the Society of Archivists* 16 (Autumn 1995): 167–171.

48. Eli M. Noam, "Electronics and the Dim Future of the University," *Bulletin of the American Society for Information Science* 22 (June/July 1996): 9.

49. Baker, "Weeds," p. 45.

50. Read, for example, Walter J. Ong, *Orality and Literacy: The Technologizing of the Word* (New York: Routledge, 1982; 1988 reprint); M. T. Clanchy, *From Memory to Written Record: England 1066–1307*, 2nd ed. (Cambridge, Mass.: Blackwell, 1993); Elizabeth L. Eisenstein, *The Printing Press as an Agent of Change: Communications and Cultural Transformations in Early-Modern Europe* (Cambridge, England: Cambridge University Press, 1979).

51. Steven Brint, *In An Age of Experts: The Changing Role of Professionals in Politics and Public Life* (Princeton, N.J.: Princeton University Press, 1994).

52. Donald Owen Case, "Collection and Organization of Written Information by Social Scientists and Humanists: A Review and Exploratory Study," *Journal of Information Science* 12 (1986): 97–104.

53. Donald Owen Case, "The Collection and Use of Information by Some American Historians: A Study of Motives and Methods," *Library Quarterly* 61: 1 (1991): 61–82.

54. Clifford A. Lynch, "The Transformation of Scholarly Communication and the Role of the Library in the Age of Networked Information," and, especially, Benton Foundation, *Buildings, Books, and Bytes: Libraries and Communities in the Digital Age* (Benton Foundation, 1996), adopting an unabashedly technocratic view of what libraries should be, available at *http://www.benton.org/Kellogg/buildings.html*. American archivists have long struggled with their interest in old records and the need to have an underlying theory and knowledge for the management of records. Setting aside for the moment the issue of whether these archivists can feel the same attachment to the newer electronic records, it is plain that for many there is an inherent romanticism at play in their work. This is not a new notion. William Hedges, in his study of the writings of Washington Irving, suggested that "Irving's picturesque feeling for ruins came close to being a concept, the one intellectual frame he had to put around his picture of the world. His sense of inevitable decay was to be his substitute for a theory of history or a philosophy"; William L. Hedges, *Washington Irving: An American Study, 1802–1832* (Baltimore: Johns Hopkins Press, 1965), p. 42. In the same vein, the American archivist's great interest in processing backlogs has come to be a substitute for any interest in the underlying knowledge supporting their work. For many, it seems that thinking of archivy as a discipline or a science is something that gets in the way of their being able to deal with their own romantic ruins.

55. Phyllis Franklin, "Scholars, Librarians, and the Future of Primary Records." The classic arguments about the need to preserve the original artifact comes from G. Thomas Tanselle; see, for example, his *Textual Criticism and Scholarly Editing* (Charlottesville: University Press of Virginia, 1991).

56. Ivan Illich, *In the Vineyard of the Text: A Commentary to Hugh's Didascadicon* (Chicago: University of Chicago Press, 1993).

57. Edward Tenner, *Why Things Bite Back: Technology and the Revenge of Unintended Consequences* (New York: Alfred A. Knopf, 1996).

Chapter Two

The Big Picture and Baker's World

Managing libraries and archives is difficult, with competing priorities and needs and too few funds to meet all the needs and to solve all the problems. They need funds, staffs, space for organizing and cataloging print and non-print sources as well as storage, facilities enabling access and ensuring security, and environmentally stable buildings. Nancy Boothe, in a posting to the Archives and Archivists listserv on April 16, 2001, reproducing the text of a letter she sent to the _New York Times Book Review,_ captured the dimension of this problem when she wondered if Mr. Baker's newspaper repository will include the services of a "staff of librarians who have cataloged all the newspapers, including item-by-item holdings, years published, and variant titles"; "a number of trained preservation folks, who do emergency—but long-lasting—repair on ailing wood-pulp paper so we researchers can handle and decipher the originals"; "a large, strong and literate crew of people who shelve the bound volumes or loose newspapers in boxes, as well as retrieve them for researchers (with a short turn-around time)"; and staff and equipment to make the appropriate copies when researchers need them. Good points.

Many probably hope that Mr. Baker holds onto his newspaper repository long enough so that he learns about the daily decisions and complicated choices that librarians and archivists have to make, but I heard rumors shortly after the book was published that he was negotiating the sale of his holdings to a major research library. What is missing from _Double Fold_ is any understanding of what libraries and archives do, how they work, the competing priorities they must wrestle with, and the resource issues they face. Or, there is little sense that there are differences between major research libraries and public libraries or between archives and historical manuscript repositories and other repositories of print and documentary resources. Or, even, that major research libraries have faced substantial challenges in keeping their programs afloat as they try to build and maintain their rare and specialized materials.[1] The notion of saving *originals*, as Baker argues, must be weighed against such matters. The irony is that these originals are in the care of *all* these kinds of repositories.

I do not want to denigrate the debate into merely a matter of I am a professional and Nicholson Baker is an amateur. Americans have loved to take shots at the notion of professionalism as being somehow elitist and antidemocratic (and there are tinges of this throughout the Baker tome— this sells books, too), and I do not want to raise this specter to cloud the issues being addressed in *Double Fold*. Yet, the essence of being an expert is in mastering a specialized body of knowledge and of using that knowledge for a public good.[2] While Nicholson Baker argues that there is a breach of trust between the public and librarians and archivists, the author of *Double Fold* makes his arguments without fully knowing what librarians and archivists do. I am not sure whether Baker really understands the distinctions between librarians and archivists. Baker notes that a "true archive must be able to tolerate years of relative inattention,"[3] neglecting to reflect on the fact that archives must be carefully monitored to ensure that mold, rodents, and other problems do not attack those precious paper documents or that archives are dealing with electronic record-keeping systems requiring intervention at the point of their creation and design and considerable monitoring and use thereafter. And, even more importantly, such a view fails in understanding that archives are repositories of evidence ensuring accountability and building and sustaining a societal memory; in other words, archives become places of "relative inattention" at the peril of a loss of the essence of what makes community, government, and nations.

In fairness to Baker, such views about archives have often been expressed. Information technologists, for example, tend to see archives as passive, purely custodial functions for obsolete information. Librarian Wayne Perryman, in ruminating on the challenges posed by information technology, suggested that "it seemed only a matter of time before libraries would become museums where books, journals, and other print formats would be venerated and preserved more for their archival or artifactual import, than for the knowledge, information, and data which they conveyed."[4] In another essay about changing employment possibilities for information professionals, the notion of the archival function was used thusly:

As more companies hire specialists to gather information from outside the firm, there is a fragmentation of the traditional functions carried out by special libraries, with the archival function staying in a room called the library and with database searching, committee work, and translation services being spun off of others.... The library itself is simply the archive for the larger information operation, and the librarian's job is viewed as being within the archival space.[5]

The more widely held notion of archives and history is that it is a "flea market, a jumble shop,"[6] where people can sort through archives as if they were their basements or attics, discovering all sorts of interesting and quaint stuff. Such views are derogatory and based on a fundamental misunderstanding of archives as old stuff or old and often unnecessary information.

Baker expresses little concern about such matters, perhaps because he has another cause or focus. This may not be an important point, because it is the public, reading *Double Fold*, which lumps all of us together. Rob Walker, reviewing the book for *The Standard*, states that the book "makes a surprisingly persuasive argument for the preservation of all kinds of old records."[7] For the public, newspapers are old records and old records must be what archivists are caring for behind their walls. In this sense, libraries and archives are like museums. Really? In yet another interview, Nicholson Baker, when asked about the role of the university research library, states:

The job of the research library is to keep the stuff that people read. And that's a very simple task, and it allows for any sort of revolution in publishing that might or might not happen. If next Tuesday everything was published electronically, the research library would have the job of keeping the stuff that people read, because people are always going to read. And it contains in it the corollary obligation to keep the stuff that people have read. We're always going to have shelves full of books because it would be monumentally expensive to scan those things.[8]

Notice, Mr. Baker believes this is a *simple* task. Yet, the increasing scholarship on reading notes how difficult it is to determine who has read what or even if something has been read at all.[9] If a research library only kept what people read, they would be very small places indeed since much of what sits on the shelves is rarely if at all consulted (at least on a regular basis). The shelves would be filled with multiple copies of popular novels, how-to manuals, "dummies" and "idiots" guides, self-help publications, and other similar currently popular materials that might not be popular or even consulted in the future because they are designed, like our computers and other electronic devices, to have short life spans. J. Peder Zane implies that Baker has missed the mark about libraries: "Baker's bogeyman, America's library system, is a straw man. Libraries are repositories, not promoters, of literature. They are keepers of the flame, but it is not their mission to make it burn more brightly for particular books or authors. It is publishers, critics, bookstores and engaged readers who decide whether a book lives in our minds or dies on our library shelves."[10] Just what is Baker going after in his book and his crusade?

This business about the preservation of books and reading has its humorous side as well. Nicholson Baker has tried to emphasize (repeatedly) that he is writing only about the most important research libraries. Many more research libraries, of all shapes and sizes, hold substantial research collections, as do public and other kinds of libraries. But who in the research or other libraries are reading books or needing access to books as artifacts? The combative social commentator Robert Hughes noted that "most American students don't read much anyway and quite a few, left to their own devices, would not read at all." A decade ago, Hughes concluded that the "majority of American households. . .did not buy one single book. . . . No American university can *assume* that its first-year students are literate in a more than technical sense."[11] While Nicholson Baker portrays American libraries and librarians betraying the public, a strong case could be made that the betrayal has occurred the other way around. While Baker perhaps confuses his own literary tastes and reading habits for the average American, I can honestly state that I have not confused my own research and needs for access to original printed and other sources with what the average citizen needs or demands. They represent different needs.

The one thing archivists or librarians cannot do is to simply label Baker as a crank and ignore him.[12] Librarians and archivists may be facing an opportunity to take their cases into the public forum in a way they have not had for years. Archivists and librarians can't afford to be dismissive or condescending of the paper prophet that has arisen in their midst. Baker already has his followers—all those people glued to the television every week watching *Antiques Road Show* or submitting their bids on e-Bay. (I plead guilty to both activities, although perhaps with less zealousness than others.) Baker himself appeals to the wisdom of the masses, believing "most people look at old books as things that are valuable and worth keeping in themselves. It's not just scholars and researchers. It's everybody. . . . You can see from *Antiques Roadshow* and architectural preservation movements and that sort of thing that we have really gotten over the idea that everything has to be torn down and new Brasilias have to be put up every ten years."[13] Again, we have some lack of analysis about what the collecting marketplace or the historic preservation movement represent. One is an irrational extension of investing and the collecting psyche, while the other is about social, economic, aesthetic, political, and even class concerns. Fortunately, both are about or involve conscious selection, not about saving everything. David Lowenthal, chronicler of the heritage movement, describes the craziness in trying to keep everything as more books are published, records accumulated, and e-mail threatens to overwhelm us. Lowenthal states: "Collecting is for many the *raison d'etre* of stewardship. We amass and hoard for pleasure, and then persuade ourselves it is good for us, for others, and for posterity." And Lowenthal notes: "In the end, the task . . . is hopeless. To collect and make available more than a tiny fraction of what is written and recorded about heritage is beyond any library's capacity."[14] When Baker backtracks and argues that he is not saying that *every* library has to save *everything*, he still misses the point about how big a task this is, about how massively coordinated this would have to be to work, and whether it really has any merit to begin with.

The irrational focus on the monetary value of *stuff*, something which Baker himself resorts to in *Double Fold*, is evident from a story by Joshua Wolf Shenk about a typewriter used by his grandfather and how we tend to assign monetary value to such items. Shenk describes the appraisal process on the *Antiques Roadshow* and the growth of eBay:

But the sugar in this oatmeal, the opium in this tea—the sweet and addictive quality of the *Antiques Roadshow*—is the transition from story to price. The segments begin with the particular, the idiosyncratic, and the obscure but within minutes yield to the impersonal, the immediate. Whatever tension and wonder have been evoked by the distance of those pioneers and immigrants collapse into a number, a precise point on the map of everything that is possible, a tag instructing how lost time, people, or feelings can be owned. The burdens of history float away, replaced by treasure chests.[15]

One feels a similar sensation in reading Nicholson Baker's description of the value of books and newspapers, where he glides from their scholarly use to marketplace values, hardly a logical transition, but certainly one recognizing that modern Americans develop identities with the objects they pursue and acquire. Historian Marilyn Halter, in a study on ethnicity and consumerism, writes: "Whereas at one time the relationship between human beings and material objects resulted in identities that were acquired with the possessions one inherited, in modern times, people most often construct their own identities and define others through the commodities they purchase."[16]

Baker also has some supporters from *within* the library and archives communities who believe that paper is the most stable medium by which to maintain documents and information or evidence found in these sources. R. Bruce Arnold, Chair of the ASTM Paper Aging Research Program, argues:

Many who think that words printed on paper are soon to become a thing of the past in this digital age may have a surprise coming. The evidence is that the current storage materials of the digital world may be likely to be even less permanent than alkaline paper. Digital technology is changing so fast that it rapidly becomes obsolete. This is true both for software and for hardware. To imagine recopying and reformatting huge numbers of electronic files in the Library of Congress and other such institutions every few years just to stay abreast of technology upgrade is hard to imagine. And it may be prohibitively costly to do. Institutions that have digitized microfilm images will be thankful that the film exists when the electronic versions become obsolete. Repositories will (and should) continue to microfilm deteriorating paper materials for preservation purposes. However, as many of my colleagues in the library, archive and museum communities tell me, it is paper that will remain the medium of choice well into the future when it comes to keeping the long-term record of civilizations.[17]

A brief article in the *LJ Academic Newswire* asked whether "administrators at the Library of Congress (LC), heavily criticized for discarding collections in Nicholson Baker's controversial" book were "attempting to mute a backlash from some of their own librarians." The publication revealed that it had a

copy of a letter written to Baker, penned by a group calling themselves "Library of Congress Librarians Who Support DOUBLE FOLD." The letter claims that "there are a number of librarians at the Library of Congress who support [Baker] wholeheartedly," and are therefore "in danger of losing our jobs." The librarians write that "the problems of storing books and newspapers are resolvable. The problems of politics and egos are another matter." The librarians go on to assert that managers at LC are not tolerant of dissent and that careers may be in jeopardy over disagreements in preservation policy.[18]

There is certainly some truth in this kind of argument, but this is very different, I believe, than the exaggerated case Nicholson Baker has built over the past few years. Reading his book reminds me when I asked a friend about the movie about Ike and Tina Turner that was released a few years ago. My friend reflected for a moment and summarized the movie this way: "Ike was very, very bad and Tina was very, very good." For Nicholson Baker, librarians, except for those who agree with him (and, sure, there are some),[19] are very, very bad, although libraries are very, very good. In the case of any letter from within any institution, we would need to consider just who these individuals are, the substance of their complaints, and what their motives might be. The library and archival communities have been ensconced happily in debates of all sorts for generations, and what Baker is alluding to here may only be a reflection of such differences of opinion.

While the charges of intolerance from dissent are serious, the fact that some librarians and archivists working at the Library of Congress agree with Baker is hardly extraordinary news. The internal debates within these disciplines and their institutions about matters such as preservation and appraisal have gone on for decades. What is extraordinary is that Baker might see such dissent as support for the rightness of *his* argument or that he would provide such lopsided evidence in his own book. That he does may reflect the fact that his *Double Fold* is not history or professional text but perhaps an example of what has been called the New Journalism (while not new anymore, it is certainly a mainstay of what sits on the front tables of the super bookstores or makes it on the bestseller lists). Such writing stresses writing style and quality without as much attention on the verifiable facts. So, we have nonfiction written like novels, with a focus on dialogue and the characters' thoughts.[20]

Not every member of the public or professional community harbors such negative views about institutions like the Library of Congress. Lawrence and Nancy Goldstone, in their third book of essays about the rare book trade, describes the Library of Congress in this way:

In many ways, a nation is known by what it chooses to protect. With all of the clamoring by so many vested interests for their share of public funds and by other interests for a reduction of the public funds for there to be a share of, it gave us a deep feeling of national pride to know that our country values this monument to humanity's constant drive for self-improvement enough to maintain the Library of Congress in all its splendor.[21]

Admittedly, this is pretty warm and fuzzy stuff, but the point here is that the Goldstones are book lovers and they possess this view of the Library of Congress. The bigger point is that Nicholson Baker's *Double Fold* and his other writings lack any balance, a characteristic of jeremiads one presumes.

The so-called Information Age has done weird things to us regarding how we perceive information and its value. Perhaps Nicholson Baker's *Double Fold* is merely a product of this strange time, when we seem to be straddled between print and digital information, between an interest in the tactile pleasures of artifacts and the convenient but sterile uses of information in unprecedented ways. On the one hand, technologists keep dreaming up ways to preserve *everything*. A project called OceanStore, as just one example, is trying to construct a "global information storage system woven into the Internet," by developing a technical process by which every computer hard drive will hold part of the vast information stores. The premise? Everything should be saved.[22] On the other hand, we have libraries and archives trying to make judicious selection decisions less they be overwhelmed by the volume of documentary sources. The premise? Not everything can be saved. But, it seems, suggesting that not everything can be saved opens up questions of why not and go against the expectations generated by this age of abundant information.

Some of this might be about the often exaggerated claims made by the digerati. As I flew to Boston in mid-May 2001 to debate Nicholson Baker, I read Mario Vargas Llosa's essay about the future of literature and the book in which he ruminated on a pronouncement by Bill Gates at a press conference that his "highest goal" is to "put an end to paper and then to books." Why? Books are "anachronistic objects," whereas "computers take up less space, and are more easily transportable." Books also are part of an ecological quagmire destroying forests, a "cataclysm that is a consequence of the paper industry." And, of course, Gates seems to rely only on the utilitarian, pragmatic use of information, prompting Llosa to state: "I cannot accept the idea that a non-functional or non-pragmatic act of reading, one that seeks neither information nor a useful and immediate communication, can integrate on a computer screen the dreams and the pleasures of words with the same sensation of intimacy, the same mental concentration and spiritual isolation, that may be achieved by the act of reading a book."[23] One does not need to agree or disagree with such an assessment, and there are many, to see that it is this kind of fear or displeasure that Baker's *Double Fold* appeals to and stirs up. However, this denies the fact that many became librarians or archivists harboring such attitudes but who develop, ultimately, a much broader view of their responsibilities or how they believe society views their mandate.

The Information Age also has thrown librarians (and archivists) into a spin about what they need to be doing. Examining the historic role of the university to promote scholarship and to preserve scholarship, classicist James J. O'Donnell has speculated: "Can we imagine a time in our universities when librarians are the well-paid principals and teachers their mere acolytes? I do not think we can or should rule out that possibility."[24] Can librarians do this and also preserve all those originals? Archivists work under a mission to identify, preserve, and make available for use records of continuing value, and this continuing value encompasses the maintenance of records for accountability, corporate or societal memory, and evidence, all to benefit and protect the citizenry. Can archivists *only* accomplish this by the preservation of originals?

Nicholson Baker defends his analysis in *Double Fold* as being restricted to research libraries (and he does mention a few repeatedly). For readers of the book this is not a very evident point, and it seems that *all* libraries and librarians are indicted by this exposé. But this may be irrelevant anyway, since the vast majority of librarians work in very different worlds than Baker seems to realize exist. Most librarians are serving constituencies who need information to make decisions and who need this information very quickly.[25] Baker would retort, I am sure, that he is writing about librarians serving scholars. But what scholars? Many researchers, in the sciences, need information quickly as well. And I doubt we could find many humanists who are not operating under deadlines or who do not care how fast they get their needed information.

Maybe Nicholson Baker is really worried about something else. And it is a concern that I can certainly have sympathy for as an author as well. Perhaps he is worried that in fifty or a hundred years his writings, his books won't be on the shelves of libraries or bookstores or in the memory banks of computers that might be supporting the roles of libraries and publishers.

Again, I remember in a conversation some time ago about the odd moments in Ray Kurzweil's book, *The Age of Spiritual Machines,* as he wistfully wrote about immortality being in reach via an injection of our consciousness into the hard drives of computers.[26] A colleague, swallowing his mouthful of food, calmly surmised that Kurzweil was beginning to think about his own mortality. Perhaps Nicholson Baker is worried that his writings will not outlast him very long, especially as he views libraries and archives being selective in what they preserve. Indeed, I know some librarians and archivists who are already testing the durability of *Double Fold's* construction and lamenting that Random House printed the book on acid-free paper.

Why can't librarians and archivists preserve all this stuff and keep it in its original forms? Well, it seems they should be able to do this, because librarians (and archivists) have been busy, very busy it seems. *Double Fold* focuses on what has been done in libraries and archives (although the emphasis is on libraries and their administration of books and newspapers), specifically the use of microfilming and the subsequent destruction of newspapers and books for their reformatting in order to preserve their content. Microfilm has been a poor choice, resulting in poor copies and leading to the massive destruction of books and newspapers. Baker's colorful language suggests that these libraries and other institutions have produced a "historical record compromised and disfigured," a "cleanout" of the libraries, and a "strip-mined history."[27] While digitization is only dealt with toward the end of the book, Baker clearly argues that digitization is more of the same and may present even greater problems because of the costs and technologies involved.[28]

Double Fold is not a mere critique of the preservation methods of librarians; instead, it looks for a conspiracy (and looks and looks). Perhaps Baker is sincere in his convictions or simply frustrated with all the hyperbole about the preservation mandate, or, maybe he knows that conspiracies sell better. Baker himself denies that he is concocting a conspiracy theory as he tells an interviewer that "it's not a conspiracy, because a conspiracy implies that all these guys are getting together and saying, 'we're going to do something sneaky.' I don't think so at all. I think they were just like-minded men who wanted libraries to move ahead quickly."[29] Baker constantly plays with the conspiracy notion. He states in another interview: "It's certainly not a conspiracy. There is a sort engine of counter reaction that's happening with the book of 'Baker is this conspiracy theorist.' But the word conspiracy never exists, I don't use it in the book. And it wasn't a conspiracy it was simply people who wanted libraries to change a certain way. And they were like-minded. And there was a certain tinge of dunce-dom in some of them."[30] But, without question, Baker employs the language of conspiracy, pointing fingers at the government, librarians, educators, and the federal government with sarcastic epithets and other inflammatory language. Pointing to the "heads of library schools and chief library administrators" as being people who "wanted to further the goals of the Cold War" or arguing that the Council on Library Resources had a "pronounced CIA flavor"[31] suggests a conspiracy—or, at least, plays on public sympathies to read into such connections a conspiracy.

Would a book critiquing library and archives preservation, minus a conspiracy theory, be featured on the pages of the leading newspapers and book review outlets? Probably not. Its fate would be to exist as an internal document, discussed and debated deep within the professional journals and conferences. Baker may have given librarians and archivists the opportunity and the motivation (indeed, the absolute necessity) to speak out in a much more public forum not merely as advocates for a particular position (Baker's main frustration may be with the intense marketing of a few dramatic, saleable points—a large portion of the print/paper heritage is on paper that becomes "brittle" and turns to "dust") but as explainers of complex and difficult responsibilities faced by librarians, archivists, and preservation administrators.

There are weaknesses in this book, and they may prove to weaken Baker's purpose. The most obvious weakness is Baker's invective against those he sees as responsible for the debacle he insists has happened. He repeatedly mentions the "incessant library propaganda" foisted on the public, policymakers, and funders, clearly arguing that they lied and, just as importantly, tried to conceal the evidence of their misdeeds.[32] Those who have been interested in public outreach in the library and archives communities have probably viewed preservation advocacy as a major, exemplary success. Baker argues that the architects of this preservation movement have been secretive, "like weapons procurers at the Department of Defense,"[33] and his constant references to the CIA, federal funding, and other like features of the preservation movement all seem rather benign or downright silly. What is missed, of course, is that the entire foundation of the information science field and computer industry was built in this era under similar circumstances. Are we participating in a conspiracy every time we use a computer to write an essay, send an electronic mail message, or look for information on the World Wide Web?[34] The Internet, shorthand for *inter*connected *net*works, which Baker obviously uses, had its origins around 1965 when the U.S. Department of Defense began to finance a limited network between some universities and military research laboratories. We have also seen the network transformed from a device for exchanging packets of information to supporting electronic mail (introduced in the early 1970s) to enabling the connection of commercial electronic mail carriers (starting in 1990) to supporting information sites such as the World Wide Web.[35]

Baker is not a Luddite, and he uses computers, as does his publisher—so I submit he is also part of a grand conspiracy hatched deep in those secret rooms in the Pentagon (and given that the original post–World War plans for that building was to turn it into a federal records center, I know that the tentacles of this conspiracy are long). If this sounds silly, so does the connecting of the use of microfilm in libraries and archives to a breach of public trust in libraries, archives, and the preservation community. Wrong decisions were probably made at times, and sloppy work done as well, but these problems may stem from all sorts of other reasons, ranging from poor funding, shortages of competently trained staff, and competing responsibilities. No one will argue that excuses should be made, but it does seem extreme to develop an explanation of what is going on in these research libraries as part of a process stretching from the Pentagon into library and information science schools.

More serious charges are leveled by Baker in *Double Fold*. Library administrators, according to Baker, have not been doing their jobs, participating in a "slow betrayal of an unknowing nation," and destroying whatever trust the public should have had in them.[36] Most importantly, Baker goes after the brittle books effort, berating both the notion of "brittle"—and the idea that books were going to turn into "dust"—and the "crisis" produced by the problem.[37] As Baker powerfully declares: "There has been no apocalypse of paper" as many seemed to predict, leading Baker to wonder what all the fuss was really about.[38] Baker may be too creative a writer for his own good when he tries to figure out how and why these decisions were being made. Perhaps his next book might be a diatribe against the entire advertising industry, because it seems that Baker is mostly upset that librarians have pushed a program that has been reasonably successful in reformatting newspapers, books, and other traditional print resources that seemed endangered and that he sees some evidence for being somewhat exaggerated. Ultimately, his anecdotal descriptions of books declared to be brittle a decade before that are found to still be in existence and, worse—that turn up with deaccession marks and command hefty prices as collectibles, really seem to miss the point that not all books are worth saving, that market prices (which are hardly rational) should play a minor role in the preservation efforts, and that libraries and archives have other priorities *and* limited funds. While the great collectors assembled collections that became major additions to research libraries and archives, much of what now passes for collecting is driven by a commodities approach with interests only in monetary values. As one commentator notes:

In this age of textual ubiquity, a bibliophilic culture has flourished. Collectors are happy to buy books without reading them, valuing them as commodities independent of their position within the intellectual culture. Other bibliomaniacs cannot resist the temptation of a bookstore for different reasons. Their obsessions bind them to printed matter not as a commodity, nor simply because of the information it contains, but because the book has the quality of captured memory. Between the covers lies a promise: the possession of a book will mystically extend the mind of the owner.[39]

How many people buy a rare book and *read* it? Probably as many that buy a rare wine and *drink* it! These are often investments and as such they are hardly evidence of some breach of faith in a covenant between librarians and the public or scholarly community.

There are various flavors in Baker's concoction. At times, one gets the sense of well-intentioned but misguided decision making operating within libraries. Baker mentions that these librarians were involved in "impetuously technophilic decisions" and often operated within a "full futuristic swing."[40] *What* libraries and *what* librarians? Yes, we know that they replaced card catalogs with online public access catalogs, but despite Nicholson Baker's pleas that civilization was ending with the loss of these printed, handwritten, and sometimes crude catalogs, most individuals seem pleased to have enhanced access to libraries across the world. These librarians bet too much on what microfilm would do for them and how well it would work.[41] More often, however, the librarians come across as evil or as dupes or just plain stupid. The source of the book's title, the test long used for determining how brittle a book's pages may be, is a good example of how Baker approaches his subject:

The fold test, as it has been institutionalized in research libraries, is often an instrument of deception, almost always of self-deception. . . . It takes no intelligence or experience to fold a corner, and yet the action radiates an air of judicious connoisseurship. Because it is so undiscriminatingly inclusive, and cheap, and quantifiable—because it can be tuned to tell administrators precisely what they want to hear—the fold test has become an easy way for libraries to free up shelves with a clear conscience.[42]

That Baker gets hot about such issues can be seen in his characterization of the double fold test as "utter horseshit and craziness."[43]

No one today will not acknowledge that mistakes were made with microfilming, especially in producing poor images, or even that some of the arguments for preservation decisions were overstated, but it is one thing to criticize and note problems and quite another to simply denounce all the intentions of what librarians and archivists were doing. At present, there are rigid technical standards in place for microfilming and preserving paper, and the existence of these standards may be the result of learning from earlier mistakes.[44] Both evidence of more recent microfilming standards and the impact of Baker's writings on the practical work of librarians and archivists are the various statements made by individual repositories in the wake of *Double Fold*. The National Library of Medicine (NLM) issued a statement that its microfilming program was "never conceived as a space saving measure" but was an effort "to create national preservation masters that will ensure access to the published medicine literature for researchers and libraries well into the future." The NLM uses the "highest technical standards. . . . Volumes that contain important illustrations are filmed on color or continuous tone film to enhance fidelity to the originals." The NLM works to build complete runs of serials, uses all sorts of safeguards to ensure excellent film, and works to ensure that all of its rare and endangered holdings are preserved in a suitable fashion."[45] If Nicholson Baker intended for his essays and books to help us continue to learn and make adjustments, its tone and message seem counterproductive. Librarians can hardly expect to embrace a plot line in which they are the villains.[46] I'm not sure what to think about archivists, since they are not even in the story.

What do librarians and archivists do? They select, provide access, organize and catalog, preserve, promote their services, and manage increasingly complicated and diverse operations. Librarians and archivists do this in the face of a lack of resources, lack of public understanding, rapidly changing technologies, societal debates and controversies, changing constituencies, internal professional debates, and new demands for services. The public may not fully understand what libraries and archives do, but they often expect services from them that stretch their resources. While Mr. Baker focuses his book on the single function of preservation, as if this is *all* libraries and archives are about, librarians and archivists have had to respond to rising expectations that everything will be readily available through digitization. Preservation and access are inexorably linked, so the focus of *Double Fold* on the maintenance of originals in cheap warehouse space is somewhat misplaced.

One of the most referenced ideas in the early reviews of Baker's book is the notion that all one needs is a large warehouse, like a Home Depot, to store everything (microfilmed, digitized, or just left alone). I shop at Home Depot, and it seems like a pretty simplistic notion. They are big but not big enough, they are not environmentally stable, they lack the amenities needed for staff and researchers, and they are trying to move a lot of goods out as fast as possible for a large profit. Libraries and archives are *not* warehouses, they are repositories for holding research and other collections that have been carefully evaluated for possessing some continuing documentary value. Librarians call it collection development and archivists term this function appraisal, but whatever it is called, the process suggests that we cannot save everything not just because there is too much (there is) but because only a portion possesses value sufficient for justifying the costs for maintaining the materials. The premise that newspapers will be kept in original form seems to resolve effectively that some newspapers require special care (because of intrinsic value—a concept Baker ridicules),[47] but *every* issue of *every* newspaper? Newspapers should be saved (in original format) when they have certain physical characteristics that cannot be captured well by reformatting, when they reflect breakthroughs in certain technological advances and changes, when there are landmark shifts in design, or when they represent certain unique social characteristics. The history of the modern newspaper is toward a rapidly disseminating news source mass-produced for expeditious use and resulting in a fairly ephemeral product, something Baker seems to be unwilling to address. He is also uninterested in the records of newspaper publishers, which are certainly equally important for understanding what these newspapers represent. This is why some library and archives administrators have tried to play with the idea of risk management in order to use their resources wisely and to ensure that the documentary sources most in need are in fact available.[48]

Double Fold takes one particular test and makes it the centerpiece of a grand conspiracy. Baker really believes that the entire preservation movement of the past couple of generations has been part of an effort merely to save shelf space—an argument he repeats at every available opportunity[49]—in which the "bones of the collection [in this instance, the one at the Library of Congress] were deformed in a deliberate squeeze."[50] This may be why Baker is so frustrated by the newspaper microfilming efforts, because once the papers were filmed it was not just the actual papers that were filmed that were destroyed but original runs of the papers in many other libraries and archives.[51] The newspaper microfilming has, according to Baker, "drained beauty and color and meaning from the landscape of the knowable."[52] And the emergence of the brittle books program was part of an effort to divert attention away from the obvious failures in microfilm.[53] Has every library tossed its original newspapers because of the availability of the microfilm? Was the brittle books program really a scheme hatched to compensate for other preservation failures? Has all of this really been part of a great effort to save shelf space? Librarians and archivists need to develop detailed responses to these (and other) charges because Baker makes it all sound so plausible and so bad. He even ignores the fact that many of these librarians and archivists are scholars in their own right, making judicious decisions in the face of difficult circumstances, and nearly all are experts building on the hardscrabble of experience. Mistakes may be made, but they are not being made as a result of some vast conspiracy, ignorance, or malfeasance.

NOTES

1. Read, for example, Kevin M. Guthrie, *The New-York Historical Society: Lessons from One Nonprofit's Long Struggle for Survival* (San Francisco: Jossey-Bass Publishers, 1996).

2. The two most influential books on my thinking about a profession and its responsibilities are William Sullivan, *Work & Integrity: The Crisis and Promise of*

Professionalism in America (New York: HarperBusiness, 1995) and Andrew Abbott, *The System of Professions: An Essay on the Division of Expert Labor* (Chicago: University of Chicago Press, 1988).

3. Baker, *Double Fold: Libraries and the Assault on Paper* (New York: Random House, 2001), p. 242.

4. Wayne R. Perryman, "The Changing Landscape of Information Access: The Impact of Technological Advances Upon the Acquisition, Ownership, and Dissemination of Informational Resources Within the Research Library Community," *Journal of Library Administration* 15: 1–2 (1991): 73.

5. Blaise Cronin, Michael Stiffler, and Dorothy Day, "The Emergent Market for Information Professionals: Educational Opportunities and Implications," *Library Trends* 42 (Fall 1993): 269.

6. Howard Mansfield, *In the Memory House* (Golden, Colo.: Fulcrum Publishing, 1993), p. 12.

7. This review is available from the April 9, 2001 issue at *http://www.thestandard.com/article/),1902,23469,00.html.*

8. Jeffrey R. Young, "Author Says Libraries Shouldn't Abandon Paper," *Chronicle of Higher Education*, May 10, 2001, available at *http://chronicle.com/free/2001/05/2001051003t.htm.*

9. For a discussion of the scholarship on reading, with direct implications for schools of library and information science, see Wayne A. Wiegand, "Out of Sight, Out of Mind: Why Don't We Have Any Schools of Library and Reading Studies?" *Journal for Education of Library and Information Science* 38 (Fall 1997): 314–326, and Janice Radway, "Beyond Mary Bailey and Old Maid Librarians: Reimagining Readers and Rethinking Reading," *Journal for Education of Library and Information Science* 35 (Fall 1994): 275–296.

10. J. Peder Zane, "Literary Life and Death," *NewsObserver*, April 29, 2001, at *http://newsobserver.com/standing/collections/zane/700000016709.html.*

11. Robert Hughes, *Culture of Complaint: The Fraying of America* (New York: Oxford University Press, 1993), p. 103.

12. Although the Archives and Archivists listserv is no clear barometer of the archival profession, it is possible to detect in the early reception of the book that this may be exactly what some archivists want to do. Posters to the list suggested that Baker lives in a "dream world," that he is a "shrill advocate," or, worse, that he is a "joke," and that he has "found a franchise—bashing libraries." Other posters suggested, more prudently, that the book will raise questions for us and that Baker raises *many* good questions. On the other hand, many useful comments were made that influenced my approach to this book. Individuals posting messages helping me were Tom Anderson, Thomas Berry, Kevin Bunker, Christine Crawford-Oppenheimer, Thomas Heard, Peter Kurilecz, Margaret Monroe, Alex Rankin, Thomas Robinson, Daniel Sokolow, Pat Timberlake, Daniel Traister, Harrison Wick, and Heather Willever-Farr.

13. "The Gutenberg Purge," *Atlantic Unbound*, May 10, 2001, available at *http://www.theatlantic.com/unbound/interviews/int2001-05-10.htm*, accessed May 15, 2001.

14. David Lowenthal, "Heritage and Its History: Menaces of the Much-Loved Past," Keynote address to the 1999 Research Libraries Group Annual Membership Meeting, available at *http://www.rlg.org/annmtg/lowenthal99.html.*

15. Joshua Wolf Shenk, "The Things We Carry: Seeking Appraisal at the *Antiques Roadshow*," *Harper's Magazine* 302 (June 2001): 46–56 (quotation, p. 47).

16. Marilyn Halter, *Shopping for Identity: The Marketing of Ethnicity* (New York: Schocken Books, 2000), p. 7.

17. R. Bruce Arnold, Chair of the ASTM Paper Aging Research Program, writes a response to Baker in this letter of July 27, 2000 to the *New Yorker*, available at *http://www.oclc.org/oclc/presres/pubpres/barnoldresponse.htm*.

18. Personal e-mail correspondence from James M. O'Toole to the author, May 18, 2001.

19. Some librarians even wrote positive reviews of the book; see Ralph Amelan, "Don't Microfilm Us!" *Jerusalem Times*, July 17, 2001, available at *http://www.jpost.com/Editions/2001/07/17/Books/Books.30590.html*, accessed on July 17, 2001.

20. Jack Fuller, *News Values: Ideas for An Information Age* (Chicago: University of Chicago Press, 1997), pp. 136–139.

21. Lawrence and Nancy Goldstone, *Warmly Inscribed: The New England Forger and Other Book Tales* (New York: Tomas Dunne Books, St. Martin's Press, 2001), p. 22.

22. Thomas E. Weber, "Berkeley Professor Has a Plan to Turn the Net into a Vast Hard Drive," *Wall Street Journal*, April 23, 2001.

23. Mario Vargas Llosa, "Why Literature? The Premature Obituary of the Book," *The New Republic*, 4504 (May 14, 2001): 33–34.

24. James J. O'Donnell, *Avatars of the Word: From Papyrus to Cyberspace* (Cambridge, Mass.: Harvard University Press, 1998), p. 90.

25. See, for example, Andy Moore, "Content, the Once and Future King: Enterprise Content Management Emerges as the Key Factor in Employee Empowerment," special supplement to *KMWorld*, May 2001, available at *http://www.kmworld.com/publications/whitepapers/ECM/moore.htm*, accessed June 13, 2001.

26. Ray Kurzweil, *The Age of Spiritual Machines: When Computers Exceed Human Intelligence* (New York: Viking, 1999).

27. Baker, *Double Fold*, pp. 15, 20, 136.

28. Baker, *Double Fold*, p. 249.

29. "The Gutenberg Purge."

30. "Nicholson Baker Talks with Robert Birnbaum," *Identity Theory*, available at *http://www.identitytheory.com/people/birnbaum12.html*, accessed June 19, 2001.

31. "The Gutenberg Purge."

32. Baker, *Double Fold*, pp. 5, 6, 18, 41, 68–69, 194, 196, 204.

33. Baker, *Double Fold*, pp. 122–123.

34. For a far more balanced view of the origins of computers, without resorting to conspiracies, see Paul N. Edwards, *The Closed World: Computers and the Politics of Discourse in Cold War America* (London: MIT Press, 1996).

35. For a good introduction to the history and nature of the Internet, see Ravi Kalakota and Andrew B. Whinston, *Frontiers of Electronic Commerce* (Reading, Mass.: Addison-Wesley Publishing Co., Inc., 1996), chapter three.

36. Baker, *Double Fold*, pp. 13, 32, 104.

37. Baker, *Double Fold*, p. 211.

38. Baker, *Double Fold*, p. 143.

39. Florian Brody, "The Medium Is the Memory," in Peter Lunenfeld, ed., *The Digital Dialetic: New Essays on New Media* (Cambridge: MIT Press, 2000).

40. Baker, *Double Fold*, pp. 83, 93.

41. Baker, *Double Fold*, pp. 14, 22.

42. Baker, *Double Fold*, p. 161.

43. Baker, *Double Fold*, p. 157.

44. See, for example, the description of standards for preserving newspapers as now used by the Library of Congress, available at *http://lcweb.loc.gov/preserv/care/newspap.html*.

45. "National Library of Medicine's Preservation Practices," at *http://www.nlm.nih.gov/psd/pcm/nlmprespract.html*, accessed April 23, 2001.

46. For a sense of the kind of response this can generate, see Barbara Quint, "Don't Burn Books! Burn Librarians!" *Searcher Magazine* 9 (June 2001), available at *http://www.infotoday.com/searcher/jun01/voice.htm*.

47. Baker, *Double Fold*, p. 224.

48. See, for example, Laura Price and Abby Smith, *Managing Cultural Assets from a Business Perspective* (Washington: Council on Library and Information Resources published in cooperation with the Library of Congress, March 2000), available at *http://www.clir.org*.

49. Baker, *Double Fold*, pp. 16, 26, 31, 35, 36, 67, 81, 82, 97, 100, 139, 181–182, 183, 233.

50. Baker, *Double Fold*, p. 140.

51. Baker, *Double Fold*, p. 255.

52. Baker, *Double Fold*, p. 259.

53. Baker, *Double Fold*, pp. 168, 171–172.

Chapter Three

Why Can't the Paper Keepers Keep All the Paper?

The fundamental weakness of Baker's argument may be his belief, more implicit than explicit, that _everything_ can and must be saved in its _original_ state. At times it seems that Mr. Baker communicates that he simply wants one copy of everything that has already been acquired by certain research libraries kept in its original pristine condition in these repositories, but I am not sure that there is fundamentally much difference in the scale he is considering from that of just saving everything (both seem impossible). How, for example, could such a vast coordination of delegating responsibility among thousands of libraries and archives for millions of books, newspapers, and other materials take place? Perhaps to the general public the notion of saving one of everything makes sense, but from my perspective this is not only not feasible because of the scale of the venture but flawed from an intellectual vantage since not everything was intended to have long-term value or actually possess such value.

As an archivist, this is my main concern with the book. Baker wants those newspapers in the original because the size of the typical newspaper is important and because microfilm projects usually do not capture all of the various editions many major urban dailies produced.[1] We need _every_ edition of _every_ newspaper? So says Baker, or at least in the book he suggests this while in interviews he says this is silly (evidence perhaps of a game Baker is playing with the public and librarians and archivists). In an interview with _Library Journal_, Baker says: "There's this idea that Nicholson Baker says we have to save every issue of every edition of every newspaper. Well, that's silly. I never say that."[2] What does Baker say? He writes: "Does microfilm successfully capture the text of the thing it locally replaces? No, often it doesn't, because big-city papers published five or ten or more editions (or 'replates') throughout a given day, and most libraries simply bound whichever ones they happened to be sent." Then, later in this chapter, Baker writes: "If collection managers in major research libraries replace their own imperfect, even badly broken original runs of a given daily paper with copies of a single filmed set that, though known to be incomplete, is 'considered complete' by indexers, and believed to be complete by trusting buyers, the replacement process necessarily leaves permanent, unfixable impairments in the documentary record."[3] Perhaps Baker does not explicitly say save every edition, but his argument certainly suggests that if this is not done then valuable information is being lost and librarians are being irresponsible.

Baker vents frustration that microfilm, at least in its heyday, was linked with destruction and with the "befuddling divergence" between conservation and preservation where one involves saving originals and the other their destruction.[4] Baker wants the paper saved because he believes that we need to study the physical history and durability of early wood-pulp paper.[5] Baker also wants the newspapers saved because of some of them having glorious color illustrations, and he concentrates on examples in the *New York World*. They are spectacular and beautiful examples, but they may be astounding exceptions to the nature of what newspapers looked like in the late nineteenth and early twentieth centuries. However, we know that the acceptance of the value of illustrations and later photographs was part of an evolutionary, and at times acrimonious, process. Barbie Zelizer's extraordinary study of Holocaust photography and its use in newspapers and news magazines reveals that the acceptance of the veracity of the photographs was tied up in changing journalistic standards and societal values. Debates about the use of the photographs revolved around debates within journalistic settings about textual versus visual information. In the case of the Holocaust, photographs were eventually relied upon because of a skeptical public's response to reports of horrific atrocities in the concentration camps.[6] But Baker brings no such analysis to his assessment of the newspapers. For him, the newspapers are neat objects, especially with their colorful illustrations, and deserve to be saved *only* for that reason. It is the flea-market approach to assessing documentation.

Archivists know, however, that saving every item is not possible—they can't even examine all the records that exist or that they believe exist (the proliferation of telecommunications has made the volume of records so great)—and the archivists and their allies have been developing selection schemes and strategies for years as a means to cope with such challenges. Even if we chose to treat original newspapers, there is still the matter of financial and other resources required that makes this less an option than what Nicholson Baker seems able to understand (perhaps because the book's message would have to become much more complex). From the Library of Congress guidelines on preserving newspapers, we have this statement:

Conservators have developed a range of treatments and techniques that stabilize and in some cases even strengthen paper made from ground wood pulp, but due to high costs the application of these techniques is normally restricted to very special items in a collection that has high intrinsic value. For libraries, archives, and historical societies that hope to allow continued use of larger collections, the most economical option is to preserve the intellectual content of the publications through reformatting.[7]

Perhaps this is merely another lie, but it seems more realistic than the idea, proposed by Mr. Baker, that simply placing these volumes into any warehouse space is all that is needed to be done. Making an argument that everything should be saved is a powerful one, and it is easier to make than trying to wrestle with who will have responsibility for selection and what criteria will be used.

More sensibly, Baker wonders why we can't have *both* the originals and copies[8]—and, of course, we can have the originals, microfilmed copies, and digitized versions on the World Wide Web, assuming librarians and archivists can find the resources to do such work. It is because of this perspective that the one true hero in *Double Fold* seems to be the bibliographer and print scholar G. Thomas Tanselle who knows that "all books are physical artifacts, without exception, just as all books are bowls of ideas."[9] So, save it *all*. Robert Darnton has reminded us, just as Tanselle and other print scholars have done, that "books are many things—objects of manufacture, works of art, articles of commercial exchange, and vehicles of ideas."[10] Other historians have weighed in and expressed their revulsion at the idea of destroying original documents, by which they include newspapers. Robert Tombs argues:

And there are two obvious reasons. One is the information that a photograph or an electronic copy cannot or might not give: the faint pencil annotations, the word skillfully scratched out and carefully rewritten, the folds in the paper, the paper and ink themselves. The other reason is the fundamental fact that one is the original, the authentic, the unique, the verifiable. No copy can be verified if the original has disappeared.

This begs the question of how many times historians must really use *original* newspapers in this way, and whether the use of the newspapers like this mandates what newspapers and how many must be kept in the original form or the impact of this on other documentary sources.[11] Tombs argues: "Newspapers are documents too: indeed, for historians of every period since the eighteenth century, they constitute surely the most important single archive. Why then treat them differently from other documents?"[12]

Why treat newspapers differently? Well, modern newspapers are moving to digital forms anyway. Jim McCue, an English journalist participating in the conference with Tombs, provided comments about the fact that newspaper publishers were adopting digital technologies in order to expedite access to their own files, forever changing the debate for newspapers of the future and demonstrating that decisions about newspaper publication are generally made in the interests of the publishers.[13] The transition to digital newspapers may also be spelling the phasing out of print newspapers, much like what happened to the LP and cassette with the arrival of the musical CD. This story appeared in the June 27, 2001 issue of *Business Wire*:

> "The Internet is fragmenting the news audience, stealing time and attention from other media, including newspapers," said John McIntyre, managing editor of *Content Intelligence*, which recently released results of a Web-based study of the role of newspapers in a digital media landscape (www.contentintelligence.com). "While newspaper subscribers haven't stopped subscribing in big numbers yet, they are spending less time reading the paper edition." According to the report, the population that uses newspapers most—ages 55 and older—say the Internet is a more important medium to them than newspapers by a margin of 52% to 37%. Further, nearly 60% of 1,400 respondents expect their overall Web usage to increase, but it will not necessarily be newspaper Web sites that capture that increase. Fewer than 25% of respondents expect their use of newspaper Web sites to increase. McIntyre said, "We found that significant numbers of those 55 and older are Web users, and their online experience affects their attitudes toward newspapers. Although they displayed the strongest newspaper readership habits of any group, they spend significantly more time each day getting information from the Internet than they spend reading the newspaper."[14]

Librarians and archivists will have to account for such shifts in the nature and use of modern newspapers, and these shifts may work against any issue of preserving *originals*, even eliminating the notion of *physical* originals. And, of course, newspapers are very different from other documents in terms of purpose and use, providing current, short-lived news rather than capturing transactions of activities (such as records) or disseminating research results or scholarship (such as printed books and journals).

Nicholson Baker has become very slippery in his notion about saving originals. In an interview we have the following exchange: "One of the 'heroes' of your book, G. Thomas Tanselle, quotes a 19th-century bibliographer, 'The most worthless book of a bygone day is a record worthy of preservation.' " Baker responds:

> Part of the reason a worthless book is worth retaining is that its worthlessness means something. If we get rid of all tabloids, all *National Enquirers* because we

think that stuff in there is garbage, then we don't know the context out of which another kind of reporting comes. But on the other hand, when you say that even the most worthless thing is worth preserving, then what the librarians who disagree with me say, "Psst, this flake Baker says we save every single scrap and he's so unrealistic." And of course we've got to make tough choices. I just don't think that I am saying that we have to keep every scrap. If you keep one copy of Joseph Pulitzer's great paper, you're keeping, not every scrap, you're keeping one millionth of every scrap because he published a million copies a day. And this was the thing in the city that everybody read.[15]

The problem? Baker simply refuses to make the *hard* decisions. Baker revels in the ordinary object, as is revealed in this interview when he states:

Yes, and in fact the obscurity of the thing is part of its beauty. The fact that it has lain untouched for all this time is part of what appeals to researchers about it. There's the place where you might find the discovery. Flipping through a volume of *The New York World*, I come to a early article about Norbert Wiener who was a cyberneticist. Here he is, a picture of him at age nine because he was a math prodigy. There's just something delightful about finding that in the context of all this muckraking.[16]

What Baker does not explain is why using the original newspapers or an idiosyncratic search method such as "flipping" through the original newspapers is crucial to this discovery. From an archival perspective, context is crucial to understanding information or evidence (in any form), but there is no reason why microfilmed or even digitized versions of newspapers or any documentary sources can't maintain context.[17]

Baker's arguments about newspapers also certainly suggest the need for us to keep originals of books, but it does not necessarily imply that we save *all* books or that we can scale this up to encompass something like newspapers. Not everything of value to some scholar far distant in the future (maybe) can be saved for posterity. Nor can everything be saved just because we imagine that someone might need it for some research. Librarians and archivists must make choices (hard as this might seem). It may be that some historians and other humanities scholars are the last true romantics when it comes to using original newspapers. Robert Schuchard, an English professor from Emory University, describes using original newspapers at the British Library as follows:

I love the Main Reading Room at Colindale, its sturdy wooden desks, the tops inlaid with blue leather, their well-crafted wooden racks: it is a high-windowed, inviting place for reading newspapers even on the greyest days. Its unique feel and atmosphere have been built up by two million readers turning folio pages for almost seventy years, and I always try to arrive early enough to claim one of the thirty-seven spacious places. With first orders in the wooden tray, I like to await delivery by observing other readers, some sitting and focused on a page, some standing and trawling, their faces giving their minds away: an intense scrutiny or a roving eye, the gradually smiling mouth, the sudden looking up, the exuberant body shifting and arm lifting that signal a private discovery made, a special piece of plankton in the sea of print found. Then you hear the unmistakable trolley coming down the lane, and at your place comes the welcome thunk, thunk, thunk, thunk of four heavy volumes. Hoisting the first onto the rack, and carefully finding an appropriate opening point, you're away on a reading spree at last. . . . For twenty years probably 95% of the papers I ordered were delivered as hard copies and returned without user's guilt. But as we came into the 1990s a creeping change had begun to take place. One day, after placing first orders, there came no trolley with my four familiar volumes but four white slips of paper, the dreaded transfers from that quiet, well-lit reading room to the dark, cacophonous dungeon of infernal microfilm projectors. I am not here to rehearse the well-known discomforts of reading microfilm: the awkward loading, the unnatural reading position, the eyestrain, the headaches, the cramped quarters, the focus problems, the broken or miswound film, the unclean gate glass and reading surfaces, the scrolling motor jumps and resultant dizziness, the poor maintenance, the repair delays, the noise of operation, the printer frustrations, not to mention the problems of the film itself: clipped filming, blurring, fading and other uneven and distracting production qualities. . . . No, I am not here *primarily* to say that this technology is an unworthy surrogate of the greater type and print technology that it purports to preserve and of the information record that it aims to transmit. I am here to say, in part, that microfilm technology, important as it is as a temporary medium of preservation, is ironically a disabler of scholarship: its severe restrictions on the reading process promote error and oversight, the primary enemies of scholarship. A great many of the discoveries that I have described in the reading of original newspapers would not have been made in a microfilm reading room.[18]

But this may be the plead of one generation of researchers. What about the next generations of researchers who may be more comfortable with microfilm, or who value the new kinds of research made possible by having quicker access to digital information?

What about the beauty of technology, and not just the kinds of technologies producing printed works on paper? The appeal to the aesthetics of the printed book or newspaper, a topic Baker grasps well in its appeal and to a certain extent scholarly importance, is a continuing matter of significance, but it does not represent the *entire* story. There is the matter of what David Gelernter calls "machine beauty." As Gelernter argues: "Many different sorts of beauty are part of this story, ranging from the austere elegance of powerful mathematics to the beautiful lines of a bridge or locomotive or a picture on a computer screen." Gelernter looks for and finds beauty in the software underlying computer work: "The geniuses of the computer field . . . are the people with the keenest aesthetic senses, the ones who are capable of creating beauty. Beauty is decisive at every level: the *most* important interfaces, the most important programming languages (the tools a person uses to build interfaces), the winning algorithms (the computing methods that underlie every piece of software) are the beautiful ones."[19] Who is to say, given that librarians and archivists have increasing responsibilities for electronic books, journals, records, and other sources, that these sources will not be more important or even considered just as or more beautiful than the printed sources Baker is concerned about? I am not arguing that we throw out one for the other, but I am certainly suggesting that librarians and archivists face complicated problems requiring hard decisions.

Nicholson Baker has stated repeatedly in interviews following the publication of *Double Fold* that he never intended to say that *everything* must be saved. It is important, however, to note that saving *everything* is the *logical* implication of what he has written and repeatedly discussed. On May 15, 2001, for example, Mr. Baker participated in a live discussion sponsored by the *Chronicle of Higher Education*. Early in the discussion he was asked who or what "should pay the considerable costs of maintaining everything in hard copy indefinitely?" Baker responded that he agreed that "not everything can be saved." He contended that "microfilming and digitization is wildly expensive compared to remote storage," arguing that "any digitization program should include as a budget item a small percentage of the total cost to go toward the safekeeping of the original item after it has been scanned." Then Nicholson Baker added, "And really big libraries, such as the Library of Congress, should *not be weeding their collections*. The national library's collection is part of its historical legacy, just as its buildings (one of which is on the National Register) are." So, he seems to be saying that only a few libraries should save *everything*. Later, in this discussion, however, he again argues that the costs of microfilming and digitizing newspapers are much higher than mere storage, adding "space costs money, of course, but poor libraries can do a very good job of keeping things if they have a will to." Later, in the same discussion, Nicholson Baker argues that the originals need to be kept because, among other things, "old things are interesting in part because they're old. Some people feel this and some people don't. We want the people who administer libraries to have this feeling, and some do." But what bubbles to the surface, here, is the *depth* of understanding by Nicholson Baker concerning libraries and archives. When asked about the differences between librarians and archivists, Baker responds that "archivists have a potentially limitless universe of things to collect, so they have to make all kinds of decisions at the outset to limit what flows in; librarians are confronted with the world of what is published, which is a more defined world."[20] Baker repeatedly avoids the matter of responsibility for making decisions about what should be saved, along with the issues of costs associated with storing all this stuff.

Yet, it is not a closed, confined world librarians or archivists work in, as is implied by the power or influence and the nature of the problems

Baker assigns to them. By necessity, because they are in the information and evidence business, archivists and librarians must make hard and informed decisions about what to acquire, how to make it accessible, and, yes, what not to acquire. Thomas H. Davenport and John C. Berk recently developed the idea that we are in an "attention economy," the challenge being how we deal with vast quantities of information confronting us in our jobs and homes. Davenport and Berk look back and note: "The Sunday *New York Times* contains more factual information in one edition than in all the written material available to a reader in the fifteenth century. In 1472, for example, the best university library in the world, at Queen's College in Cambridge, housed 199 books." But here is the clincher:

But now it's difficult to imagine how we could possibly devote enough attention to all the information in our society. Think about all the text in those 60,000 new books that spew out of U.S. presses every year, or the more than 300,000 books published worldwide. Think about the more than 18,000 magazines published in the United States alone—up almost 600 from the year before—with more than 225 billion pages of editorial content. There were more than 20 billion pages of magazine editorial content about food and nutrition alone! Consider the 1.6 trillion pieces of paper that circulate through U.S. offices each year. Try scanning the 400,000 scholarly journals published annually around the world. If you prefer lighter reading, peruse some of the 15 billion catalogs delivered to U.S. homes in 1999, or the 87.2 billion pieces of direct mail that reached U.S. mailboxes in 1998.[21]

This is the world librarians and records professionals work in. Now, along comes Baker who sees the work of librarians and archivists as largely running warehouses.

Archivists and librarians grapple with complexities. Assuming, for example, that these professionals must make selection choices (which they must), what does this entail? The business of *future* use, who will use *what* or *when* they will use it, is a chimera the writer Llosa, in reflecting on the printed book's future, muses over:

The social and political effects of a poem, a play, or a novel cannot be foreseen, because they are not collectively made or collectively experienced. They are created by individuals and they are read by individuals, who vary enormously in the conclusions that they draw from their writing and their reading. For this reason, it is difficult, or even impossible, to establish precise patterns. Moreover, the social consequences of a work of literature may have little to do with its aesthetic quality.[22]

What are libraries or archivists to do? Save everything ever printed or written, which seems deceptively easy. But, given the enormity of the documentary or informational universe, including both print and nonprint materials, archivists and librarians *must* be engaged in selection. Looking at the convincing arguments that scholars like Llosa make, how is this selection to be done?

Baker's hero, Tanselle, does make compelling arguments for why scholars need original objects, print and manuscript (I have read and used his writings for more than a decade myself), but the fact is that libraries and archives have many other competing priorities with limited resources. Besides, the fact that *some* scholarship requires original artifacts does not mean that it can be completely accommodated—that is, everything saved in its original state (just as monks needed to copy over manuscripts a millennium ago to preserve the text, modern-day librarians and archivists also must make decisions about reformatting).[23] What about other challenges, such as the digitally-born objects and records systems, and the other research and purposes served by records that extend far beyond the scholarship on books, printing, and other related matters? Government archives are saving records to ensure accountability. Corporate records management programs are administering record-keeping systems to ensure legal and regulatory compliance. The world, at least for libraries and archives, may be a bit more complex than Nicholson Baker knows or cares to consider. This gets us back to the point Robert Darnton made about the "prosecutorial" tone of *Double Fold*. Mr. Baker would be a good attorney. And, as a result, the library and archives community needs some good defense attorneys too (and, perhaps like O. J., we need a defense team to answer all the charges).

Archivists know that saving everything is simply impossible, yet this point of Baker's may be what has the most resonance with the public. Malcolm Jones, general editor of *Newsweek*, was willing to concede that Baker is a "zealot and a polemicist," *but* he continued: "He has one towering and inarguable fact on his side: when it comes to books and especially newspapers, nothing beats the original. Historians know this. Librarians, who are after all curators of physical objects, ought to. The real lunatics in this story are the bibliobureaucrats who've come close to destroying the nation's libraries in the name of saving them."[24] Mr. Baker wades in, pleading: "Leave the books alone, I say, leave them alone, leave alone."[25] And by the time you finish the book, you want the librarians and archivists to leave everything alone as well. But consider the weakness of this. Just letting everything accumulate, and leaving it there in its original form, assumes that libraries and archives do not make selections to begin with (Baker constantly focuses on the Library of Congress as serving as a repository for *all* printed, copyrighted books), that there are not accidents and catastrophes that weed out such natural accumulations, or that many (most) books and archives will not be used for decades or more (or, perhaps, not used at all). Even more critical, do researchers really want everything, every residue of past activity? No, unless there was some guaranteed means of having ready access to these documentary sources, quick means of navigating through the many layers of sources (and, while librarians and archivists can provide such access in improved means, there is still no such speedy search technologies for finding particular, desired documents in a comprehensive universe of all documents).

There are many problems with what we find in *Double Fold*. We cannot keep everything (and whether this is what Nicholson Baker is saying or not, it is what people are responding to), and the mere act of trying to do so weakens our ability to keep anything. Regardless of what some might argue, not every book, pamphlet, newspaper, or document is important enough to merit perpetual care. And librarians and archivists, even if they were *just* in the business of running warehouses, could not store everything or even a substantial portion of everything published or created. While Mr. Baker provides some simple cost estimates that deserve to be answered, the problem with his estimates is that he does not factor in all of the resources or kinds of resources that would be needed. Specialized staff, adequate storage facilities, reading rooms, equipment for copying, and other similar items and functions are not considered in the pages of *Double Fold*. Nicholson Baker's libraries are simpler places than they are or ever have been in the real world. *Double Fold* dotes on costs of microfilming, digitizing, and storing originals. Baker reads the professional literature of librarians, preservation administrators, and to a lesser degree, archivists, and reports back many of the doubts and concerns raised by librarians and preservation administrators and others about how to calculate or justify the costs of reformatting. What is missing, of course, is any sense on Baker's part of how preservation fits into all the *other* responsibilities and functions of libraries and archives, especially the comprehension that there are many demands pushing librarians and archivists that compete for financial, staff, and intellectual resources. It is imperative, I believe, that librarians and archivists respond to these monetary criticisms, but that they also do so in a way that indicates that preservation is expensive and that preservation that assumes the maintenance of all originals is expensive beyond our (or Baker's) wildest dreams.

In addition, *Double Fold*, what some are calling a history (perhaps because it has footnotes), describes many procedures, policies, and processes that date back many years and that have been corrected, updated, or replaced with better approaches. It is just as likely that what we have experienced over the past half century, both successes and failures, have prepared us for new approaches that might not have come into play if we had not stumbled about looking for and experimenting.[26] Preservation Technologies, for example, employing the Bookkeeper® process, deacidifies books and other paper materials without use of solvents or gasses and without necessitating the disassembly of the materials. Would we have gotten to such a technology if we had not experimented with other, even if cruder, approaches first? We can say the same for any kind of technology; think of automobiles, airplanes, trains, as just examples. In their earlier forms, all were primitive, fraught with problems, and, at times, dangerous. Or, let's get closer to libraries and archives, and consider the evolution of personal computers. Earlier computers, while promising great advances in mathematical calculations, statistical applications, and other uses, were often compromised by technical problems, poor software, and other basic problems that can look just as silly, if portrayed in the same way as Baker does early experimental uses of mass preservation/conservation techniques.[27]

Viewing *Double Fold* as some sort of history of library and archives preservation gives it a credibility that it does not deserve. Baker likes to draw on anecdotal evidence rather than looking at the substantial evidence accumulated through several generations of library and archival work. In my debate with Mr. Baker in May 2001, he, on several occasions, tried to say that he only "reported" what librarians and archivists told him. Other than the most obvious question, *what* librarians and archivists (not all operate with identical knowledge levels nor would Nicholson Baker necessarily be able to sort out such professional nuances), there is the matter of conflicting anecdotal evidence. I can chat with my colleagues in the faculty lounge about any particular topic, receive extremely conflicting opinions, and I certainly cannot then say I have done research. In a *Village Voice* article, Jessica Winter reported an interview with David Walls, Yale's assistant head of preservation, that contradicts Baker's worldview of libraries: "I don't see anything like what Baker describes. The paper continues to get more and more brittle until it can't even support its own weight. We have material in the stacks that is fragile that when the shelvers come in and scoot the books over, the movement simply crushes the paper and destroys it. If you pick up the edge of a page, it snaps off."[28] Do we simply issue a report full of such firsthand observation in order to provide a more balanced view of what Baker is discussing?

Nicholson Baker actually may possess a low view of libraries and archives, despite all his protestations to the contrary. While Baker boils everything down to low-cost, unattractive, functional warehouse buildings, art museums in the United States are announcing major new building plans by major architects with a focus on "architecture as spectacle," a "chance to create or commission great art." This trend reveals that "Museums realize that an engaged public expects not only new galleries but also grander lobbies and more lecture halls, libraries, cafes, and shops, all of which may help to further engage the public—including potential donors."[29] Imagine, instead, the Home Depot-like warehouse structures Nicholson Baker imagines for libraries and archives. Even if these structures are intended to be the overfill, offsite storage facilities (and Baker never clarifies this, as he is fixated with storage), there are still the problems associated with proper environmental and other quality storage features, the kind of matters that a Home Depot does not need to worry about.

For Baker, it is all much simpler. He agrees with the problems of predicting future use: "There's never a way to predict what will become interesting to a library user, and that's why research libraries have to be indiscriminate." For him, the Library of Congress should save a copy of *everything.* "Put it on the shelf," he urges. "It isn't that hard. If you've driven up and down I-95 you've seen warehouse after warehouse. America is fantastically talented at building warehouses, and it would only take a few of those hundreds of thousands of warehouses to hold all the things that libraries have mistakenly gotten rid of."[30] But, of course, libraries are *not* warehouses or vice versa. And, what's more, it is not just a *few* warehouses involved. While I don't want to guess or speculate about how many newspapers or printed books you could store in a Home Depot-like warehouse, I am reasonably sure that in relation to the quantity of titles and the actual physical volume of these objects that such warehouses would fill up quickly, perhaps holding no more than a year or two of all titles printed (remember, I am following Baker's admonition to save a copy of everything). And I have not even considered the matter of printed ephemera (brochures, pamphlets, junk mail, advertisements) or other items, such as maps, requiring special and usually oversize storage containers.

While one might easily interpret from *Double Fold* that librarians and archivists should proceed with caution, especially as future technologies might help resolve some of the challenges of preserving originals, the lesson not appreciated is the complexity of the responsibilities faced by librarians and archivists. It must also be recognized that librarians and archivists will make decisions about treating objects like newspapers based on changing technologies and what vendors and others are doing to provide access to such information sources. In early June 2001, the National Newspapers Association announced that it planned to "archive some 20,000 community newspapers dating back to the 1690s," by transferring the newspapers from microfiche to digital formats, with expectations "to market the online archives to historians, journalists, researchers, sports writers and students" and to public repositories.[31] Bell and Howell changed itself into ProQuest in early 2001, with plans to market its vast content: according to the company it has the "world's largest commercial archive of content, including 7,000 newspapers and 20,000 periodicals, and nearly 6 billion pages of information on microfilm." The consequences for newspapers are immense as the company builds its newspaper holdings by offering to digitize the newspapers (including advertisements and searchable databases), offering specialized products such as genealogical aids, and sustaining its proven microfilming of newspapers (noting that four thousand libraries alone acquired the *New York Times* in 2000 on microfilm).[32] How institutions will need to refocus their efforts to preserve selectively original newspapers will certainly be affected by services such as these (and they should be affected, since libraries and archives do not operate in a closed system).

Nicholson Baker and *Double Fold* needs and deserves responses that reexamine the scientific evidence for brittle paper, the history of microfilming and brittle book programs (both what they have accomplished and the failures), the responses of researchers and other users (especially considering the use of microfilmed newspapers and the uses of original papers), the economics of preservation (and libraries and archives in general), the need for and types of selection criteria for devoting extraordinary resources to preserving particular originals, the need for and effectiveness of preservation and conservation education, and numerous other such topics. Librarians and archivists need to respond carefully to the many levels of Baker's arguments, and his arguments are seemingly complex and comprehensive. Baker's arguments also appeal to the emotions. Our gut reactions are, yes, save all these artifacts. As I write these words I am surrounded by several thousand printed books, vintage photographs, a few antique office objects—so I know just how appealing such artifacts can be.

Throughout *Double Fold* Baker urges caution in what librarians and others do when they undertake preservation. In one encounter with a preservation administrator who argues that they needed to do something, Baker says that "when trying, does far more harm than not trying, don't try. Go slow. Keep what you have."[33] Perhaps it would not be a bad idea to call a moratorium on the major reformatting projects for a brief period so we can discuss these issues, do some study, and consider *all* the options. At the least, why not divert some of the millions of federal and foundation funding to study some of the kinds of questions Baker has raised? Or, perhaps Nicholson Baker can help us tap into the foundation funding sources that he needed to support his own newspaper archive? However, librarians and archivists ought not to retreat to positions, in light of the seeming public outcry caused by this book, that jeopardize their capacity to preserve books and archival materials. It is possible that the public attention will be short-lived.

And, yes, it is ironic that the criticisms Baker makes about the external government funding to support the insidious microfilming and brittle books projects does not direct attention to the responsibilities of newspaper and book publishers for creating generations of cheap, poorly manufactured, and ephemeral objects. Why target librarians and archivists who have been stuck with these objects rather than their manufacturers, especially since the former, because of their campaigns, have managed to get better products? Why target librarians and archivists when they are the ones trying now to work with the computer hardware and software manufacturers so that better, more durable e-books and digital records systems are available? Why target librarians and archivists who campaigned and managed to convince book publishers to use acid-free paper (such as is now used in the publication of books like *Double Fold*) and who had an influence on a paper manufacturing industry that not too many years ago hardly produced such archival paper?

In ruminating about such questions, it would be easy for librarians and archivists to lose their way. The scholarship on reading, for example, suggests that a "book becomes a different book every time we read it" and that, for this reason, readers have no "confidence" in library cataloging.[34] So, should librarians stop cataloging? Or, should librarians see cataloging as some insidious, wrongheaded approach to classifying information and texts that reveal peculiar preoccupations about gender, race, nationality, and so forth? Even though we can admit that library cataloging has had just such problems, I doubt anyone seriously would argue that cataloging should be abandoned. Revised, yes. Improved, yes again.

Study and careful analysis is what we need, not hyperbole nor unsubstantiated charges. Is it an exaggeration that brittle paper will literally turn books into dust? Of course. So what? Baker provides a lot of anecdotal evidence (mostly from his own personal experience and observation), some of it quite compelling, but we need to examine in analytical, if not scientific, fashion the extent of deterioration of paper. Hyperbole on both sides of the debate will not resolve this issue. While it appears that the proponents of reformatting books and newspapers may have overstated their case, it is also possible that Baker has overstated his (I certainly believe he has). Preserving original newspapers across the world does seem excessive, unless undertaken as a very selective exercise. Do some researchers complain about using microfilm? Yes. Do some researchers complain if they have to travel hundreds or thousands of miles to use original newspapers because they have not been microfilmed? Yes, again.

This business of saving an original of each newspaper is incredibly complex. Ronald Milne, director of the Research Support Libraries Programs in the United Kingdom, gives us a glimpse into the conundrum: "I think newspapers do have value as artifacts—it is self-evident that a reader of a microfilm does not experience a newspaper as a physical artifact in the same way as a reader who has direct access to the original. It is also true that no form of reproduction will be 100% satisfactory for all readers. So for those reasons as well as others, I believe we should keep at least one hard copy of a newspaper."[35] But where does one stop? Henry Woudhuysen has rightly pointed out in his article in the *TLS* that newspapers do not exist in single identical copies for each day. He asserts that "a paper which puts out three or four different issues a day, which may include different headlines, leaders and features, ought to be preserved in multiple editions or states." Woudhuysen continues:

I suspect the matter is even more complex, where the current technology allows different emphases in news reporting according to the part of the country in which the newspaper is being sold. The copy of the *Times* I buy in Edinburgh is, in effect, if not in name, a Scottish edition, with different emphases in news reporting from the copy I might buy in London. To the best of my knowledge, copies of different states of newspapers have never been preserved by research libraries. I'm afraid the idea is simply impractical and, furthermore, the nation cannot afford the luxury. It is also a bibliographical nightmare. We do have to adopt a pragmatic view in the management of newspaper collections.[36]

Such statements are overwhelmingly positive, because they suggest that every bit of information may be invaluable to someone, somewhere, at sometime, and because we have that appeal of the original object in full view. But counter to such perspectives, we have this comment by a preservation librarian:

Even today, many scholars tell us they prefer the ease and accessibility of microfilms to the use of the artifact. In a recent U.S. survey conducted by NINCH (National Initiative for a Networked Cultural Heritage), most academic respondents reported regular use of surrogates and a few reported that they never, or only rarely, used original material. An historian from UCLA tells me that newspaper surrogates have been essential to his work. He says that he "could not have written as well or as expeditiously without microfilms."[37]

Such an assessment ought to bring us back to earth, making us realize that we need to be selective and that we need to have an eye on practical usage, from academic scholars to journalists to local historians, genealogists, schoolchildren, and community activists.

We really do not know the actual impact of either microfilm or digitization on scholarship and the providing of information in general to genealogists, amateur historians, hobbyists, journalists, citizens groups, and the public. I have talked to archivists who tell me of patrons complaining about having to use original newspapers, so I (and others) can also compile such anecdotal evidence on the other side of the argument as well. That we do not know the nature of use is, of course, another criticism that could be weighed in support of Baker. It does seem that the marketing in support of brittle books and other such efforts preceded extensive fact gathering, although those that built the campaign were certainly well-intentioned and committed to rectifying or retarding the potential loss of our documentary heritage. Moreover, some people engaged in such projects as a means to study changing styles of usage as for any other reason. On the other hand, what is the evidence to suggest that microfilming complete runs of newspapers did in fact enhance scholarship and research more broadly defined? Will librarians and archivists compile, effectively, the evidence about the use of digital materials on the World Wide Web? In responding to Baker, archivists and librarians have to be more serious about studying what they do and communicating the nature of their work to researchers, funders, and policymakers.

A minor theme in Baker's book, although no less emotional or intense, is the role of education in the crisis he is describing. Baker muses over the fact that the book conservator, the one most likely to save the original artifact, must go through a "slow apprenticeship" while the preservation administrator, the one making those reformatting decisions, "needs but an extra year of library-science courses to earn the right to decide, or help decide, what to do with a stackful of artifacts about which he or she might know almost nothing."[38] At another point, Baker asserts that "there is a direct correlation between the spread of preservation administration as a career and the widening toll in old books."[39] Well, enough said, librarians and archivists need to rethink education, but archivists and librarians need to be doing (and they do) that as a regular activity *anyway*. Some of this is nothing more than the typical tension between education and practice that most professions debate, almost continuously.[40] The most interesting comment by Baker here is, of course, his concern about how librarians (and maybe archivists) are being educated to deal with the "stackful of artifacts." It is not just artifacts they are being prepared to work with, but documentary materials, evidence, and information sources. Again, this is a very different and more comprehensive viewpoint of what these professionals must be equipped to care for and manage.

Some of this is the general aversion toward professional education. Cognitive scientist Thomas Landauer, looking at Boolean search processes, for example, laments that its designers knew little about how individuals use language. He caustically remarks that this kind of problem has given rise to the "information specialist," an individual "who always knows less than you do about what you want."[41] On the other hand, Clifford Lynch's article on searching the Internet reveals that those who want to use the Internet and the World Wide Web need information scientists, archivists, and as many other experts as they can get to help. As Lynch contends, the "Internet . . . was not designed to support the organized publication and retrieval of information, as libraries are." However, he also notes that if the Net is to "continue to grow and thrive as a new means of communication, something very much like traditional library services will be needed to organize, access and preserve networked information."[42]

However, most librarians and archivists have operated on a different level regarding preservation, assuming the main problem was that there were too few trained preservation administrators out there in the first place (except, remember, Baker simply believes you can put these books and newspapers on shelves and forget about them). Of course, adopting Baker's argument that we should just leave the books in the stacks and not bother with them suggests eliminating the education that we already have in place. Becoming a conservator does require a long and tedious apprenticeship, but there are other implications Mr. Baker does not address. Even preserving originals brings changes, ranging from less obtrusive cleanings to more substantive rebindings, resizing, and other treatments to stabilize and make these documents usable for future generations. We persistently make compromises to preserve what we can of books and manuscripts for as long as we can, realizing that while we lose some of the information provided by the object in its original state that this is still better than a complete loss.[43]

Someone needs to be educated, us or Baker and, most certainly, the public and funders. I believe archivists and librarians have a major educational venture before them, but not merely in retraining new kinds of preservation administrators but in explaining to the public and policymakers the nature of library and archival preservation. They need to be able to educate their friends too, people like Mr. Baker who declare that they love libraries and archives. Again, James J. O'Donnell predicts that the "real roles of the professor in an information-rich world will be not to provide information but to advise, guide, and encourage students wading through the deep waters of the information flood. Professors in this environment will thrive as mentors, tutors, backseat drivers, and coaches."[44] Librarians and archivists also need such coaches and tutors in working with public figures who influence funding and other support for libraries and archives.

In order to do this, librarians and archivists must examine in detail all of the arguments Mr. Baker makes. While it is impossible to accomplish this in a modest volume such as this (a kind of preliminary response to Baker and his followers), I would like to take one example in a bit more detail—in this case, Nicholson Baker's arguments about newspapers. It is really in the discussion about newspapers that Baker's view of libraries and archives as a refuge for paper come to the forefront. Librarians and archivists could consider the newspapers as part of their context, such as how the costs and services devoted to them fit into *all* the costs and services supported by archives and libraries. Faced with the choice (and librarians and archivists encounter choices every day) of preserving an original newspaper and an original set of letters by a significant literary figure (perhaps those of Mr. Baker himself?), what decision would they make? In considering the case of newspapers (indeed, of *any* sources), librarians and archivists must still recognize that preservation, whether involving high-cost reformatting such as microfilming or digitizing or just storing the originals in repositories, is a form of appraisal (selection). Libraries and archives must have criteria by which they determine *what* newspapers will be preserved and this must be judged in the context of the universe of documentation (all print, organizational and government records, and personal papers) that newspapers are merely a part of.

In Baker's most recent article before the explosive arrival of his book, "Deadline: the author's desperate bid to save America's past," published in the July 24, 2000, *New Yorker* and weaved into *Double Fold*, he argues that a lie has been foisted upon the public about the care of newspapers, the insidious destruction of original newspapers, the resultant loss of trust

by the public in libraries and archives, and a set of wrong priorities leading
to the misguided microfilming and destruction of newspapers. The essay
had quick reactions throughout the library community. The British Library
suspended its sales of newspapers after the "public outcry" stemming from
Mr. Baker's article.[45] Baker created a "good old days" of newspaper preservation when he writes:

> If American libraries had been doing the job we trusted that they were doing over
> the past several decades, then the British Library's decision to auction off millions
> of pages of urban life, although it would mark a low point of cultural husbandry,
> would not be the sort of disastrous loss to future historians that it threatened to
> become when I found out about it. Fifty years ago, there were bound sets, even
> double sets, of all the major metropolitan dailies safely stored in libraries around
> the United States.[46]

Such rhetoric was bound to obtain media attention.[47] Archival and library
listservs lit up with reactions, ranging from highly defensive to highly critical. Newspapers and news magazines ran photographs of Mr. Baker in
protective mode with a stack of original bound newspapers, warding off
those vandals (the librarians and archivists). We have the image of David
versus Goliath, the outgunned good guy versus the bad guys, or of Martin
Luther nailing those theses on the door. In other words, we have all the
makings of a good story.

Baker declares that while we know that newsprint left in the sun "quickly
turns yellow and brittle," we also know that wood-pulp newspapers of fifty
and a hundred years ago are often surprisingly well preserved."[48] As a
result, Baker asks: "Why not find out what's happened to the newspapers?"[49] Here, Baker also injects the notion of a lie. He agrees that newsprint can become brittle and fragile "if it is stored, say, on the cement floor
of a library basement, near heating pipes, for a few decades. But there has
never been a long-term study that attempted to plot an actual loss-of-
strength curve for samples of naturally aging newsprint or, indeed, for samples of any paper."[50] In other words, America's repositories are being
irresponsible. Baker believes, however, that it was more than irresponsibil-
ity. Instead, he speculates that even after librarians learned that newsprint
was not deteriorating as fast as predicted, they remained wedded to microfilm because of other issues, such as space savings[51] (also a major theme of
the *Double Fold* book). One problem with his assessment is, of course, that
space *is* a problem and that space is not always as easily obtained as Mr.
Baker claims it can be. His speculation that librarians grabbed onto microfilm and the destruction of newspapers as a rationale for cleaning out their
stacks is no more than an extension of the dilemma that these professionals
face with limited resources and the press of many *other* responsibilities.

If American libraries and other repositories have been engaged in fabricating a lie, it is truly one of immense proportions (and certainly Nicholson Baker believes this *is* the case). For one thing, the Library of Congress started worrying about newspaper deterioration in the 1890s and commenced actively working on the solution via microfilming in the 1930s. Within three decades, the Library of Congress newspaper program was nearly exclusively one utilizing microfilm.[52] Moreover, other nations have looked to the United States as providing exemplary leadership in the preservation of newspapers' content. Helmuth Bergmann describes the situation in his own country of Austria where very few newspapers are microfilmed, loaning is problematic because of the bulk of the originals, and there is little bibliographic control over titles and runs so it is difficult to track down titles.[53] Baker's desperation to *save* America's newspaper heritage may seem a bit odd to others in foreign nations where less has been done to gain control of newspaper collections. If one only views the maintaining of original newspapers as the objective, then there is room for objection. However, such preservation must be put into the context of other priorities, bibliographic control, access, and other such matters faced by the repositories holding newspapers.

The pervasive use of microfilming newspapers does cause some consternation within the preservation community, leading to mixed opinions with some attesting to the scientific research on newsprint and others contending that at least some originals of these papers should be saved. Winston Tabb, at the Library of Congress, argues that Baker simply has it all wrong. He writes: "Unfortunately, the chemical 'vice' of certain formats, such as the acidic and impermanent newsprint on which most of the world's news is printed, limits what libraries can retain in original format." Tabb relates that "In asserting that newsprint will last indefinitely, Mr. Baker is overlooking several decades of scientific research that contradicts the linchpin of his argument. Library of Congress experts shared that information, as well as more recent unpublished scientific data, with Mr. Baker when he visited the Library in December 1998." Microfilm may have problems, but it is still the best solution, according to Tabb:

Microfilming, while not perfect, has proven to be an effective technology for rescuing brittle paper and for facilitating shared access to endangered research materials. Microfilm created in accordance with international standards has succeeded in preserving millions of newspaper pages that would otherwise have crumbled into uselessness. It has also enabled innumerable numbers of readers in distant locations to gain access to the content of newspapers that they otherwise could not have used.[54]

Other preservation experts hold different perspectives. Ellen McCrady, a longtime leader in preservation work, sides with Baker. She believes newsprint can be kept strong if stored in the proper environment, keeping it from "prolonged exposure to sunlight," "temperature elevations sustained above 60 deg.-70 deg. F," "high prolonged humidity combined with heat," and "heavy continued and careless reading or referral use of the publication." The problem, according to McCrady, comes from the problems with how the tests on newsprint have been done:

Our ideas of newsprint permanence come from accelerated aging tests using heat, and from direct observation of tattered clippings in scrapbooks and cookbooks. We have heard that deacidification can extend the life of newsprint almost as far as that of ordinary book paper. However, a report of research based on accelerated aging using light, not heat, was recently published in *Restaurator*. It found that the achilles' heel of newsprint was not heat, but light.

McCrady makes a similar emotional appeal as we find in Baker's article:

I don't think Mr. Tabb should be as disturbed about Nicholson Baker's comments or descriptions of the Library of Congress's actions as he is. Those newspapers are, after all, part of my heritage, and the heritage of others who don't like to see them disappear. In the past, I have watched, aghast, as the guillotine at the Library of Congress cut off the backs of bound newspaper volumes so that they could be microfilmed. . . . Since it is the Library of Congress's duty to preserve the American heritage, there should be some way for Americans to express our preferences to the Library of Congress without our being criticized for speaking up.[55]

Here we have an age-old problem about the tension between saving information that is inherent in the original format of any source, such as newspapers, and that the information may be completely lost if nothing is done or partially destroyed if actions such as microfilming are carried out. Even those that may worry about the deteriorating condition of newspapers have worried just as much about the quality of microfilm or the loss of *all* originals. Colin Webb, Director of the Preservation Services Branch in the National Library of Australia, believes Baker's article is worth some reflection. Webb has "often been dismayed to see the results of rapid deterioration, but just as often we've been surprised to see 100 year old issues that were just fine." Webb also worries about the unevenness of quality of microfilm and argues that his own institution is continuing to rely on microfilming while "raising the standard of filming, project design, specifications and project management." Webb muses that Baker's article "seems unfair at a number of points," but it "reminds us that as well as quality issues, even at its best microfilm can't be said to replicate all the values of the 'original.'" He suggests

[O]ur preservation profession has sometimes found it easier to enlist support by telling half-truths (probably nine-tenth truths). We did it with environmental conditions for storing collections, we probably did it with accelerated aging, and it looks like we might have done it with microfilming. We can see the same phenomenon with digitization, although the "digitization preservation" lobby is largely coming from outside the preservation profession.[56]

Donald Farren describes how he had some years before (in a 1989 conference) proposed that "national libraries should assume the responsibility (distributed countrywide as appropriate) to Conserve in Original Form at Least One Copy of Every Newspaper," lamenting that there was little support for the idea. "As Nicholson Baker's piece suggests," Farren chided, "time will tell, and public opinion will decide, which policy—elective (at least) conservation or mass microfilming—is the wisest."[57] It is true that at times compromises have to be made to preserve content apart from its artifactual carrier in order to save *something*.

This is, however, merely the beginning of the challenge when dealing with newspaper preservation, as the next chapter demonstrates.

NOTES

1. Baker, *Double Fold: Libraries and the Assault on Paper* (New York: Random House, 2001), pp. 24, 47.

2. Andrew Richard Albanese, "Double-Edged: Is Nicholson Baker a Friend of Libraries?" *Library Journal*, 126 (June 1, 2001): 104.

3. Baker, *Double Fold*, pp. 47, 52.

4. Baker, *Double Fold*, pp. 25, 107–108, 145.

5. Baker, *Double Fold*, p. 58.

6. Barbie Zelizer, *Remembering to Forget: Holocaust Memory Through the Camera's Eye* (Chicago: University of Chicago Press, 1998).

7. The document is at *http://lcweb.loc.gov/preserv/care/newspap.html*.

8. Baker, *Double Fold*, p. 67.

9. Baker, *Double Fold*, p. 224. Tanselle has written numerous articles about the immense value of the original document or book as the purveyor of information. Many of his most recent writings have been conveniently collected in his *Literature and Artifacts* (Charlottesville: Bibliographical Society of the University of Virginia, 1998).

10. Robert Darnton, *The Forbidden Best-Sellers of Pre-Revolutionary France* (New York: W. W. Norton and Co., 1995), p. 181.

11. Another historian at this conference, Peter Mandler, made just these points; see his "Scholars v. Library: Grounds for a Truce," paper presented at the University of London conference, March 2001, available at *http://www.sas.ac.uk/Ies/RCHB/News%20Mandler.htm*.

12. Robert Tombs, "The French Newspaper Collection at the British Library," paper presented at the University of London conference, March 2001, available at *http://www.sas.ac.uk/Ies/RCHB/News%20Tombs.htm*.

13. Jim McCue, "Newspapers and Archives," paper presented at the University of London conference, March 2001, available at *http://www.sas.ac.uk/Ies/RCHB/News%20McCue.htm*.

14. This article is from *http://news.excite.com/news/bw/010627/ma-content-intelligence*.

15. "Nicholson Baker Talks with Robert Birnbaum," *Identity Theory*, available at *http://www.identitytheory.com/people/birnbaum12.html*, accessed June 19, 2001.

16. Ibid.

17. I discuss context repeatedly in my own *Managing Records as Evidence and Information* (Westport, Conn: Quorum Books, 2001).

18. Robert Schuchard, "Why I Go to Colindale," paper presented at the University of London conference, March 2001, available at http://www.sas.ac.uk/Ies/RCHB/News%20Schuch.html.

19. David Gelernter, *Machine Beauty: Elegance and the Heart of Technology* (New York: Basic Books, 1998), pp. 4, 50.

20. "Technology and the Future of Academic Libraries: A Live Discussion with Nicholson Baker," available at *http://chronicle.com/colloquylive/2001/05/library/*.

21. Thomas H. Davenport and John C. Berk, "The Attention Economy," *Ubiquity* 2 (May 22–28, 2001), available at http://www.acm.org/ubiquity/book/tdavenport2.html.

22. Mario Vargas Llosa, "Why Literature? The Premature Obituary of the Book," *The New Republic*, 4504 (May 14, 2001): 34.

23. For a popular treatment of this, see Thomas Cahill, *How the Irish Saved Civilization: The Untold Story of Ireland's Heroic Role from the Fall of Rome to the Rise of Medieval Europe* (New York: Anchor Books, Doubleday, 1995).

24. Malcolm Jones, "Paper Tiger: Taking Librarians to Task," *Newsweek*, April 16, 2001, *http://www.msnbc.com/news/556235.asp*.

25. Baker, *Double Fold*, p. 135.

26. Information about this process can be found at *http://ptlp.com/book.htm*.

27. Read, for example, Thomas K. Landauer, *The Trouble with Computers: Usefulness, Usability, and Productivity* (Cambridge: MIT Press, 1995).

28. Jessica Winter, "Secrets from the Staxxx: New Haven Vice," April 11–17, 2001, available at *http://www.villagevoice.com/issues/0115/edwinter.shtml*, accessed May 5, 2001.

29. Ann Wilson Lloyd, "Architecture for Art's Sake," *Atlantic Monthly* 287 (June 2001): 85–88 (quotations, pp. 85, 86).

30. "The Gutenberg Purge," *Atlantic Unbound*, May 10, 2001, available at *http://www.theatlantic.com/unbound/interviews/int2001–05–10.htm*, accessed May 15, 2001.

31. "Breaking News," *Washington Business Journal*, June 11, 2001, available at *http://washington.bcentral.com/washington/stories/2001/06/11/daily7.html*, accessed June 16, 2001.

32. "Bell & Howell Becomes Proquest: Company to Expand Digital Archiving Effort," *E&P Online*, June 13, 2001, available at *http://www.mediainfo.com/ephome/news/newshtm/stories/061301n4.htm*, accessed June 19, 2001. See also Ross Kerber, "New Move to Put Century-Old Newspapers' Archives Online," *Boston Globe*, June 18, 2001, available at *http://www.boston.com/dailyglobe2/169/*

business/New move to put century old newspapers archives online+.shtml, accessed June 21, 2001.

33. Baker, *Double Fold*, p. 260.

34. Alberto Manguel, *Into the Looking-Glass Wood: Essays on Books, Reading, and the World* (New York: Harcourt, Inc., 1998), pp. 10, 27.

35. Ronald Milne, "Joint Solutions: The Research Support Libraries Programme, the Distributed National Collection, and the Importance of Cross-Sectoral Collaboration," paper presented at the University of London conference, March 2001, available at *http://www.sas.ac.uk/Ies/RCHB/News%20Milne.htm*.

36. H. R. Woudhuysen, "Vandals of Colindale," *Times Literary Supplement*, August 18, 2000, 14–15.

37. Karin Wittenborg, "A Librarian Looks at Preservation," paper presented at the University of London conference, March 2001, available at *http://www.sas.ac.uk/Ies/RCHB/News%20Wittenborg.htm*.

38. Baker, *Double Fold*, p. 108.

39. Baker, *Double Fold*, p. 212.

40. See, for example, Jack Fuller, *News Value: Ideas for an Information Age* (Chicago: University of Chicago Press, 1997), pp. 180–181, 183, critiquing the education of journalists that is eerily reminiscent of the kind of debate about education in the library and archives disciplines.

41. Landauer, *The Trouble with Computers*, p. 147.

42. Clifford Lynch, "Searching the Internet," *Scientific American* 276 (March 1997): 52. In the same issue, see the articles by Michael Lesk, "Going Digital," pp. 58–60, and Brewster Kahle, "Preserving the Internet," pp. 82–83.

43. For a personal and intriguing description of such issues generated by those doing book conservation, refer to Annie Tremmel Wilcox, *A Degree of Mastery: A Journey Through Book Arts Apprenticeship* (New York: Penguin Books, 1999).

44. James O'Donnell, *Avatars of the Word: From Papyrus to Cyberspace* (Cambridge: Harvard University Press, 1998), p. 156. O'Donnell also argues that "we teachers do not automatically deserve a future. We must earn it by the skill with which we disorient our students, energize them, and inculcate in them a taste for the hard discipline of seeing and thinking" (p. 123). This is precisely why Nicholson Baker's writings are so useful to me as an educator. They disabuse the students of their assumptions about why they are pursuing careers as librarians and archivists.

45. Nigel Reynolds, "Library to Halt Sale of Historic Journals," *Electronic Telegraph*, November 24, 2000; John Ezard, "British Library Halts Dumping of Newspapers," *Manchester Guardian*, November 24, 2000, available at *http://www.guardian.co.uk/Archive/Article/0,4273,4095735,00.html*, accessed July 10, 2001.

46. Nicholson Baker, "Deadline: The Author's Desperate Bid to Save America's Past," *New Yorker*, July 24, 20002, p. 45.

47. Although some questioned a policy that had the British Library saving American newspapers that Americans themselves were not interested in preserving, at least in their original state; see Brian MacArthur, "The Debt We Owe History," *The Times*, March 16, 2001, available at http://www.thetimes.co.uk/article/0,,66–99778,00.html, accessed July 10, 2001.

48. Baker, "Deadline," p. 45.

49. Baker, "Deadline," p. 44.

50. Baker, "Deadline," p. 48.

51. Baker, "Deadline," p. 47.

52. S. Branson Marley, Jr., "Newspapers and the Library of Congress," *Quarterly Journal of the Library of Congress* 30 (1975): 207–237 (see pp. 222–225, 232).

53. Helmuth Bergmann, "Newspaper Interlending: Back to Library Tourism?" *Resource Sharing & Information Networks* 12: 1 (1996): 55–58.

54. This is from a letter Tabb wrote to the *New Yorker*, posted on the Conservation *DistList* (*consdistlindy.stanford.edu*) on Saturday, October 14, 2000 (PDT).

55. Ellen McCrady is the president of Abbey Publications, Inc. in Austin, Texas. Her comments were posted on the Conservation *DistList* (*consdistlindy. stanford.edu*) on Monday, October 16, 2000 (PDT). Her reference is to Vladimir Bukovsky, "The Influence of Light on Ageing of Newsprint Paper," *Restaurator*, 21 (2000), pp. 55–76. See also Victor Bukovsky, "Is Deacidification a Stop to the Rescue of Historic Newspapers?" *Restaurator*, 20: 2 (1999), pp. 77–96 and "Yellowing of Newspaper After Deacidification with Methyl Magnesium Carbonate," *Restaurator*, 18: 1 (1997), pp. 25–38, studies suggesting that the durability of the individual newspapers largely depends on the initial quality of the paper.

56. Colin Webb, Conservation *DistList*, October 23, 2000 (PDT).

57. Donald Farren, Conservation *DistList*, October 23, 2000 (PDT).

Chapter Four

Newspaper Warehouses

A major focus of Nicholson Baker has been his appeal for the preservation of original newspapers, quite evident by the attractive full-color reproductions of stunning examples of some of these newspapers in his book. When I debated him in May 2001, after he gave a formal presentation on his position about libraries and preservation as depicted in *Double Fold*, the author devoted equal time to showing slides of the colorful *New York World* pages interspersed with black and white images of the same newspaper as captured by inadequate microfilm. It was an emotional and compelling description of the tragic loss of this part of our heritage. How could librarians do this to us, and even the audience of mostly librarians and archivists he was facing seemed to be shaking their heads in sad agreement.

While individuals are responding to Baker's arguments, obviously being moved by them, others have written before about newspaper preservation in a way that challenges Baker's interest in the preservation of *original* newspapers. Englishman David Stoker wrote in 1999 that microfilming activities are needed now

due to the urgency of the preservation problem, which necessitates some form of action now, before more titles are lost forever, and the inadequacies of existing OCR technology to cope with the rough and ready printing quality found in local newspapers. Newspapers were never intended by their producers to be a permanent means of storing textual information, and the recognition that they contain a mass of valuable information not available elsewhere, is only a comparatively recent phenomenon.[1]

This statement suggests something Baker does not consider, that the manner in which not only librarians and archivists but society as a whole have looked at newspapers has been transformed. The poor examples of microfilm produced of some of these newspapers used by Baker date from a half century ago, in an era when many may have doted far less attention on them as artifact than as a common source of information. More importantly, for such individuals as Stoker, then, there is a timing issue; if we do not move now, we will lose most or much of the newspapers, not just because of the paper quality but because the original newspapers are often stored in substandard environmental conditions (a recognition that the vast bulk of the newspapers are scattered about in moderate and small repositories in older facilities and with limited financial resources) and because these newspapers might be heavily used by researchers (and for some of the most fragile newspapers, "heavy" might constitute a few turns of the pages).

Nicholson Baker's second issue about newspaper microfilming is even more insidious, namely that the process of microfilming for preservation actually destroys the newspapers—an immense contradiction and one not openly discussed, according to this author (he uses the same argument in dealing with the reformatting of brittle books in *Double Fold* as well). Baker admits that there is "nothing intrinsically wrong with microfilming," except that right from the beginning, it has been "intimately linked" with the destruction of newspapers.[2] One of the reasons Baker's article and book elicits such emotional responses is his graphic descriptions of how the old newspapers are being disposed of. Baker recounts how many of the newspapers are being sold to dealers like Timothy Hughes Rare Newspapers where the papers are cut up and sold for their "eye-catching headline issues" or "issues containing primordial Coke ads or Thomas Nast illustrations, shrink-wrapped against white cardboard, at paper shows . . . or from his catalogue or his Web site."[3] With this issue, Baker reaches far to make his point. His assessment, that "not since the monk-harassments of sixteenth-century England has a government tolerated, indeed stimulated, the methodological eradication of so much primary source material," seems a bit outlandish but the image is indeed powerful.[4] Baker also seeks sympathy in his revelation that he is, at great personal expense, buying newspapers and storing the originals in order to save these newspapers, an activity that has generated as much attention as any other matter in the reviews of *Double Fold*.[5] A first response to Baker's personal sacrifice might be nothing more than how foolish this seems, until we remember that sometimes the origins of important documentary collections stem from the personal acquisitions of what many consider to be of no or secondary value.[6] Still, there is always a thin line between farsightedness in such collecting and basic, sometimes quirky, psychological needs fulfilled by such collecting.[7]

In discussing spending his life savings to establish a repository for original newspapers, perhaps the aspect most gaining public sympathy for Baker's perspective, Baker sarcastically notes: "Maybe someday a research library will want to take responsibility for these things, or maybe not—whatever happens, at least they aren't going to be cut up and sold as birthday presents."[8] This ignores that the kind of responsibility Baker expects such programs to assume must be evaluated against many other responsibilities, a matter that weakens Baker's longer discussion in *Double Fold*. It also ignores that the same basic instinct leading him to gather up these original newspapers is what drives individuals to buy these newspaper fragments as souvenirs, the same impulses that sometimes threaten rare book and antique map collections because of their illustrations.[9] Saving every original newspaper seems a bit excessive, especially since this limits their use to those who can come to the repository and ignores other problems such as how much these newspapers will cost to maintain given their prospective use. In a description of Baker's American Newspaper Repository, Peter Terzian notes: "To view one of the last collections of 20th-century newspapers in the country, you must come to this anonymous-looking red brick building in this unpretentious New Hampshire mill town."[10] And how many researchers are going to make this pilgrimage? There is also some speculation that Mr. Baker has carefully purchased just newspapers that are in good condition and that he is banking on the fact that use will be low.[11] The fact that Baker sought and secured funds from the MacArthur and Knight Foundations to support his repository is also ironic given his critical attitudes toward the use of grant funds by libraries and archives and his argument that these institutions should just secure additional space to store all originals.

Baker fails to understand that the issue of storing such papers and then making them available for use has long been a problem. The Library of Congress started acquiring newspapers from its beginning, and it began to acquire newspapers much more systematically in 1874. The problem of the massive volume associated with newspapers leads to a need to rethink their maintenance, and this issue has long been known, leading to reports more than a hundred years ago decrying the problems caused by the massive quantities of the newspapers and the challenges posed by the size and quality of the paper. The Librarian of Congress, in his 1875 report, wrote:

Though carefully preserved and promptly bound for preservation, there is no longer the possibility even of receiving half the issues of these representative journals, so important in our current history and politics; and the time will soon come when the legislator in search of a fact, a date, a political article, or a table of statistics known to be in a certain newspaper at a certain date, will find it only at the bottom of a lofty pile of journals, all of which must be displaced before it can be reached. Besides the issues of the daily press, the periodicals which are taken under the copyright law or by subscription, embracing most of the monthly and quarterly magazines and reviews, accumulate with such rapidity that no device yet invented will long avail to produce them when wanted.[12]

A quarter of a century later, in the 1901 report, things were still bleak at the Library in terms of its newspaper collections:

When the collection was moved into the new building these files were only in part bound, or in condition to be placed on the shelves or even assorted. The newspapers, piled upon the floor filled aisles and alcoves of seven of the nine decks of the south stack. The unbound mass, which could be estimated only by tons, occupied three large rooms. . . . It was also piled upon the floors 6 feet deep, with but narrow aisles along the walls. It was the accumulation of nearly half a century. In fact it had been tied in bundles, but the strings had broken in handling.[13]

These problems can be found in other smaller repositories, local historical societies, and public libraries, for example, but posing just as daunting challenges to these institutions because of the volume, condition, and other aspects of newspapers.

The sheer size of all of the newspapers ever printed makes for a staggering image of what would be required in maintaining and servicing original newspaper issues. David Stoker's contention, that newspapers were viewed as ephemeral by their creators and most of their readers, seems lost in such an argument, unless we assume that all those old newspapers held onto as keepsakes is anything more meaningful than normal human nature's impulse to collect stuff. Saving everything in original form seems almost the old antiquarian sensibility (delighting in the often deteriorated look and feel of the artifact) rather than a result of a more informed opinion that careful selection and employment of technologies can work together to save a representative sample of the original newspapers while making the content of most of the newspapers more accessible to researchers. The massive microfilming efforts of the past half century now make it possible for a researcher to compare newspaper accounts from multiple newspapers around the country and make reasonable copies without having to handle oversized volumes on photocopiers or by paying for expensive photographs of the desired pages.[14] We know, for instance, that "From the beginning, the Librarian [of Congress] and staff recognized that the institution could not house more than a sampling of American newspapers and that the collection must be guided by general research requirements."[15] I have been told, for example, that if the Library of Congress bound all of its current newspapers, that this institution would accumulate more than fifty thousand volumes each year.[16]

One of the early reviewers of Baker's book brought up the problem with selection versus saving everything, although with no resolution. Jay Tolson ended his review with this:

> But how feasible is it for libraries to save every original source when, says Mark Sweeney, head of his institution's newspaper division, the Library of Congress gets 1,000 newspapers a day? G. Thomas Tanselle, vice president of the John Simon Guggenheim Memorial Foundation, insists that it is the only "intellectually responsible" policy, since no one knows what will be important in the future. Destroy the object, he says, and you lose, among other things, a sense of how people read and reacted to the information in the past.[17]

There are so many problems with such views that they threaten to stranglehold our ability to manage the documentary heritage. Do we need every object to develop a "sense" of how people read? Does possessing the object enable us to understand how people actually "reacted" to information in the past? If we believe this, does this mean that we must save every local television newscast, every vacation postcard, every letter ever written, or even every piece of junk mail sent to our homes? And, what are the implications for electronic mail and the World Wide Web?

Nicholson Baker's focus on even keeping one copy of each newspaper ever published begs the question about who will maintain what would be a huge quantity of newspapers, as well as stretches the imagination about what the variety of newspapers would entail. Baker is fixated by a few major and historically important dailies, but the universe of newspapers includes thousands of local newspapers, many with interest to that locality but hardly needing to be maintained in the original. When I was in Boston for the Baker debate I read the new issue of the weekly *Milton Times*, a local newspaper possessing no color advertisements, featuring a lead story about the results of the fishing tournament, and carrying news of activities of the town of potential interest only to the town's residents. The newspaper suggested nothing about its design, content, or any other aspect that cries out for some repository to maintain a run of original newspapers. The author of *Double Fold* provides little guidance about such matters as these, precisely the kinds of issues faced on a regular basis by archivists and librarians.

That Nicholson Baker easily loses his perspective can be seen in his argument that every edition of every newspaper should be saved. At my debate with Mr. Baker in May 2001, he denied that this is what he meant as he has in subsequent interviews with the media. But it is clearly stated in his book, and others have picked up on it. Barbara Quint, in her strong response to *Double Fold*, writes:

> In one chapter, not satisfied with indicting libraries for having switched to microfilm instead of keeping decade upon decade upon century of daily newspapers, he ex-

pands his demands into the need to keep every edition of every daily. That's right—the morning edition, the evening edition, the "valley" edition, the "mountain" edition. Mr. Baker apparently does not believe in the concept of "issue of record," which even newspaper publishers have traditionally aspired to. Actually, however, this is a problem that time and technology have solved, at least for future issues. Most newspaper publishers now consider electronic databases the "issue of record." For example, if you search *The Los Angeles Times* database on any of its many outlets, you will get all the original content which the *Times* owns, regardless of the edition in which it was published. This gift of full available archive exists—and, practically speaking, can only exist—in the "bottomless newshole" of electronic database environments. Of course, we do lose layout and ads and.... [18]

These are all good criticisms of what Baker is suggesting, and they move us back to the difference between understanding what newspapers represent as a documentary source and an emotional appeal to them as an artifact.

Much of Baker's essay on newspapers and *Double Fold* also turns on a third theme, a loss of trust by the public in what libraries, archives, and other repositories are doing with resources like newspaper collections. This loss of trust may be more due to public misunderstanding about the responsibilities of libraries and archives than the malfeasance suggested by Nicholson Baker. The decision to use microfilm is again presented almost as if it is part of a vast coordinated conspiracy. In the face of a great quantity of poor microfilm, "All the major American newspaper repositories have long since bet the farm on film and given away, sold, or thrown out most of their original volumes published after 1880 or so."[19] No one will argue that mistakes have been made or that problems have occurred, but this is true for *every* aspect of library or archival work—not part of a conspiracy.[20] Some of this assumes that all of the newspaper collections are tucked securely away in repositories like libraries and archives, but we know that newspapers are still being turned up in barns, attics, flea markets, and other places where they were not accessible and subjected to even poorer care than the kind Mr. Baker describes in his essay and *Double Fold.* Is his warehouse in New Hampshire being outfitted with the latest technologies to ensure stable environmental conditions necessary for storing paper? Certainly it is not given the modest sums of money he generally mentions related to this operation.

There was, of course, *no* grand era for managing and preserving newspapers. The durable bound sets Baker refers to may have been in pristine shape because they were infrequently used and, of course, such newspapers—the "major metropolitan dailies"—represented only a small portion of the many thousands of titles published in every region of the nation. Anecdotal evidence, the kind Mr. Baker most frequently presents in his writings, also suggests that many newspapers had few uses or even one use left before they would be damaged and become unusable for subsequent researchers—suggesting the need for microfilming as a best or desperate approach to at least saving the newspaper's content. But it is not just the microfilming of the papers or even the quality of paper they are printed on that is to blame for the matter of the use of the newspapers. The publishers of the newspapers saw their ventures as being extremely time-bound, possessing value to them and society for periods of time measured in days and even hours. This is why their accuracy is often questionable, and why, as historical documents, newspapers must be used with caution. English librarian David Stoker writes:

newspapers ... provide a unique and readily accessible glimpse of the unfolding nature of events. They indicate that state of knowledge or of public opinion at a given time, that no amount of subsequent analysis and more considered reflection can provide. Newspapers are not merely historical sources for academics, but have an equally important role in education and for all that are interested in the past. Of course any reasonably sophisticated reader knows that all newspapers are at times inaccurate or else select, interpret, and at times distort the events they report. Indeed some newspapers even today will print what amounts to little more than barefaced lies. They must therefore be used with care—yet this must apply to any historical source.[21]

Another librarian interested in the preservation of newspapers adds:

By studying a community's newspaper over an extended period, one has a better chance of bringing that world back to life. For those of us trying to trace our ancestors, we have the opportunity to discover not only that they bought a particular piece of property, but we also have a chance to see what they might have built on that property, how their house might have been furnished, what they wore, what ailments they were subject to, and how they and their neighbors felt about the events occurring around them. The social scientists might find clues to a community's attitude toward suicide by noting its appearance in, and then sudden disappearance from, death notices. The economist will show how the ban on DDT in Mississippi altered local commerce from cotton-growing to catfish farming. The fashion designer will study ads and illustrations for new ideas. Finally, the careful researcher will be able to confirm that the Alliance Aviators humiliated the Massillon Tigers by a score of 46–0 in the fall of 1962 in Ohio, in the rain.[22]

What do such statements suggest other than the fact that librarians and archivists must balance how they use their resources in preserving a range of documentary sources, of which newspapers are only part and not always the best or most important source. Pulling any single document out of its broader documentary universe and asking the public to react to it distorts the preservation decision making that is involved because it transforms the document into a museum piece or collectible, qualities that actually may be of less consequence than its information.

Commentators on newspapers often write of not facts but claims as reported in these sources, and they reflect on the newspaper's general inco-
herence as it rushes to get daily news out. Carlin Romano argues:
"Newspaper facts tend to be unchallenged claims rather than unchalleng-
able ones." James Carey suggests: "Journalists present to the world not a
mirror image of truth but a coherent narrative of the world that serves
particular purposes. . . . As a rule, the newspaper presents a disconnected
and often incoherent narrative." And James Allen Paulos, in a biting analysis of the use of numbers in newspapers, comments: "Whether in television
(where it's more extreme) or in newspapers, the obvious weakness of news
stories' inverted-pyramid structure is that encapsulation necessarily tends
to obscure complexity."[23] In other words, newspapers, like most information sources, are useful *if* carefully scrutinized by the researchers. They can
be flawed, misleading, incomplete, biased, and of lesser value than other
documentary sources, a critical sense Nicholson Baker ignores as he builds
a case for their preservation as glorious historical artifacts.

We must be careful not to paint a picture of historical evidence that
suggests that newspapers are the keystones of such documentation. There
are problems with the accuracy of the information found in any newspaper,
compounding whatever challenges may come from using microfilm. English
sociologist John Scott notes that "there is a common presumption that
newspapers are not subject to a high level of distortion or falsification. . . .
Undoubtedly the major source of insincerity in newspaper and television
reporting is the influence of owners and controllers acting on the basis of
the perceived political or financial interests of themselves or of external
bodies." Scott sees that the problem of accuracy is much more pervasive.

The most common problem of credibility in newspaper and television reports, however, derives not from a lack of personal sincerity on the part of the journalist or
of those with whom he or she deals, but from the administrative routines of news-
making that affect its accuracy. Apparently factual reports are frequently compiled
from press releases, with journalists checking the basic story and following up one
or two points.

Scott mentions how quotes are made up, understood by journalists but
often not by readers. "Researchers using such sources must apply an understanding of the conventions of the press release as a way of inferring
the meaning of the text."[24] Now, I am certainly not implying that newspapers should be destroyed, but I also think that tending to romanticize
them as critical to American history and society also does a disservice,
clouding the real need for selectivity. The typical newspaper's ratio of relevant information per linear or cubic foot of library or archive shelf space
may be much lower than many other evidence sources. In many cases,
resources used to preserve these sources may not be available for use for

other sources. We need to remember that we must develop carefully selected priorities that will enable us to preserve the most important historical
sources in the most efficient manner possible. It is not just about whether
we preserve some old newspapers in their original form or via reformatting,
but it concerns how well we manage the entire documentary heritage of
which newspapers are only a small part (at least in terms of importance if
not in their volume). One might argue, for example, that far more attention
needs to be given to electronic records (digitally-born sources) and the
maintenance of items digitized through migration, emulation, and other
strategies.

It is easy to imagine the kinds of issues librarians and archivists face
when considering newspapers by constructing some typical scenarios. Suppose you are the head of the library or archives at a local historical society,
in a modest urban area where one daily newspaper was published for the
past century. Consider that the newspaper's design is nothing special, lack-
ing color reproductions save for a few special issues (the ending of World
War Two or the assassination of John F. Kennedy). Do these newspapers
need to be saved in their original form or could they be reproduced via
microfilm following archival standards and produced by careful checking
to ensure that no issues are missed in the filming? Perhaps a small number
of special issues are preserved for exhibitions, but most likely reformatting
will be an excellent option in order to ease storage demands so other unique
sources can be preserved (family papers and local business and institutional
records) and because the intrinsic value of the newspapers is low. Suppose
that you are the head of a university library's special collections unit with
the mandate to document an aspect of ethnic history. You would certainly
wish to acquire various newspapers focused on these ethnic groups, but the
decision of whether you preserve them in the originals certainly has to be
weighed against these newspapers' intrinsic value, condition, optimum use,
and other needs and concerns of the repository in acquiring other source
materials.

Opening the discussion up to electronic sources also raises specific questions about the recommendations being made by Nicholson Baker regarding newspapers, since his exclusive focus or case is on "paper" newspapers.
Yet, newspapers are the product of technologies and they are changing.
Geographer Mark Monmonier, examining weather maps—a form of information at least partly associated with the newspaper—notes their development is the result of the "triumphant collaboration of science,
technology, bureaucracy, and cartography." Looking more specifically at
newspapers' publication of weather maps, Monmonier argues that their use
and appearance are "embedded in the publication's overall design, where
it serves as both news and packaging." Predicting the future of the weather
map, the geographer says that the future is not the "rigid printed page"
but a "flexible and intelligent graphic interface supporting many maps,

some animated and most interactive."[25] While Baker would undoubtedly argue that the influence of *USA Today* in publishing color weather maps mandates saving original newspapers using such color representations, the issue is hardly so straightforward. Librarians and archivists have responsibility for archiving weather data in manuscript, print, and digital forms—posing many larger questions and issues that will influence how the newspapers' representation of weather will be handled on a long-term basis.

Electronic information and records sources also complicate the issue of preserving other paper documents. Will the librarian or archivist at the local historical society use his or her resources to preserve original newspapers or endeavor to deal with digital records being created in the region by individuals and institutions? Will the head of the university special collections documenting an ethnic group focus on original newspapers or try to divert some resources to deal with electronic records and other information sources being created by or about the ethnic group? The individual who argues that all of this has to be done may be ignoring the reality librarians and archivists face, where they must make choices and divert financial and staff resources to emphasize shifting priorities. In the perfect world Nicholson Baker describes, such difficult choices never have to be faced. Librarians and archivists have all the resources they need, all the power to make their decisions, and no difficult decisions to make.

Baker often makes huge leaps in order to make his impassioned plea for the preservation of newspapers in their original form. Complaining about the inconveniences of using microfilm is one example: "Historians don't read the old papers because their libraries don't keep the old papers to read, and microfilm is a brain-poaching, gorge-lifting trial to browse."[26] Really? I have heard many people complain about using microfilm, but I have heard many more praise the increased access that microfilm provides to them. Richard Atlick, in his classic volume on literary research, suggested that microfilm has enabled "even libraries of fairly modest proportions to acquire immense quantities of rare books and periodicals [and newspapers]."[27] For Baker, it is his juxtaposition of complaints about the quality of microfilm with the possibility that institutions are disposing still usable original newspapers that raises the specter of a huge breach of trust. "Everything goes wrong in time," Baker muses, but the

germane question is whether the Library of Congress, and the many institutions that followed its example, got rid of things that were, at the time of their jettisoning, both usable and valuable. I bought, on eBay, a 1908 volume of the Panama City *Star & Herald* (published in English during the building of the Panama Canal); it has the Library of Congress's oval stamp on the spine. From a dealer, I bought a volume of the New York *Post* for April, 1943, also spine-stamped by the Library of Congress. Both these objects are in excellent fettle; they can be opened and the pages turned with impunity.[28]

Such anecdotal evidence hardly makes the case Baker thinks it does, especially when it seems to be the basis for a national indictment of what librarians and archivists have been doing with newspaper collections. Indeed, I would argue that the case could be made *only* if most newspapers microfilmed were still usable, even though microfilming might be the preferred approach because it saves most of the content of newspapers in a form less expensive and more accessible than other approaches.

Baker knows there is an emotional, romantic perspective associated with using newspapers in their original form. A few months after his *New Yorker* essay, other newspapers were picking up the story, complaining about the inability to use the papers, problems with microfilm, and the high costs and slow process associated with digitizing the newspaper files. When *Double Fold* hit the bookstores, reviews of it also appealed to the same sentimentality. Kevin Fagin of the *San Francisco Chronicle* writes: "Papers create a space crunch for newspapers and public libraries alike, and around the nation over the past half-century, archivists have had to grit their teeth and throw away huge rooms of bound volumes in favor of microfilm." He continues, "Many still long for the authenticity of a real, printed newspaper—and that longing becomes especially acute when considering that microfilm, the answer thought to be so perfect from about 1950 onward, has proven fallible."[29] It is difficult to argue with people who think in this way, because at the root of such conviction is an emotional response to the object at the expense of a more rational viewpoint about documentary sources.

Here, perhaps, we have the real issue—a desire, in this virtual age, to experience what original newspapers were like. However laudatory this may seem, there are simply not the resources to preserve all originals and, as well, the preservation of newspapers in this way actually limits access to the crucial information found in such sources. Some readers or researchers love the smell of decaying books or the allure of dark and dusty archives, but this does not suggest we should create such environments as these, ones obviously threatening the survival of books, other print material, and manuscripts. Such concerns have become even more important in our modern technocratic society. As society becomes ever more dependent on computers and information, with increasing demands to crunch numbers and information ever faster and with more emphasis on questioning every task and datum as to its relevance to the here and now—the bottom profit line—it seems that we could risk losing something about the past. Why save all this stuff? Does it really help us do anything?

Well, something is going on. A few years ago, a major survey about Americans' interest in the past concluded that most were interested in history. Most talked about "documenting the past." "Almost one third wrote in diaries or journals. More than four fifths documented historical memories by taking photos or videos, and many shot their photos with a clear

archival purpose."[30] E-bay, the *Antiques Roadshow*, Martha Stewart's dec-
orating emphasis utilizing antiques, and the production and sales of inexpensive collectibles by Bombay and the Pottery Barn all reflect such
interests. Indeed, it is possible that what Mr. Baker is appealing to is a kind
of *religious* notion of experience and knowledge found in symbolic and
sacred objects and texts. Karen Armstrong provides some understanding of
this:

People have turned to their holy books not to acquire information but to have an
experience. . . . But the knowledge sought by Adam and Eve was not information.
They were not seeking new facts, new truths, a new science. . . . What Adam and
Eve sought from the tree of knowledge was not the philosophic or scientific knowledge desired by the Greeks but the practical wisdom that would give them blessing
and fulfillment.[31]

This is fine, but it certainly seems misplaced if it is extended to encompass
newspapers. Are newspapers the holy writ of the twentieth century? Baker
might argue, of course, that archivists and librarians, in their efforts to
reformat newspapers, are only after a kind of mundane, practical, technocratic information that eliminates beauty, interest, and the pleasures of
print. Librarians and archivists can counter that they are weighing the options in how to best conserve a range of documentary sources that are
multifaceted, complex, and full of many diverse challenges.
    Librarians and archivists have long known about the challenges associ-
ated with newspapers, but they have often had to make the best choices
open to them in light of physical, financial, and other criteria. We know,
for example, that if a researcher uses a newspaper by searching on a CD-
ROM or on microfilm that different search results may come. Lorre Smith,
an academic serials librarian, studied the differences between using microfilm and a CD-ROM version of one newspaper. Smith found that using the
different indexes produced different end results. "The equipment that is
used to provide physical access to the information in microform and in
compact disc format result in considerably distinct experiences for users."[32]
A staff member of the British Library, now under attack for selling off
some of its newspaper holdings, wrote that the

biggest problem for users of hard copy and microfilm newspaper collections is the
difficulty of subject access: unless the newspaper is one of the few to which a subject
index is published or unless an index to a title or group of titles has been created
locally, then finding articles on a particular topic is very time consuming, unless
one has a precise knowledge of the dates on which relevant articles were likely to
have been published.

This individual also noted the limitations of online versions of newspapers
when the publisher is selective, excluding

items for which the newspaper concerned does not hold copyright, e.g., press agency material, signed articles by individual columnists, as well as the photographs, advertisements, cartoons, crosswords and much other material which give the text articles their context and which give individual character to the titles concerned. The user does not see the page on which the article appeared, so that the size of the headline, the prominence given to the particular article, the accompanying photographs are all lost.[33]

These are real problems needing to be resolved.

Archivists and librarians also have been aware of the limitations of microfilm, but, unlike Baker and other critics, they realize that the conditions of newspapers required decisions to be made about the copying of their contents. David Stoker, Senior Lecturer in the Department of Information and Library Studies, University of Wales Aberystwyth, writes about the decision to use microfilm:

A more difficult question to answer is why the project should have chosen to persevere with the use of micrographic technology at a time when the rest of the world seems to be moving in the direction of the digital storage and transmission of texts. Arguably, this is the use of a mid-twentieth century technology to solve a preservation problem stretching into the new millennium. Micrographic formats may offer considerable advantages in terms of their compactness of storage, and they are inevitably far more robust and stable than the poor quality newsprint used for provincial newspapers, especially those from the nineteenth century which are deteriorating at an alarming rate. Yet they are by no means a permanent answer to preservation problems, and they offer many disadvantages in access and usability of the texts. Microfilm in particular has never been popular among information users compared with the originals in hard copy. It requires expensive and cumbersome equipment that impedes rapid scanning and browsing, which is an important element in accessing the text on any newspaper page.[34]

The issue is presented well here, noting that there are disadvantages with any information migration system, but that the most important issue is the possibility of more rapid information loss or lower use if reformatting is not done. Baker will respond that the newspapers (like the books) are not deteriorating that rapidly, if at all. But there is a caveat in the basis of Nicholson Baker's perspective.

Although Mr. Baker believes that the role of a library or archives is to keep everything just in case someone might want to use it or might need it, this is not the mission of such repositories. A library or archives, for example, must not only be concerned with older sources but with new and emerging information technologies. Actually, preservation does include destruction, either in the stuff that the librarians and archivists never see or because of the decisions they make not to assume responsibility for certain kinds of materials; of course, these same institutions have saved lots of

original materials as well. I have long taught future archivists that one key
to being a good archivist is being a good destroyer, otherwise society would
be drowning in information and evidence. Some have argued that a problem with the so-called Information Age is that we have too much information, and I agree.[35] Shirley K. Baker, president of the Association of
Research Libraries, has written a letter to the *New York Review of Books*
with the following data:

Research libraries in North America have almost 500 million print volumes in their
collections and add another 10 million volumes each year. In a recent year, they
spent over $83 million on a wide range of preservation strategies. Almost 3.5 mil-
lion volumes were bound, 1 million volumes were restored through conservation
treatment, 115,000 items were deacidified, and 156,000 items were placed in protective enclosures. In addition, 110,000 volumes were reformatted through microfilming or photocopying. Almost 50% of ARL's 122 member libraries report
significant improvements in environmental conditions in their buildings over the
past three years—controlled temperature and humidity being one of the most effective ways to prolong the life of library resources. Could libraries do more to
preserve original artifacts? Of course, with additional funding, more materials could
be preserved. Will this happen? Only with greater public commitment to preservation of the historical record.[36]

The scale of the documentary universe is immense, and this has an impact
on how librarians and archivists approach the preservation of sources like
newspapers.

This suggests that archivists and librarians must find ways of incorporating the new digital versions of newspapers. The old communal act of
everyone in a particular community reading the same paper has been transformed by an increasing number of people customizing online newspapers
with the implications that each person may be reading different things following their own interests. In other words, the notion of the newspaper
has changed. And there is no guarantee that the newspaper will survive.
Mitchell Stephens reminds us: "Those who argue that books or newspapers
will long endure like to point to other forms of communication that have
survived the arrival of new competitors; radio is their favorite example.
They do not, however, mention clay tablets, papyrus scrolls, handwritten
books, printed ballads, town criers, the camera obscura, vaudeville, tele-
grams, typewriters, phonograph records or the magic lantern."[37] The demise of the printed newspaper, if this does occur, will suggest to librarians
and archivists that they should want to save some examples, but the emphasis here is on *some*.

There are, however, even more basic concerns that critics like Nicholson
Baker tend to overlook when assessing how libraries and other repositories
have maintained their newspaper collections, a recognition that preservation is at best a difficult function because of costs, the loss of some evidence,

use difficulties, and other, similar tenacious matters. While there is debate about the future of the print newspaper, there is little question that the changing technology of the newspaper is transforming how, who, and when we use newspapers. Jack Fuller, an expert on the newspaper industry, writes:

The printed newspaper will be around for a long time, and not only because people's habits change slowly. The new media are showing us advantages of communication on paper that we never thought about before we began to see the alternatives—portability, disposability, ease of browsing, and so forth. There is a reason why the paper-less office did not immediately follow the spread of computers through the workplace. But it would be a mistake to underestimate how much the new communications technology will affect the way we live and learn or to over estimate our ability to predict its ultimate consequences.[38]

In other words, it is possible that we will have print newspapers, but that these might cost extra in the future, as we subscribe to an online, digital news service that we can customize to match our interests. The point here is that we will need to rethink what the "object" is or how we study how people read and use text and information of all sorts. The original newspapers Baker stresses in his crusade are only part of the overall responsibilities librarians have to manage information and archivists to administer evidence and the documentary heritage. D. T. Max, writing about the implications of the e-book, argues that at present

No one knows exactly what books I have in my house—and no one cares. The risk of buying electronic books is not really censorship. It is the end of informal information dissemination—pressing a book on a friend, picking up a paperback at a rummage sale, handing a dollar to the guy on the sidewalk who's selling books off a blanket. This is the way ideas move through the culture. There's an accidentalness to reading—one of its pleasures—that the computer world doesn't think much about.[39]

In this discussion, the real point is that librarians and archivists will have to think about how to manage and preserve these new information approaches, alongside of whatever other responsibilities they have for preserving originals. So much for the image of stripped-down warehouses.

One of the greatest challenges not addressed by Baker is the immensity of the intellectual control over the thousands of newspaper titles published and the volatility of titles, runs, and other aspects of their publication. Baker, in assailing the turn to microfilm, ignores that the *first* step of the U.S. Newspaper Program was creating accurate union lists of all American newspapers, from national and regional publications to the most local imprints.[40] What Baker misses in his romanticizing of preserving the originals is the enormity of the task involved in maintaining accurate bibliographic control or even in acquiring complete runs of most newspapers; it has been through the process of trying to create complete microfilm runs that both bibliographic control and more complete archives of the newspapers have been developed. One individual describing the U.S. Newspaper Program (USNP) writes: "[E]ven though at least one institution in nearly every state has maintained a large collection of titles published in that state, USNP project teams will discover anywhere from 25 percent to 50 percent of the titles published in the state have not been collected, and an additional 10 percent have not been previously identified." Sometimes even the files of a single newspaper "may be broken up and scattered through the state."[41] The U.S. Newspaper Program expects to catalog over 245,000 different newspaper titles and to microfilm 55 million pages, and many of these titles are quite complex in terms of their control and creation of full runs. Two Michigan newspapers "went through 18 title changes and five mergers" in their existence,[42] and this is not at all an unusual occurrence. Without some national attention to such matters, most often manifested as parts of projects to reformat the contents of newspapers for greater access, it is unlikely that any researchers would be able to use with confidence original runs of newspapers. It has been only more recently that any reliable bibliographic control has been established enabling researchers to find the newspapers to begin with.

We have seen, in fact, a revolution in how we deal with newspapers, a stark contrast to Baker's lamentations about their destruction. The problem with intellectual control over American newspapers has been a continuing problem, and one that has been faced for a long time. Although historians recognized the value of newspapers as a historical source a long time ago (John Bach McMaster published a history of the United States based on newspaper accounts in 1883, and in 1923 Lucy Salmon published her *The Newspaper and the Historian*) and institutions have long collected newspapers (Isaiah Thomas donated a large collection of newspapers to the American Antiquarian Society in 1812), by the 1970s, when the U.S. Newspaper Program got started, bibliographic control over newspapers was very poor. In fact, all of this latter activity should be seen as a positive thing: "The great burst of activity in that decade, manifest in such developments as the reorganization and coordination of national preservation efforts at the Library of Congress, the formation of the U.S. Newspaper Program with its emphasis on bibliographic control, and the introduction of several online newspaper indexes, pointed for the first time to the possibility of total research assess to all newspapers."[43] Why, now, someone like Nicholson Baker comes forward and criticizes the microfilming of newspapers seems a bit strange, except that we can see such outbursts as part of an uneasy living within the newly emerging Digital Age. Diary writing, scrapbooking, and hunting through flea markets all have grown enormously in popularity in the past decade, partly because of the need for people to touch originals as so much becomes virtual. However, to transform such concerns to an assault on librarians and archivists as a means to compensate for the foibles of our modern era seems to go too far and to miss the mark.

NOTES

1. David Stoker, "Should Newspaper Preservation Be a Lottery?" *Journal of Librarianship and Information Science* 31 (September 1999): 131–134 (quotation, p. 132).

2. Baker, "Deadline: The Author's Desperate Bid to Save America's Past," *New Yorker*, July 24, 2000, p. 49.

3. Baker, "Deadline," p. 44.

4. Baker, "Deadline," p. 50.

5. Baker, "Deadline," pp. 59–61.

6. Examples of this can be found in Nicholas A. Basbanes, *A Gentle Madness: Bibliophiles, Bibliomanes, and the Eternal Passion for Books* (New York: Henry Holt and Co., 1995).

7. See, for example, Werner Muensterberger, *Collecting: An Unruly Passion; Psychological Perspectives* (Princeton: Princeton University Press, 1994).

8. Nicholson Baker, "Discards," *New Yorker*, April 4, 1994, p. 61.

9. See, for example, Miles Harvey, *The Island of Lost Maps: A True Story of Cartographic Crime* (New York: Random House, 2000).

10. Peter Terzian, "Newspaper Crusader," *New York Times*, April 16, 2001.

11. Harrison Wick, working in the preservation department at Indiana University, posted this message to the Archives and Archivists listserv on April 25, 2001:

I recently conducted a search through OCLC and RLIN of the newspapers that Nicholson Baker has at his repository. . . . You will notice that most of these are incomplete runs, and he claims that they are in excellent usable condition, well this is because he only purchased those that were in good non-brittle condition to substantiate his objective. He claims that his collection represents newspapers that are not available to the public, but I have found that of the 101 newspaper titles he has, 85% of them are incomplete runs. Less than 22% are owned by less than 5 repositories in their original format and 33% were available from more than 10 repositories in paper.

For a long article about the Baker newspaper repository, see the article by Doug Hubley, "Old News: Fighting to Save a Historic Newspaper Collection, Author Nicholson Baker Makes His Stand on the Banks of the Salmon Falls River," *Portland Phoenix*, November 9–16, 2000, available at *http://www.portland phoenix.com/archive/features/00/11/10/PAPER.html*. This article features a photograph of Mr. Baker, standing with his arms folded in a defiant gesture before pallets of old newspapers, with the caption "Paper Savior." There is a Web site for the American Newspaper Repository at *http://www.gwi.net/dnb/newsrep.html*.

12. S. Branson Marley, Jr., "Newspapers and the Library of Congress," *Quarterly Journal of the Library of Congress* 30 (1975): 211.

13. Marley, "Newspapers and the Library of Congress," p. 212.

14. The United States Newspaper Program maintains statistics at *http://www.neh.gov/preservation/usnp.html*.

15. Marley, "Newspapers and the Library of Congress," p. 219.

16. Conversation with Bob Harriman, April 19, 2001.

17. Jay Tolson, "Is the Library a Good Place for Books?" *U.S. News.Com*, April 23, 2001, available at *http://www.usnews.com/usnews/issue/010423/library.htm*, accessed April 24, 2001.

18. Barbara Quint, "Don't Burn Books! Burn Librarians!! A Review of Nicholson Baker's *Double Fold: Libraries and the Assault on Paper*," *Searcher* 9 (June 2001), available at *http://www.infotoday.com/searcher/jun01/voice.htm*, accessed May 5, 2001.

19. Baker, "Deadline," p. 45.

20. Mistakes do occur in the appraisal or selection of library or archival materials. See, for example, *Inquiry into the Disposal of Records of the Naval Research Laboratory Stored at the Washington National Records Center in Suitland, Maryland*, NARA Bulletin 99–03 (Washington, D.C.: National Archives and Records Administration, April 24, 1998), available at *http://www.nara.gov/records/nrlrpt.htm*.

21. Stoker, "Should Newspaper Preservation Be a Lottery?" p. 133.

22. Robert Harriman, "The World's Biggest Paper Drive," *Inform* 5 (October 1991): 21.

23. The Romano and Carey comments are in Robert Karl Manoff and Michael Schudson, eds., *Reading the News: A Pantheon Guide to Popular Culture* (New York: Pantheon Books, 1987), pp. 73, 161. The other statement is in Paulos's book, *A Mathematician Reads the Newspaper* (New York: BasicBooks, 1993), p. 28.

24. John Scott, *A Matter of Record: Documentary Sources in Social Research* (Cambridge, Mass.: Polity Press, 1990), pp. 145, 146.

25. Mark Monmonier, *Air Apparent: How Meteorologists Learned to Map, Predict, and Dramatize Weather* (Chicago: University of Chicago Press, 1999), pp. 7, 174, 230–231.

26. Baker, "Deadline," p. 55.

27. Richard D. Atlick, *The Art of Literary Research* (New York: Norton, 1963), pp. 140–141.

28. Baker, "Deadline," p. 54.

29. Kevin Fagan, "Battling to preserve remnants of history; newspaper archives expensive and complex," *San Francisco Chronicle*, (November 2, 2000), available at *http://www.sfgate.com/cgi-bin/article.cgi?file/chronicle/archive/2000/11/02/MN111401.DTL*, accessed November 6, 2000.

30. Roy Rosenzweig and David Thelen, *The Presence of the Past: Popular Uses of History in American Life* (New York: Columbia University Press, 1998), p. 24.

31. Karen Armstrong, *In the Beginning: A New Interpretation of Genesis* (New York: Alfred A. Knopf, 1996), pp. 4, 26, 27.

32. Lorre Smith, "Access to Full Text in Microform vs. Optical Disc: A Newspaper Closely Examined," *Microform Review* 22 (Winter 1993): 31–36 (quotation, p. 35).

33. Geoff Smith, "Access to Newspaper Collections and Content in a Time of Change," *IFLA Journal* 21 (1995): 282–286 (quotations, p. 283).

34. Stoker, "Should Newspaper Preservation Be a Lottery?" p. 132.

35. See, for example, David Shenk, *Data Smog: Surviving the Information Glut*, rev. ed. (San Francisco: Harper SanFrancisco, 1998).

36. I appreciate Rush Miller, director of the University of Pittsburgh Library System, making me aware of the letter.

37. Mitchell Stephens, *The Rise of the Image The Fall of the Word* (New York: Oxford University Press, 1998).

38. Jack Fuller, *News Values: Ideas for An Information Age* (Chicago: University of Chicago Press, 1997), p. 218. Indeed, newspapers and their informational content have always been evolving; see, for example, Herbert J. Gans, *Deciding What's News: A Study of CBS Evening News, NBC Nightly News, Newsweek, and Time* (New York: Vintage Books, 1980); Robert Karl Manoff and Michael Schudson, eds., *Reading the News*; and Michael Schudson, *The Power of News* (Cambridge, Mass.: Harvard University Press, 1995).

39. D. T. Max, "The Last Book: If Computers Finally Replace Trusted Hardcovers and Paperbacks, Will Our Culture Ever Be the Same?," *Utne Reader Online*, available at *http://www.utne.com/bBooks.tmpl?command§earch&db†Article. db&eqheadlinedata^he%20Last%20Book*, accessed May 22, 2001.

40. See, for example, Robert P. Holley, "The Preservation Microfilming Aspects of the United States Newspaper Program: A Preliminary Study," *Microform Review* 19 (Summer 1990): 124–132.

41. Robert Harriman, "The World's Biggest Paper Drive," p. 22.

42. Lise Hedlin, Margaret Mering, and Linda M. Pitts, "Newspapers: Yesterday, Today, Tomorrow," *Serials Librarian* 34: 3–4 (1998): 307–312 (quotation, p. 309).

43. T. F. Mills, "Preserving Yesterday's News for Today's Historian: A Brief History of Newspaper Preservation, Bibliography, and Indexing," *Journal of Library History* 16 (Summer 1981), pp. 463–487 (quotation, p. 482).

Chapter Five

Wrong Priorities

Nicholson Baker makes a lot about his view that our libraries and archives are working under the wrong priorities, a major theme in his *Double Fold* book and in all his essays. Baker drops little bombshells about just what libraries are doing these days, such as "Like missile defense, leading edge library automation is a money pit."[1] But Baker saves his most critical assessments for the largest libraries. About the Library of Congress and its efforts to offer older runs of original newspapers, Baker writes: "Increasingly, there were no takers, because such is the prestige of our biggest library that whatever its in-house theoreticians come to believe—however anathematic to the ideals of reasoned stewardship—other research libraries will soon believe as well."[2] And Baker continues to assert that it is not just because of the ill-guided notions of the Library of Congress's "theoreticians" that such poor decisions are being made, but something even more insidious that it is difficult to pinpoint: "Lack of money isn't the problem. The library has spent huge sums on microfilming, and its preservation budget is more than eleven million dollars a year—enough to build and out fit a warehouse the size of a Home Depot, which would hold a century of newsprint."[3]

Baker's perspective on newspapers is a case study in how he critiques librarians and archivists making decisions and setting priorities. A century of newsprint from *what* newspapers is, of course, the major question, because such a warehouse could *not* hold all of the newspapers nor even all the major urban dailies from the past century. Baker, as I have noted, is even more critical of the British Library, prompting a public furor about that institution's policy regarding its newspapers. In reference to this institution, he speculates: "Apparently, it was a matter of indifference to the library's managers whether the newspaper collection held rarities or not; they were perfectly willing to act in a way that would all but guarantee its quietus at the hands of the paper knackers. They wanted the money."[4] Baker ignores the tremendous space needed to maintain originals, just one of many issues he does not consider (and precisely the kinds of issues librarians and archivists *must* consider). Geoff Smith, writing about the challenges faced by the British Library some years before the Baker article, described the situation in this way: "For anyone collecting and preserving newspapers in original hard copy form, the first essential requirement is for a great deal of storage space. The British Library Newspaper Library's 600,000 bound volumes and parcels of newspapers and 300,000 reels of positive microfilm occupy some 18 linear miles . . . of shelving."[5]

Baker's inclusion of the British Library in his writings about American libraries came about because of his discovery that that library was selling off its American newspapers, some of which he arranged to purchase. Baker's article caught the attention of the British, and an article accusing the British Library of betraying the public's trust appeared in the *Times Literary Supplement*. In this later article, most of Baker's arguments are repeated, although the author extends his worry that if the British Library will destroy original newspapers after microfilming, what is to prevent it from doing the same to books. Again, most of this argument revolves about the unique values of originals, problems with the production of microfilm, and a sense that librarians and archivists are assumed to be responsible for maintaining newspapers (and books) in their original form.[6]

As I have suggested throughout this extended review of *Double Fold*, we need to keep one eye on the cynical ways Nicholson Baker describes librarians and archivists and another on the substance of what he has to say about how libraries and archives are working with books, newspapers, and other materials in their care. In the early weeks of the appearance of Baker's book, a few reviews tried to strike some balance like this. Jeffrey Young, in the *Chronicle of Higher Education*, provided an opportunity for both Baker and leading librarians to voice their opinions about Baker's themes in *Double Fold*. The librarians featured in the Young article stated that Baker's views were "unbalanced and distorted"; that his views were no more than a "misrepresentation"; that the story is simplistic, ignoring other responsibilities faced by librarians; and that it is an inaccurate accounting from a historical perspective since it often stresses practices no longer used. Baker disagreed, of course. He contends that his is a truthful account. He made, Baker asserts, no "purposeful misrepresentations," continuing, "I tell the truth. Certainly libraries need money, but they need it to go for reasonable things [rather than for microfilming]. Libraries need more money for unglamorous things like storage space, reference staff, and book repair." Then, Baker adds this note: "Historians are just going to look back on . . . these people as—I don't want to say as destroyers—as diminishers of the past. They're not going to feel any gratitude."[7] It is in the latter statement, however, that we can now turn to and ruminate about. Would historians feel any "gratitude" for how Mr. Baker would select originals to be kept or for how and where these originals would be kept? Is there any selection involved in Nicholson Baker's approach? Would historians be grateful for a landscape where one of everything has been kept in the original form and in some repository?

Nicholson Baker has drawn the public's attention to the challenge of preserving books and newspapers, and perhaps to the larger challenges associated with all library and archival preservation. The strength of his essays and his book is that people can understand one aspect of the difficulty in preserving any information document, that there are never any easy answers and, at best, solutions may bring as many additional problems with them as what they are supposedly resolving. Yet, it is incumbent upon librarians and archivists to speak up about such matters because they will add the complexities. The appeal of *Double Fold* and Nicholson Baker's writings and interviews for the public may be his rather simplified version of what librarians and archivists do—they are supposed to keep all this paper, no more or no less. In this light, librarians and archivists face the same problem that history museums have discovered in the 1980s and 1990s—the difficulties of interpreting the past when the public wants to gaze at objects and be entertained at the same time.[8] Even if it is at best a false hope that we should save all original newspapers (perhaps even one original of each newspaper ever published—given the immense number and the scattered runs of many of these papers), just as it was somewhat off kilter that we should save all those old library catalogs, *how* will we explain this to the public?

In this regard, librarians and archivists have been trumped by Nicholson Baker because he provides a simple but compelling story that suggests that the task is easy. Reading Baker's book and essays makes one wonder about other things. Should we also save *all* old buildings, old books, and printed ephemera? Should everything always be saved in the original form? Or, is this a misunderstanding of just what the responsibility of librarians and archivists represent? Indeed, it is a gross misunderstanding, but it is one that the public may more easily buy into than the tale of difficult decisions, compromises, successes, and failures that archivists and librarians must consider.

Archivists have always operated on the premise that they must be selective, saving most of their internal professional debates not to focus on the question of original versus reproduction but rather on just what the criteria for selection might be. Arguments have been made to suggest that use, multi-institutional selection plans, theoretical models, and even the preferences of records creators should serve as the foundation of the appraisal approaches. While there are many camps within the modern archival community about just what criteria should be used, there appears to be consensus about the fact that archivists destroy more records than they preserve.[9] Some have even argued that not *all* archival records can be saved; the immensity of the challenge is such that we know there will be losses, either through mistakes or by virtue of the fact that there are too few archivists and too many records. Too many people might believe that these records will be saved because of their experiences at flea markets, auctions, and what they see happening on *Antiques Roadshow*. But what we experience here is nostalgia, not scholarship or a service to the public promising evidence and information (in other words, what librarians and archivists do).

The problem with the question of newspaper microfilming is that neither the library or preservation communities have been as open about developing criteria for selection, until very recently. I was involved in discussions between archivists and conservators concerning such criteria, and I know these discussions had a modest impact on librarians, archivists, and preservation administrators and certainly no effect on the public.[10] Perhaps the reasons for this has been due to the problems generated by telling a complex tale in ways that can be understood, but it is clear that all professionals involved with the preservation of the documentary heritage and artifacts need to improve how they communicate with the public. It has only been in recent years (the past two decades) that the preservation community has worked on focusing on selection criteria anywhere close to rivaling the schemes suggested by various archivists, but this may be due to the fact that the library and archives preservation administrator corps also has only developed within this same time period.[11]

Paul Conway is one who has been most forceful in pushing a selection approach, perhaps because he moved from the archival profession to the preservation community. Conway argues:

[P]reservation adds value through selection. Choice involves defining value, recognizing it in something, and then deciding to address preservation needs in the way most appropriate to that value. Selection in archives and research libraries was once thought to be primarily a one-time decision about the potential for future use, made near the time of publication or when the documents ceased to serve the primary purposes for which they had been created originally. Over decades the act of preservation has evolved from saving material from oblivion and assembling it in secure buildings to encompass more sophisticated condition, value, and use assessments on the already-collected. Preservation selection in libraries has been dictated largely by the need to stretch limited resources in as wise a fashion as possible, resulting in the dictum that "no item shall be reformatted twice." The end result is a growing "virtual" special collection of items preserved using a variety of techniques, most notably by microfilming. Selection is perhaps the most difficult of undertakings precisely because it is static and conceived by practitioners as either completely divorced from present use or completely driven by demand.[12]

Now, basic textbooks in preservation feature considerable discussion about selection concerns.[13] The development of digital means for reformatting, meaning the addition of another reformatting approach, has prompted more serious discussion about selection criteria. In the case of newspapers and their microfilming, librarians and archivists have focused on reformatting the content of *all* newspapers without much regard for the possible selection of *some* newspapers that might deserve to be maintained in their original format. The problem here is that this approach emerged long before more sophisticated selection approaches began to be discussed. The emphasis on microfilming newspapers started shortly after the Second World War and was ingrained by the 1970s and the start of the U.S. Newspaper Program (USNP). Discussions about preservation selection issues seem to have commenced in the 1980s, with writings by Ross Atkinson, Margaret Child, and Christinger Tomer.[14]

We can have the best of both worlds, the microfilming approach to ease storage and enhance access while freezing the deterioration of the information found in newspapers with a highly selective saving of original newspapers. Baker commenced his *New Yorker* essay with laments about the loss of the earliest color printed comics. I see no reason why such newspapers should not be saved in their original form, as long as we are not contending that this can only be done if *all* newspapers are saved or if we cannot safely predict such unique features leading to a need to be comprehensive in saving all newspapers in their original form. All newspapers are not rare and thus not deserving of being maintained in original form; do we need millions of original newspapers to study an array of typographic design, paper manufacturing, and other technologies? In being selective, we need to have a plan in mind, a sense of what it is we would need to save. Such typographic breakthroughs as the first color comics could be identified and dealt with in a meaningful way. Beyond that we would need to work on developing criteria about what newspapers would be saved to document certain aspects, such as landmarks in newspaper publishing and journalism, particular historic events, and aspects of local community developments. Clearly doing this would have another benefit—opening up the process of developing mechanisms for preserving the content of newspapers and the small percentage of newspapers needing to be saved in their original formats. The Baker essay might be the result of an effort to preserve newspapers that has simply ignored communicating to the public not just *how* but *why*.

Librarians and archivists need to experiment more with determining just what original newspapers should be saved. Librarians and preservation administrators, in attacking the brittle book and other large-scale preservation

problems, experimented with a series of selection processes. According to
Abby Smith, Director of Programs at the Council on Library and Information Resources, first, they tried the "great collections" approach, but
they found serious problems with this method: "But selecting those titles
and volumes, and only those, that are both valuable intellectually and fragile physically is a very labor-intensive activity. It would have meant choos-
ing items for preservation literally title by title." Then, librarians and their
allies tried the "bibliographical model" where they "used a series of titles
or a body of literature identified by a bibliographer or scholarly editorial
board as a basis for selection, thus assembling a single metacollection that
exists only in surrogate form." This, too, had limitations:

It was generally acknowledged that this method could only be effective in those
academic fields that had a highly evolved bibliographical consensus, such as classics,
agriculture, theology, and some area studies. It is simply impractical for newer or
more dynamic fields that are evolving too quickly for consensus to emerge, or for
fields such as history, in which the size of the source base precludes the idea of
comprehensiveness.

Another approach based on use was experimented with as a selection
method: "Use-driven selection takes an approach opposite to that of the
collections- or subject-based methods. This is an essentially passive form of
identification, in which any item that is called for use is treated if it is in
bad condition." Here both scholarly and political limitations emerge:

That this approach has not been widely adopted is due in part to the fact that
NEH, the primary source of funding for preservation microfilming, endorses only
the collections- and subject-based methods. User-driven selection is seen as ineffec-
tive in helping to rescue endangered information within a national, rather than
local, context. By focusing on commonly used materials, it has been argued, one
would end up creating a so-called national collection that is randomly selected, not
a coherent body of literature.

In looking at the range of possibilities, Abby Smith concludes:

Preservation is the art of managing risk to the intellectual and physical heritage of
a community and all members of that community have a stake in it. Risk management is dynamic, and, in practice, preservation becomes an ever-changing assessment of value and endangerment. A collaboration between scholars, who can advise
about the intellectual value of collection items, and librarians, who can make judgments about the physical risk that threatens collections, is the best and most responsible way to ensure that the legacy we have inherited, and to which we
contribute, will survive into the future.[15]

Perhaps being very selective and identifying a small percentage of newspapers with what archivists term "intrinsic value" to be maintained in original form makes far more sense. Intrinsic value

has long been used by archivists to describe historical materials that should be retained in their original form rather than as copies. . . . Intrinsic value is the archival term that is applied to permanently valuable records that have qualities and characteristics that make the records in their original physical form the only archivally acceptable form for preservation. Although all records in their original physical form have qualities and characteristics that would not be preserved in copies, records with intrinsic value have them to such a significant degree that the originals must be saved.[16]

The sample of newspapers the Library of Congress has acquired needs to be reevaluated in light of more rigorous selection criteria, especially about what newspapers it microfilms or maintains in original form. The need for selection, especially in a universe of documentation as large as what is represented by newspapers, is an issue often missed by outside commentators, not just in libraries and archives but in all fields with some responsibility for aspects of the documentary heritage.[17]

In considering the development of selection criteria for determining what newspapers should be saved as *originals,* much of the emphasis has to be on understanding that the rise of the newspaper industry is largely the product of changing technologies (and the same can be said about books and other printed sources as well). From the first newspaper in Boston at the end of the seventeenth century to the proliferation of thousands of newspapers by the mid-nineteenth century to the use of telecommunications supporting the rapid relaying of millions of words a day, the nature (content and physical features) has been closely intertwined with technology.[18] We might want to save the original newspapers in which color represented landmark innovations, especially since color is a physical aspect that cannot be captured well by the usual reformatting approaches. An example might be when the *New York Times* started color ads on September 15, 1997, ending New York's run as the last major city without color ads.[19] Another example is when (in 1975) the *Wall Street Journal* became the "first true national newspaper, beaming page layouts to printing plants around the country" via satellite transmission. We might want to save the first of these newspapers.[20]

Preserving original newspapers is not as easy as merely declaring that we should save them. We might wish to save original editions or newspapers documenting certain technological advances or major transformations, such as when photocomposition took over typesetting in the 1950s. Rene Higonnet, a French engineer and amateur photographer, combined typesetting and photography in the photocomposition machine.[21] We might want to

select certain original issues because they document certain design landmarks, such as in the 1920s and 1930s when the newspapers shifted to
"modern designs" from the "crowded, chaotic pages" and expressed the
"new professional authority of journalists and designers."[22] Perhaps original copies of newspapers might be needed to document the social aspects
and impact of newspapers, such as occurred in the 1870s with improved
technology and distribution of papers, their more affordable prices, the
shifting content for a broader appeal (a more general orientation), and the
rise of advertising and consumerism. As one historian suggests:

> In most general terms, the newspaper trends of the 1870s suggested the emergence
> of a more popular form of communication. With improved technology and re-
> sources for distribution (improvements in communication, printing, production,
> and transportation); increased accessibility (greater number of newspapers and af-
> fordable subscription prices); broader appeal (the move away from factionalism of
> partisanship toward a less political and a more general orientation); and a stronger
> base of economic support (the rise of advertising and consumerism as more per-
> vasive forms of funding compared to political patronage), newspapers were carving
> out a new social, political, and economic role for themselves.[23]

The interest in advertising, for example, has prompted the creation of
services, such as the Historic Photo Archive, whereby old discarded newspapers are rescued so that good photographic copies of advertisements and
even texts can be made for commercial and scholarly use. This does not
necessarily mean that *all* originals should be saved or that libraries and
archives should assume this role, but it does suggest a level of sensitivity
needed when libraries and archives make deaccessioning decisions and
opens the possibility for some cooperative ventures that can meet a variety
of needs.[24] Archivists and librarians need to reflect on how such dramatic
and significant shifts in publishing should be documented by the artifacts
of publication. What newspapers assist us to understand such changes, and
do we need to preserve examples of the originals of such newspapers?

With all of the above examples, however, there are implications extending far beyond merely saving original newspaper issues. What about saving
equipment used to support the various technological advances or the other
artifacts generated, such as the plates produced by the new photocomposition process? Concerning various landmark shifts in time, do we just need
the actual newspapers to understand what these changes signify? What
about the correspondence, business records, sketches, and even trial and
errors documenting the process of change? What about other sources of
documentation that help us to understand the historical, cultural, social,
and other aspects of the context in which newspapers were established,
grew in importance, and were periodically transformed or challenged?

In approaching the notion of considering if and how to preserve some select original newspapers, another issue does emerge and it is one that Nicholson Baker does not address in his *New Yorker* article or *Double Fold*. There is merit in saving originals of the pioneering illustrated newspapers, such as *Frank Leslie's Illustrated Newspaper* (starting in 1855 as America's first illustrated newspaper) and following the establishment by Leslie in 1848 of his *Illustrated London News*, the first illustrated news venture in the world. However, as has been discovered, the manner in which the images were used suggest considerable differences between the final printed and original images created for the use of the newspapers and news magazines. As one historian suggests: "Because news illustrations were so important to publishers and readers of the period, the relative merit of *Frank Leslie's Illustrated Newspaper* and *Harper's Weekly* must be assessed primarily for their contributions to pictorial reporting. But this has not happened. Scholars have judged the papers only on the quality of their texts." This suggests, as Nicholson Baker argues, the value of saving originals. The historian continues:

Leslie's published Civil War images, and those of other illustrated papers of the day, however, were not always exact copies of the "special" artists' original sketches. Changes made in the images usually can be attributed to difficulties in delivering the artists' drawings to the publishers. Wartime travel was laborious; sketches could take anywhere from one to eight weeks to reach the home office, three to four weeks on the average. By the time the drawings arrived at the publishing houses, the scenes that they related might have happened so far in the past that they were no longer pertinent. In these cases, publishers occasionally changed details in the drawings in order to make the images seem more timely. They did not announce the changes to the public, however. Thus, contemporary readers had no way of knowing that publishers ever altered the artists' initial drawings. The published engravings seemed as truthful to journal subscribers as the artists' original sketches.[25]

Such concerns mimic the debate that occurred as a result of the debates about documentary filmmaker Ken Burns's use of images in his *Civil War* television series.[26]

This causes one to wonder about who has been taking responsibility for the business records of the newspaper publishers. What about the responsibility of the publishers for preserving the newspapers *and* the records supporting the daily reporting of news? What about the records that will enable a fuller understanding of the newspapers themselves as businesses, reflection of contemporary events, and as historical sources? This is precisely the kind of issues librarians and archivists must consider, reflecting again the complicated nature of the responsibilities they face.[27] Nicholson Baker's earlier discourse on the destruction of library card catalogs was also limited in that it focused exclusively on these cards as a kind of cultural record while ignoring the problems faced in the management of library records and archives.[28]

That other sources from newspaper publishers may be as vitally important as the newspapers themselves can be seen by considering their morgues (classified newspaper clippings). Catherine Covert, two decades ago, argued that the morgues themselves provide critical evidence about particular societal views:

Morgues of dead newspapers (stored in libraries if you are lucky and in inaccessible warehouses if you are not) provide an archaelogical expedition to the mind of past decades, with clippings in neatly-titled yellow envelopes, filed according to the conceptual patterns of the communities involved, and sometimes still laid down within the envelopes in geological layers of crumbling newsprint. Infrequently used by historians anywhere, these morgues provide, I believe, one of our culture's richest troves of historic evidence as to past patterns of thought, neatly filed according to subject, accessible on demand, and rarely used.[29]

Understanding newspapers develops, then, from not just some romantic reaction to their content and visceral qualities, but it comes from comprehending how newspapers are constructed, that they are products of a business, and that they are the result of the work of professional journalists, among many things.

One point on which I agree with Nicholson Baker regards his criticism of the zeal by which librarians and archivists may have embraced microfilming as *the* solution to the preservation problems they face with printed sources. Regarding newspapers and their microfilming, there are many questions needing to be reconsidered: Why do we microfilm newspapers? Why would we want to preserve original newspapers? Where are newspapers in the overall priorities of historical documentation? How do we bring together archival appraisal approaches with preservation initiatives? The best means by which to approach such questions is to develop criteria for saving original newspapers that balance the artifactual and informational values of the papers (and books as well). This can be accomplished by bringing together journalists, historians, and others with expertise about the newspaper industry, and it can best be done by encompassing not just the newspapers but the publishers, the papers of leading journalists and media leaders, and newspaper morgues and other business records of the publishers. The matter of preserving original newspaper runs might be the *last* matter to be considered.

All involved in preserving our documentary heritage have to be committed to educating the public. The preservation community thought it had done a good job with films like *Slow Fires: On the Preservation of the Human Record* and *Into the Future: On the Preservation of Knowledge in the Information Age,* both sponsored by the Council on Library and Information Resources. The films raised public awareness about the threat of the technologies used in the creation of the documentary sources to the content of books, various print media, and electronic sources.[30] Obviously, archivists and librarians have not done well enough. In the *Times Literary Supplement* essay about the British Library newspapers, reference was made to the fact that the British Library was enamored with "new technologies, so much more exciting and so much more expensive than old ones . . . simply superior to printed material, which is seen as disposable."[31] Nicholson Baker perceived the films as part of a massive, misguided propaganda effort on the part of librarians and archivists. They are certainly a mix of propaganda and education, because they are public relations devices. The films were produced in order to grab public attention and to persuade policymakers about library and archives preservation matters. These films may seem misguided due to their zealous messages because they were designed to win political and monetary support.

In effect, Nicholson Baker's writings are really a lament about the loss of an older sensibility to original newspapers, one generated by our immersion into and acceptance of copies via the Internet/World Wide Web that he and others worry may have dulled our senses about the value of original objects. Technologies of all sorts have long sought to create facsimiles, fakes, and forgeries, all raising many questions about authenticity in our modern era.[32] Baker's article and book are much like Sven Birkerts's worry about the demise of both the printed book and linear reading.[33] Baker worries that the loss or reduction of printed objects in our libraries will remove a crucial aspect of our civilization. However, one can believe in the continuing utility of print and the value of maintaining books and some newspapers in their original condition, while recognizing that the ultimate preservation demands require mechanisms like microfilming and digitization projects. I know, because I (and many others) see the need for both.[34] There is no conspiracy or even tragic problem with our libraries and archives, other than the fact that they have immense challenges and limited resources. Nicholson Baker might think of himself as a Greek hero, calling others to join in his epic quest to save America's past. But, at best, Baker will only save a miniscule portion and perhaps even divert the public's attention from the greater issues facing the preservation of the books, documents, newspapers, and other artifacts of the past. If he is taken seriously, and if *Double Fold* has an impact on how libraries and archives function, the resources for preserving our documentary heritage might actually be diminished. Baker reminds me, unfortunately, of Sisyphus.

Sisyphus rolled his rock with determination and passion, but his activity is also the symbolism of futility. Baker's book is very much like the ancient Greek myth. Stephanie Zacharek's review of *Double Fold* described it as a "passionate" read, one that moved the reviewer to "tears more than once."

Zacharek even suggests that the passion is more important than the book's content, although she believes it to be well-researched:

And Baker does care far beyond the realm of what might be considered normal, which is precisely the point. Some people (librarians especially) are sure to accuse Baker of being too heated, of not having enough distance from his subject to write a balanced treatise. To hell with *that* kind of balance. Baker gives us something much rarer. His passion is bound up in the very fibers of the pages; it's as concrete as the binding. Baker could have written a wholesome, boring, respectable tome about how the fate of the nation's books and newspapers hangs perilously in the balance. As it is, Baker's research is tireless and sound, and yet the tone of *Double Fold* is its own best argument: It's as close as a book can come to a living, breathing being.

Baker's passion makes this reviewer passionate as well. Using the book, the reviewer mentions the "careless logic" of archivists and librarians and the "creepy doublespeak of 'preservation' and 'conservation,'" two terms that library administrators use interchangeably to bamboozle the public, even though they mean very different things."[35] Such responses to the book and Baker's crusade is what worries most librarians and archivists, not the fact that mistakes have been made. Nicholson Baker provides plenty of passion but not much more than a simplistic analysis of library and archival preservation. Such reviews also ignore the passion that librarians and archivists bring to their work and careers, as well as the fact that Baker is often so critical of librarians and preservation administrators who express passion about their views about saving books and newspapers.

The simplicity of Baker's own work is evident in his own recommendations—publishing discard lists "so that the public has some way of determining which of them are acting responsibly on behalf of their collectors," having the Library of Congress "lease or build a large building" for holding everything, persuading "several libraries around the country" to "begin to save the country's current newspaper output in bound form," and seeing that the U.S. Newspaper Program and the Brittle Book Program are abolished or require that "all microfilming and digital scanning be nondestructable" and "all originals be saved afterward."[36] I have no problems with including these recommendations into a list of issues for study, but I believe that some more fundamental matters about Baker's argument, research, and assumptions need to be considered first. Baker believes that all *originals* must be saved, but I do not believe this necessarily follows or is possible. And, of course, Baker believes that librarians and archivists were involved in a great effort to deceive the American public. His skewed historical analysis and his recommendations provide us only a superficial assessment of library and archival preservation, making little difference as to whether it is passionately argued or not. Yet, at least in the early stages of the public reception of the book, a lot of damage has been done by Baker to libraries and archives. Another reviewer, Michael Upchurch, concludes that Baker "goes into degrees of detail that may try some readers' patience, but there's no mistaking the passion and intelligence he brings to his task or the fiery zest with which he relays his most damning anecdotes." Now, here's the clicker: "On some deep level, the follies the book describes seem merely one more symptom of a bewildering national flaw. If *Double Fold* finds enough readers to do its intended job, it may fix more than libraries."[37]

What all this leads up to is the need to use the same standards for evaluating Baker's book, writings, and other critiques that he himself employs to evaluate library and archives preservation efforts (and other library and archival functions he decides to become a critic of) of the past half century. Baker assesses the early 1990s film *Slow Fires* in this fashion: "It would be a better film if what it was saying happened to be truth and not head-slapping exaggeration—then its use of crisis language . . . would have some justification."[38] The same applies, of course, to determining just how exaggerated the claims made by Baker in *Double Fold* and elsewhere may be. Certainly Baker thinks a "crisis" also exists. I think the exaggeration comes in Baker's characterization of some individuals and the more conspiratorial aspects of his arguments. The truth rests somewhere in his arguments about the massive microfilming and digitization of books that may not be as endangered as we were led to believe. Other problems stem from Baker's blinders to examine only this aspect of libraries (and archives), ignoring their other responsibilities, now including what they will do with e-journals, e-books, and the information and evidence resting on the ever-changing World Wide Web.

Despite whatever problems or weaknesses exist in *Double Fold*, librarians, archivists, and preservation administrators better read it carefully and determine how (not if) they will respond. The book is receiving favorable reviews, drawing lots of attention, and this will undoubtedly lead some archivists and librarians to start getting some hard questions by their bosses and the public about what they are doing. Despite whatever one's personal reactions may be to the book, archivists and librarians need to take it very seriously. That is my intention in this book.

NOTES

1. Baker, "Deadline: The Author's Desperate Bid to Save America's Past," *New Yorker*, July 24, 2000, p. 48.

2. Baker, "Deadline," p. 50.

3. Baker, "Deadline," pp. 53–54.

4. Baker, "Deadline," p. 52.

5. Geoff Smith, "Access to Newspaper Collections and Content in a Time of Change," *IFLA Journal* 21 (1995): 282–286 (quotation, p. 282).

6. H. R. Woudhuysen, "Vandals of Colindale: Why the British Library is Discarding Newspapers," *Times Literary Supplement*, 5081 (August 18, 2000), pp. 14–15.

7. Jeffrey R. Young, "A Novelist's New Book About Libraries and Technology Outrages Librarians," *Chronicle of Higher Education*, May 1, 2001, available at *http://chronicle.com/free/2001/05/2001050101t.htm*, accessed May 1, 2001.

8. See Michael Kammen, *American Culture, American Taste: Social Change and the 20th Century* (New York: Basic Books, 1999), chapter nine.

9. The literature about archival appraisal, especially in the past decade, is very rich and contentious, although the contentious aspects have nothing to do with the question of selection but more about criteria for that selection. For the best writings representing both the debates and the main points of consensus, see the series of articles by Terry Cook, "Mind Over Matter: Towards a New Theory of Archival Appraisal," in Barbara L. Craig, ed., *The Archival Imagination: Essays in honour of Hugh A. Taylor* (Ottawa: Association of Canadian Archivists, 1992), pp. 38–70; "Many are Called but Few are Chosen: Appraisal Guidelines for Sampling and Selecting Case Files," *Archivaria*, 32 (Summer 1991): 25–50; *The Archival Appraisal of Records Containing Personal Information: A RAMP Study with Guidelines*, PGI-91/WS/3 (Paris: UNESCO, April 1991), at *http://www.unesco.org/webworld/ramp/html/r9103e/r9103e00.htmContents*. For other examples of the debate about criteria refer to Terry Eastwood, "Toward a Social Theory of Appraisal," in Craig, ed., *The Archival Imagination*, pp. 71–89; Mark Greene, " 'The Surest Proof': A Utilitarian Approach to Appraisal," *Archivaria* 45 (Winter 1998): 126–169; Jennifer A. Marshall, "Documentation Strategies in the Twenty-First Century?: Rethinking Institutional Priorities and Professional Limitations," *Archival Issues* 23: 1 (1998): 59–74; Terry Abraham, "Collection Policy or Documentation Strategy: Theory and Practice," *American Archivist* 54 (Winter 1991): 44–52 and his "Documentation Strategies: A Decade (or more) Later," paper presented to the Society of American Archivists annual meeting, August 31, 1995, available at *http://www.uidaho.edu/special-collections/papers/docstr10.htm*; Timothy L. Ericson, " 'To Approximate June Pasture': The Documentation Strategy in the Real World," *Archival Issues* 22: 1 (1997): 5–20; Leonard Rapport, "No Grandfather Clause: Reappraising Accessioned Records," *American Archivist* 44 (Spring 1981): 143–150; Karen Benedict, "Invitation to a Bonfire: Reappraisal and Deaccessioning of Records as Collection Management Tools in an Archives—A Reply to Leonard Rapport," *American Archivist* 47 (Winter 1984): 43–49; Luciana Duranti, "The Concept of Appraisal and Archival Theory," *American Archivist* 57 (Spring 1994): 328–344; Frank Boles and Mark A. Greene, "Et Tu Schellenberg? Thoughts on the Dagger of American Appraisal Theory," *American Archivist* 59 (Summer 1996): 298–310; and Richard J. Cox, "The Documentation Strategy and Archival Appraisal Principles: A Different Perspective," *Archivaria* 38 (Fall 1994), pp. 11–36.

10. Despite extensive meetings, only a brief report resulted with little practical recommendations; see *The Preservation of Archival Materials. Report of the Task Forces on Archival Selection* (Washington, D.C.: Council on Preservation and Access, April 1993), available at *http://www.clir.org/pubs/reports/arcrept/arcrept.html*.

11. See, for example, Michele V. Cloonan and Patricia C. Norcott, "Evolution of Preservation Librarianship as Reflected in Job Descriptions from 1975 through

1987," *College and Research Libraries* 50 (November 1989): 646–656 for the slow development of such professional positions.

12. Paul Conway, *Preservation in the Digital World* (Washington, D.C.: Council on Library and Information Resources, March 1996), available at *http:// www.clir.org/cpa/reports/conway2/*. Archival appraisal is included in Anne J. Gilliland-Swetland, *Enduring Paradigm, New Opportunities: The Value of the Archival Perspective in the Digital Environment* (Washington, D.C.: Council on Library and Information Resources, February 2000), available at *http:// www.clir.org/pubs/reports/pub89/contents.html*.

13. See Carolyn Harris, "Selection for Preservation," in Paul N. Banks and Roberta Pilette, eds., *Preservation: Issues and Planning* (Chicago: American Library Association, 2000), pp. 206–224.

14. See the bibliography appended to the Carolyn Harris essay, "Selection for Preservation." Archivists were asked to share their viewpoints gained from their appraisal experiences, such as my essay jointly authored with Lynn W. Cox, "Selecting Information of Enduring Value for Preservation: Contending With the Hydra-Headed Monster," in *Rethinking the Library in the Information Age: Issues in Library Research:Proposals for the 1990s* (Washington, D.C.: U.S. Government Printing Office, 2000), pp. 115–130.

15. Abby Smith, *The Future of the Past: Preservation in American Research Libraries* (Washington, D.C.: Council on Library and Information Resources, April 1999), available at *http://www.clir.org/pubs/reports/pub82/pub82text.html #national*.

16. *Intrinsic Value in Archival Material*, Staff Information Paper Number 21 (Washington, D.C.: National Archives and Records Administration, 1982), available at *http://www.nara.gov/arch/techinfo/intrin.html*. Specifically, the attributes related to intrinsic value are as follows:

1. Physical form that may be the subject for study if the records provide meaningful documentation or significant examples of the form

2. Aesthetic or artistic quality

3. Unique or curious physical features

4. Age that provides a quality of uniqueness

5. Value for use in exhibits

6. Questionable authenticity, date, author, or other characteristic that is significant and ascertainable by physical examination

7. General and substantial public interest because of direct association with famous or historically significant people, places, things, issues, or events

8. Significance as documentation of the establishment or continuing legal basis of an agency or institution

9. Significance as documentation of the formulation of policy at the highest executive levels when the policy has significance and broad effect throughout or beyond the agency or institution.

17. The most logical framework for reflecting about this is the recent scholarship on the concept of public memory. Patrick H. Hutton, *History as an Art of Memory* (Hanover: University of Vermont Press, 1993) provides a good introduction to the nature of the recent scholarship. Kenneth E. Foote, *Shadowed Ground: America's*

Landscapes of Violence and Tragedy (Austin: University of Texas Press, 1997) is a good example of the different societal and other variables affecting historic sites, one that could be easily transposed for thinking about how artifacts, books, and archives survive. In most cases, the general public, even avid museum visitors or library users, do not think about how collections are established and evolve.

18. A good source for understanding the development of newspapers is Phil Barber, "A Brief History of Newspapers" at *http://www.historicpages.com/nprhist.htm.*

19. See Dori Perrucci, "Color Storms N.Y. Ad Market; Old Gray Lady No More, N. Y. Times Sprouts Color on Ad and News Pages; Daily News Close Behind," *Editor & Publisher* 130 (September 27, 1997): 12–13.

20. Richard Reeves, *What the People Know: Freedom and the Press* (Cambridge, Mass.: Harvard University Press, 1998), p. 40.

21. The photocomposition machine created columns of type, which were then arranged and pasted into a full newspaper page, photographed, and the negative sent to the platemaking department. The negative was placed between glass and photosensitive metal or plastic plate, developed in a chemical solution. Elizabeth MacIver Neiva, "Chain Building: The Consolidation of the American Newspaper Industry, 1953–1980," *Business History Review* 70 (Spring 1996): 22–26.

22. See John Nerone and Kevin G. Barnhurst, "Visual Mapping and Cultural Authority: Design Changes in U.S. Newspapers, 1920–1940," *Journal of Communication* 45 (Spring 1995): 9–43.

23. Jeffrey B. Rutenbeck, "Newspaper Trends in the 1870s: Proliferation, Popularization, and Political Independence," *Journalism & Mass Communication Quarterly* 72 (Summer 1995): 361–375 (quotation, p. 371).

24. Information about the commercial archives can be found at *http://www.historicphotoarchive.com/.*

25. Andrea G. Pearson, *"Frank Leslie's Illustrated Newspaper* and *Harper's Weekly:* Innovation and Imitation in Nineteenth-Century American Pictorial Reporting," *Journal of Popular Culture* 23 (Spring 1990): 81–111 (quotations, pp. 81, 89–90).

26. See Robert Brent Toplin, ed., *Ken Burns's The Civil War: Historians Respond* (New York: Oxford University Press, 1996).

27. Newspaper publishers have tried to digitize and market their "morgues." See "The Morgue Morphs," *Editor & Publisher* 131 (April 25, 1998): 17.

28. See my "Library History and Library Archives," *Libraries & Culture* 26 (Fall 1991): 569–593.

29. Catherine L. Covert, "The Newspaper and Intellectual History: A New Approach," paper presented to the History Division, Association for Education in Journalism Annual Convention, Houston, Texas, August 1979, EDRS ED 179983.

30. Information about these films can be found at *http://www.clir.org/pubs/film/film.html.*

31. Woudhuysen, "Vandals of Colindale," p. 15.

32. See, for example, Hillel Schwartz, *The Culture of the Copy: Striking Likenesses, Unreasonable Facsimiles* (New York: Zone Books, 1996).

33. See Sven Birkerts, *The Gutenberg Elegies: The Fate of Reading in an Electronic Age* (Boston: Faber and Faber, 1994); *Readings* (Saint Paul, Minn.: Graywolf

Press, 1999); and *Tolstoy's Dictaphone: Technology and the Muse* (Saint Paul, Minn.: Graywolf Press, 1996).

34. For example, see my "Selecting Historical Records for Microfilming: Some Suggested Procedures for Repositories," *Library & Archival Security* 9: 2 (1989): 21–41 and "Debating the Future of the Book," *American Libraries* 28 (February 1997), pp. 52–55, along with my other essays cited here. The *American Libraries* article is incorporated into Chapter six of this book.

35. Stephanie Zacharek, "*Double Fold* by Nicholson Baker," *Salon.com*, April 27, 2001, available at *http://www.salon.com/books/review/2001/04/27/baker/index.html*, accessed April 27, 2001.

36. Nicholson Baker, *Double Fold: Libraries and the Assault on Paper* (New York: Random House, 2001), p. 270.

37. Michael Upchurch, "A Bibliophile Defends the Printed Page: *Double Fold* Suggests What a Gizmo-Gullible Country We Live In," *Chicago Tribune*, April 1, 2001, available at *http://chicagotribune.com/leisure/books/article/0.2669,SAV-0103310030,FF.html*, accessed April 18, 2001.

38. Baker, *Double Fold*, pp. 186–187.

Chapter Six

The Real Thing

Washington Post book reviewer Michael Dirda provided yet one more positive review of Nicholson Baker's _Double Fold_ shortly after the book was released by its publisher. Unlike many of the other early reviewers Dirda made some criticism of Baker's perspective, but it was also clear that Dirda was sympathetic to the arguments advanced in _Double Fold_. The reviewer writes: "I do suspect that Baker may be Utopian in asking our cultural institutions to preserve literally everything, but at the very least the decision to discard should be made only after careful reflection by scholars and librarians." Dirda affirmed that microfilming or digitization "does reduce wear and tear on the original," but he was cautious about such technologies. "Let us hope, too, that those accountable for the guardianship of our books and intellectual heritage always remember that no copy can ever replace the real thing." Dirda cautioned: "Perhaps our preservation administrators and similar library honchos need a daily reaffirmation of their own Hippocratic oath: First and last, do no harm."[1] Perhaps authors and book reviewers also need such an oath, as well.

Michael Dirda, like most of the early reviewers of _Double Fold_, is a book lover and because he loves books Dirda, like Baker, thinks he understands libraries and librarians. In one of his essays, Dirda provides us with his view of the librarian: "Most of all, I daydream about possessing enormous wealth so that I could employ a personal librarian, someone to catalogue my books properly, answer my correspondence, delicately bring to my attention one or two choice items coming up for auction at Sotheby's."[2] Dirda's view of the librarian is straight out of the nineteenth century, or from *Masterpiece Theatre*, possessing very little resemblance to the modern librarian of the twenty-first century (except, perhaps, for the small group who work in the rare books collections of university libraries, museums, and other cultural institutions). Like Baker, Dirda also possesses a view of the book and reading that most librarians, while they may worry about such matters, often do not have the luxury to promote:

More and more, I sense that focused reading, the valuing of the kind of scholarship achieved only through years spent in libraries, is no longer central to our culture. We absorb information, often in bits and pieces and sound bites; but the slow, steady interaction with a book, while seated quietly in a chair, the passion for story that good novels generate in a reader, what has been called the pleasure of the text—this entire approach to learning seems increasingly, to use a pop phrase, "at risk."[3]

Most librarians probably concur with this statement, and, as well, they would love to see such readers in their facilities. Honestly, however, librarians are in the *information* business, and books are only *one* means for getting information. Archivists are in both the information and *evidence* business, making their position in such a discussion as offered by critics like Baker or Dirda even more difficult to ascertain.

Nicholson Baker revels in such traditional views about libraries and librarians, longing for a different era and certainly a different purpose than what most librarians have to face on a daily basis. In one of his interviews, Baker states:

It doesn't strike me as particularly eccentric or Quixotic to want to keep one or even two original runs of artifacts that whole populations once paid money to read every day. We understand why old flags and old presidential letters are valuable as things—we don't believe that taking a photograph of Plymouth Rock amounts to a "reformatting" of Plymouth Rock—and we're even doing better with old mills and old train stations. But many of the great libraries are still in Cold War mode; they haven't grasped the fact that their collections are historical landmarks, not heaps of words that can be squeezed down with the help of expensive hardware.[4]

The problem with this statement, among other things, is that libraries are not just about books and all books are not artifacts in the traditional sense. Books, like most information or textual sources, are changing.

Sitting in the comfort of your easy chair (as Michael Dirda longs to do), stretching out on the blanket on the beach, or killing time waiting for the airplane to depart are all activities enhanced by the reading of the latest John Grisham thriller or popular biography by David McCullough. For most of us, books, magazines, and newspapers are an inescapable and invaluable part of our lives. We use them to entertain and to inform ourselves. Yet many are speculating that the inexpensive, portable, and convenient paperback book or magazine may all but disappear from our society in the next generation. Others are even predicting, because of this, the end of the traditional library facility and its replacement by a virtual library with electronic texts. Nicholson Baker's lamentation about the stripping of printed books and newspapers from the libraries is really only a side debate in a difficult transitional era from print to digital, or so it seems. Some reviewers, such as Michiko Kakutani, picked up on such concerns, especially Baker's notion about why both the copies and originals can't be saved: "Whether the reader agrees with all of Mr. Baker's arguments, his provocative book addresses an important and all too frequently overlooked subject: the future of our libraries in the digital age and the fate of the printed word."[5] Yes, indeed, although Baker never makes much of a case about *why* the situation he is describing would be part of a major cultural shift; Baker spends so much time focused on the peculiar personalities and quirky decisions he finds in his investigation.

Long before *Double Fold* appeared, scholars and social commentators were arguing about the future of the printed book. A veritable publishing industry has emerged with the appearance of a genre of writing of speculations about the future of the book and other printed materials. The writings are thought provoking, irritating, fun, and often confusing. They also represent what I go looking for first in my weekly visits to the local bookstores, displaying the same eagerness that my wife has as she searches out the latest mystery by one of her favorite writers. In these futurist writings we can discover much that stimulates questioning about the nature, importance, and continuing impact of both the printed word and the library. There is a difference with this earlier debate, pitting futurists against traditionalists, than with the debate generated by Nicholson Baker's writings. Within a week of the official release of *Double Fold*, one newspaper columnist declared that the debate was over: "Signs within America's bibliophile establishment indicate Baker's book has not only sounded the alarm but won the debate. The Washington-based Council of Library and Information Resources issued a draft report this month [April 2001] rescinding decades of received wisdom by recommending a nationwide effort to save original copies of books and newspapers."[6] This is, of course, not true. Librarians and archivists have worked for a long time on developing criteria for identifying which items should be saved in their original state, with archivists leading the way twenty years ago developing the concept of intrinsic value (a concept Nicholson Baker scorns).

Ironic as it might seem that speculations on whether the book has a future in society have been largely confined to the publishing industry, these speculations are at least testimony to the fact that the book, at present, is alive and well, especially as it is used to meditate on its own place in society. Of course, the Baker book provides a startling contrast to this by suggesting that books are not safe in libraries. In effect, these writings and their authors (including Baker) are providing a commentary on our society—fast-paced, diverse, schismatic, constantly transforming, a new age of information (a Knowledge Age?). Or, these authors might be taking advantage of confusion and change, stirring the same feelings one has when walking through the business section of a bookstore with titles such as *How to Get Rich on the Information Highway*—the one who is getting rich is the person who got this book to the bookstores first. One might wonder just what Nicholson Baker's motivation was in writing *Double Fold*. Earning his livelihood by writing suggests that he will try to write on topics that will sell books, and the irony of libraries and librarians destroying books and other documentary materials seems dramatic enough to catch the public's attention and imagination (and judging by the early reviews, it has).

What are the predictions and conclusions of these authors writing on the book and its future? Who are these authors and why are they writing these volumes? Why should we read and pay any attention to what they have to say? These are all good questions, the central aspect of the kind of education academician Neil Postman writes about, especially in his *The End of Education: Redefining the Value of School,*[7] in which students (and, really, all of us since Postman's book concerns the need for continuing education in society and at the workplace) are encouraged to question, to probe, to poke about, and to provoke encounters in which knowledge is gained and wisdom might ensue. As a university professor teaching future librarians, archivists, and information professionals, what better way to get these future knowledge workers engaged than to have them speculate on how that knowledge will be packaged? Even, as I must admit, if I have to force many of these students to move from thinking about what they do to the how's and why's of being part of the twenty-first century's information professions—to focus on knowledge with long-term value rather than skills with a short-term shelf life. We could assume that Nicholson Baker's *Double Fold* will be an excellent stimulant to the classroom and for students planning to work as librarians and archivists, except that Baker's indulgence in vitriolic language and the musings of a conspiracy theory make *Double Fold* more difficult to use in this way than in most of the other books and writings on related topics mentioned here. Still, I believe if used carefully, Baker's book is a great device for engaging library science, archives, and preservation management students in reflecting on the future of books and records, libraries and archives, the mission of librarians, archivists, and preservation administrators, and other critical and controversial matters.

The amazing variety of texts on the future of the book sends a variety of mixed messages to us, and, for me at least, that is what stimulates me to introduce these works into the classroom but also to engage my own thinking about my own assumptions. My assumption, my primary one at least, is that the published book, the artifact of human manufacture that has been the most effective means of disseminating information and knowledge for four centuries, will continue to have a role in the constantly evolving Information Age of the twenty-first century. I still read books, while navigating through the Internet. I still write books, while mounting electronic texts on the World Wide Web. I still browse bookstores, while scanning electronic library catalogs. I still enjoy reading the traditional newspaper delivered to my door while relying heavily on access to newspapers on the World Wide Web. I believe traditional printed sources will be manufactured for a very long time into the future, and their manufacture will produce books and other publications far more durable than the majority produced during the past century.

And there is precedence for such mutual coexistence. Despite the clear advantages of the codex, the codex existed side by side with rolls for centuries, probably because of the ancient readers' comfort with using rolls and the availability of apparatus for copying and maintaining rolls.[8] And, as some now argue, it is just as likely that the digital book will exist alongside the printed book or vice versa for a very long time, although the issues this coexistence raises for libraries is much more complex than ever faced before because the control of books changes along with the economics of authorship, printing, and, of course, uses of technologies and preservation implications. Clifford Lynch provides numerous examples and cases for the depth of such challenges. The move to online, updateable dictionaries and encyclopedias might lead to where "we stand to lose the ability to have snapshots of the state of knowledge and understanding, and of cultural biases that scholars can revisit from later epochs as we move away from editions to continually updated databases." The shift to digital publications also raises new challenges for building research collections. Lynch writes:

If one looks at the history of the collecting and preservation of cultural materials over the last century, one finds again and again situations in which individual private collectors built up collections of contemporary materials that virtually all libraries overlooked or chose to ignore, and decades later libraries and archives built their collections of these materials (which proved to be vital raw materials for scholarship and cultural history) through acquisitions or donations from these private collectors. Research libraries are often driven by scholarly needs, and it can take decades to develop canons and to legitimize new fields of scholarly inquiry. Individual collectors preserve and protect potentially significant materials while these changes in scholarship occur. It is vital that individual consumers, and not just cultural memory institutions, have the capability to retain indefinitely the works that they acquire and to preserve them.[9]

Notice, however, that this still differs from Nicholson Baker's perspective that all printed artifacts must be preserved in their original format. The utility of print does not translate into meaning that either it must be universally preserved or that it is the best means by which to maintain information or evidence.

But this is not an assumption shared by everyone. And it is not something we can or should take for granted. The Internet, electronic books, books on demand, and the nonlinear quality of hypermedia, among other things, all seem like potential rivals to what now exists. And we need to understand that what now suffices as a publishing industry, primarily the cost-effective paperback, is an innovation primarily of the twentieth century, not of Gutenberg and his peers who produced costly, bulky books so valuable (and still so rare) that they were chained down to the reading tables of the libraries in which they resided. Think about the transition to what Nicholson Baker and his allies seem to suggest. If every book or newspaper or printed text needs to be preserved in its original format, does this not suggest the need of chaining down every text? Henry Petroski notes that the techniques of chaining books is "generally not known to younger librarians. They did not share my interest in the history of libraries."[10] While it is true that the history of libraries and librarianship has deteriorated in the graduate programs educating future librarians (although I believe it is beginning to reemerge because of the kinds of broader issues being discussed here), we also can extend this lack of history to the critics, like Baker, of modern libraries and librarians. Baker's criticisms return us to the age of the laboriously produced manuscript or hand typeset books, but such criticisms also miss the point that these were small libraries, not the library behemoths of the modern age.

While some of the debate lapses into the most academic and arcane, the average person ought to take stock of his or her own uses of the book and print as sources of information and entertainment because it is very likely that these sources may irrevocably change in the next decade or so. In fact, the cybernauts already view the traditional printed book as equivalent to the old, rare, and cumbersome incunabula (the printed books of the first fifty years after Gutenberg's first printing endeavor) that were usually chained to the monks' desks. Getting future librarians and information professionals to understand the historic context of the current debate is essential if they are to make decisions about the design and use of the libraries they will work in. Possessing a broader historical knowledge of print and texts certainly will aid librarians and others in determining what books to save and how to save them. Acquiring this knowledge will not mean, however, that *all* books will need to be saved as artifacts. In fact, studying the book suggests quite the opposite, providing some additional tools by which informed selection of the books needing to be saved as objects can be made.

Two authors offer compelling, though contrasting, speculations about the printed book. Nicholas Negroponte's *Being Digital*[11] (1995) and Barry Sanders' *A Is for Ox: Violence, Electronic Media, and the Silencing of the Written Word*[12] (1994), books written from opposite perspectives and predictions. Negroponte, MIT professor and internationally known as the founder of the Media Lab (MIT's innovative think tank in the use of electronic information technology) and columnist in the hippest Information Age journal (*Wired*), has constructed a wild roller-coaster ride of predictions about where the computer will take us as a society and culture (the book almost reads as if he dictated the text to a transcriber, perhaps itself a reflection of an individual more accustomed to the more oral, informal nature of cyberspace). As Negroponte argues: "Computing is not about computers any more. It is about living."[13] Couldn't we have said that about reading and the paperback book as well?

Negroponte predicts new communities, new businesses, new ways of disseminating information, new notions of copyright and intellectual property ownership, new expressions of creativity, more friendly and accessible computing, innovation in the manner in which information is supplied to you, and the end of the book as traditionally defined. The apparent irony of publishing a book such as this, given its subject, is that, as he says, the "written word sparks images and evokes metaphors that get much of their meaning from the reader's imagination and experiences" rather than multimedia software.[14] Or, as Negroponte later writes: "Right now it is hard, but not impossible, to compete with the qualities of a printed book."[15] The future, Negroponte fantasizes, will be a post-information age in which "Everything is made to order, and information is extremely personalized."[16] Where are books, reading, and literacy in this new world? Will the next book Negroponte writes really be digital? Will he even bother to write a book? While Nicholson Baker relishes the object, Nicholas Negroponte stresses the content and its delivery. The point in all this, ignoring whether or how rapidly society embraces Negroponte's vision, is that the librarian and archivist will have to navigate their way through such diverse perspectives and manage objects *and* systems. Resources, ranging from financial to appropriate storage and usage spaces to technical expertise, will have much to say about how well the information and evidence embedded in texts is managed.

If Negroponte's work is a personal, nearly autobiographical musing on the electronic world (telling us as much about his encounters with digitization as about anything), then Sanders' book seems to be a more impersonal, scholarly account of the impact of electronic information technology on our world. It is more book-like, at least in the traditional sense. It reads like a book before books were seen to be questionable artifacts of an earlier, pre-information age. Appearances can be deceptive. Sanders, a university professor in English, has argued that although "Human beings as we know them are products of literacy,"[17] the new electronic wizardry has worked to block the possibilities of literacy. Armed with the standard scholarly apparatus of long discourses on particular studies and footnoted authorities, Sanders carefully works his way from oral societies to the advent of writing and printing up to the present. But there is a very personal tone to this book, with its laying at the doorstop of technology many of the ills of our contemporary society. Crime, social unrest, political malaise, and educational decline are all, in one way or another, connected to the ways in which electronic information technology is being used. It is a view Nicholson Baker might easily embrace, as he lays so much blame on earlier librarians and their mindless adopting of various information technologies.

Sanders and Negroponte are not alone with their thoughts about the future of the book, writing, and reading, or their efforts to convey them to us. The books coming out on the future of the book are quite remarkable, as is the pace of publication. I mention two other books as examples of this rich array of thinking about the future of information, writing, and print. Sven Birkerts's, *The Gutenberg Elegies: The Fate of Reading in an Electronic Age*[18] is similar in tone and purpose to the Sanders book, and in it the author struggles to look at the gains and losses of the new technocratic order, but winds up lamenting the actual and potential losses. Like Sanders, Birkerts worries about the fate of reading and the nature of literacy, and the impact of the decline of these activities and skills on our society. In an eloquent phrasing, Birkerts notes that "language is the soul's ozone layer and we thin it at our peril."[19] Indeed. If the book disappeared, would this change constitute a part of this thinning? In many ways, as I have mentioned before, Birkerts' book is the soul mate of Baker's *Double Fold*, both viewing the printed book as the linchpin of civilization, often with somewhat exaggerated claims. Birkerts writes, for example: "The depth of field that is our sense of the past is not only a linguistic construct, but is in some essential way represented by the book and the physical accumulation of books in library spaces. In the contemplation of the single volume, or mass of volumes, we form a picture of time past as a growing deposit of sediment; we capture a sense of its depth and dimensionality."[20] It is easy to imagine the dialogue between Birkerts, with this view, and Baker, lamenting the removal of books and newspapers and their replacements by digital or microfilm surrogates. One can value the traditional printed book without elevating it to a place where anything less is seen as unacceptable. For some reason, however, I liked the Birkerts book much better, perhaps because the tone was more restrained and there were no conspiracies floating about its pages. Perhaps, on the other hand, I am just a little older and more of a curmudgeon.

Richard Lanham's *The Electronic Word: Democracy, Technology, and the Arts*[21] (1993) has a similar subject, but an altogether different theme— indicated in his early statement in the book that "I think electronic expression has come not to destroy the Western arts and letters, but to fulfill them."[22] He sees disciplinary boundaries dissolving, new means of access opening up, new creative forces about to be leashed, and better opportunities for raising the general level of literacy in our society. Upon finishing the book you might feel like applauding the level of optimism, while remembering some of the realities of how the world is actually changing. Would I miss the book as artifact? Is there something that I would like to hold onto, physically, while I read or scan information? Are there certain books that I would perhaps like to see published electronically, such as a history of cinema or a discourse on the metaphysics of the photograph, because the format would be an improvement over even the best designed, flat, printed text? Lanham's volume probably represents the kind of scary thinking Nicholson Baker worries librarians and archivists have adopted. In the first sentence of his first chapter, Lanham states: "Perhaps the real question for literary study now is not whether our students will be reading Great Traditional Books or Relevant Modern ones in the future, but whether they will be reading books at all."[23] Yipes. There is little reason to be concerned, I suspect, since the reasons librarians and archivists have tried to develop efficient reformatting processes has more to do with the realities of the resources available to them and their commitment to access to the information found in books, newspapers, and other documentary materials. While archivists and librarians often engage in debates about the future and nature of print, the book, the document, the text—just as I am doing now—they rarely have the luxury to try to institutionalize or make operational their dreams. This is just one reason why my repeated reading of Baker's writings continues to upset me—he assigns so much more power and imagination and resources to librarians and archivists than they have time for in their daily work.

The real issue emerging for me, as an educator, is how to present these contrasting views in the classroom. How do we get students engaged in these topics so that they are prepared to face them in their new workplaces? How do we turn on vocationally focused students to the intellectually stimulating ideas and debates represented in the writings about the book and its future? But, in actuality, the same concerns exist outside the academy. How do we get the average person, walking through the airport or rushing to catch a taxicab and caught up in all the daily bustle characterizing life in the late twentieth century, to reflect on what is really the future of information and with that the future of work, home, and play? I always come back to two approaches, hinted at in other volumes on education.

The first is remembering that my task is education, not training (a topic itself currently being argued about strenuously in the academy and the professions). The matter can be summarized as the difference between thinking and merely reacting. In the aforementioned book by Neil Postman, he describes this issue as the difference between "technology education" and technical training. He argues that students (and he is discussing students at the high school and college level) need to be able to answer certain basic questions about technology, such as knowing "where the alphabet comes from, something of its development, and anything about its psychic and social effects" or for knowing "anything about illuminated manuscripts, about the origin of the printing press and its role in reshaping Western culture, about the origins of newspapers and magazines." In other words, technology education "is about how the meanings of information and education change as new technologies intrude upon a culture, how the meanings of truth, law, and intelligence differ among oral cultures, writing cultures, printing cultures, electronic cultures. Technology education is not a technical subject. It is a branch of the humanities."[24] I am sure Nicholson Baker would agree with this assessment, as his own estimation of the education of librarians reflects a concern that it is technocratic and absent broader perspectives one would find in the humanities. It is another reason why using *Double Fold* in the classroom makes sense, even if used by one like me who has so many quibbles with its arguments and evidence. Presenting a diversity of opinions is, for Postman, the essence of education, and I agree.

Reflecting upon the future of the book is really reflecting on the future of our society and culture. And while some are prone to use Postman's writings as being part of a technophobic backlash to the increasing importance of and dependence on the computer, how can anyone disagree with his arguments that we must educate people to understand—meaning being able to evaluate what the technology represents—what that computer sitting on the desk means in terms of technological innovation, political and economic efforts, and marketing and capitalistic endeavors? In effect, Nicholson Baker seems in sympathy with such a view, except that he made no effort to understand the culture of librarians and archivists, their professional missions and mandates, and the societal and organizational contexts in which they work.

These kinds of writings about the future of the book enable these discussions to ensue. We can use them to set up the debate, less about the future of the book and writing and more about how we view technology, stimulating thinking and leading to knowledge. Using these books as point-counterpoint, the second approach, is reminiscent of some of the more levelheaded arguments that have emerged from the debate about multiculturalism in education, probably the most divisive aspect of our modern society, connected as it is to racism, immigration, relativism, religion, postmodernist theories, and other radically divisive themes. It is precisely what historian Peter Stearns is arguing in his book, *Meaning Over Memory: Recasting the Teaching of Culture and History*[25] (1993), where we look at process rather than teach doctrine, where we discuss competing ideas rather than present a fixed canon. This reflects, of course, the challenge of using Nicholson Baker's book in the classroom or for any other kind of educational venture involving the future of books and publishing or libraries and librarianship. The often vitriolic tone of *Double Fold* distracts from the more reasoned arguments Baker advances about such issues as the book as artifact or the durability of paper. While one can suggest readings with different perspectives about the science of paper or the notion of content versus its carrier, it is far more difficult to contend with such silly arguments as the CIA involvement in library preservation or the other conspiratorial tones of *Double Fold*.

Perhaps the best known of these writings is Gerald Graff's *Beyond the Culture Wars: How Teaching the Conflicts Can Revitalize American Education*[26] (1992), winner of a 1993 American Book Award. Graff's thesis is summarized in his title. Graff ruminates on the "deeply contradictory mission" of the university: "The university is expected to preserve, transmit, and honor our traditions, yet at the same time it is supposed to produce new knowledge, which means questioning received ideas and perpetually revising traditional ways of thinking."[27] Drawing on his own discipline of English literature, an area beset by multicultural, postmodernist debates (explaining why much of the writing about these topics as well as the future of the book has come from this discipline), Graff simply argues that competing views, perspectives, and interpretations be put to play in the classroom in order to get students to think about and to appreciate the wide range of views that exist about virtually any topic, including whether the book has a future. In this sense, Baker's *Double Fold* certainly provides a different perspective, especially since one of its assumptions is that a source of the problem is the education of librarians and the knowledge base that underpins library and information science. The weakness of *Double Fold* is, of course, that its author makes no real effort to understand librarians or archivists or the institutions and collections they manage. The other weakness is that using *Double Fold* may lead to devoting too much time dissecting the perspective of the author, rather than understanding the nature of preservation management issues facing librarians and archivists. Still, neither of these may be insurmountable problems in the classroom, since students (presumably) are there to be challenged and learn. These weaknesses become more serious with the book's discussion out in the public forum, where there often seems to be little opportunity for exchanges between social critics and librarians or archivists.

Nicholson Baker's qualifications as a novelist may get him into trouble here, and it certainly poses challenges for librarians and archivists as they grapple with the future of paper, print, and traditional information and evidence sources. There are many similarities in writing history and historical fiction, but only one purports to make an effort to provide an accurate representation of the past. Novelist Russell Banks writes:

I assume . . . that when a reader opens my novel, he or she will do so knowing that I have not written it as a biographer or historian, as one who . . . relies solely on his interpretation of data, fact, testimony, documentation, and primary and secondary sources. No, the word "novel" declares, as if it were a contract between me and my reader, that I have written this book solely under the restrictions, obligations, and responsibilities, and with all the freedoms, that control and liberate a fiction writer, more properly a *storyteller*.[28]

So, has Nicholson Baker given us fiction or nonfiction, or primarily just a good story, with his *Double Fold?* Will we get so immersed in his story, especially the stranger dimensions of it, that whatever good points he is making about library and archives preservation will be lost?

Where am I in all of this? I mean, I sat down and wrote this essay as much to think aloud about my perspectives in order to understand my current approach as to convince anyone that they should think in a similar fashion. I teach in a school of library and information science, a school reflecting a constellation of information professions all of which are in a constant state of flux due to the rapid changes in technology, the changing expectations of society about how to use information, and the various social issues about copyright and ownership bubbling to the top in discussions about the so-called Information Highway or Digital Era or whatever new moniker comes along. How do we prepare the future information workers to navigate on this highway? Do we confidently tell them that the book is dead? Do we bravely announce the arrival of the digital or virtual library? Or, do we instill in them an intellectual curiosity about the social, technological, and economic history of the book that prepares them to know how to approach the multitude of decisions they will face in their careers? I think we opt for the latter. And Negroponte, Sanders, Birkerts, Lanham, and others (even Baker's writings) all have something to offer in the education of librarians, archivists, and other information workers, as well as offering us something to think about in our current position in an increasingly complex and fast changing society.

The point to all this is really rather simple. Whether the book is a physical object or electronic shadow is almost beside the point. The real matter is that we understand, regardless of what might replace the book, the nature of information (evidence for archivists) and knowledge in our society. It is what any society or culture is held together by, the book being a part of the symbols and memories of a society. It is indeed what distinguishes us as human. We think, and the book, printed artifact or electronic and virtual, is a reflection of and crucial to the work of our minds. Of course, none of this necessarily translates into saving all printed books. Alexander Star, in a sympathetic review of *Double Fold*, still perceived this as a major weakness of Nicholson Baker's arguments: "But in arguing so eloquently for the preservation of original sources, Baker leaves open the question of how many original copies of a book or newspaper must be kept, and by whom. For most libraries, this is the essential question. . . . Should nobody ever discard a bound volume of anything? Baker seems to imply that everything is worth keeping." And more to the point:

It is this intense effort to extract meaning from even the most ephemeral things, and to turn willfully away from the reality of oblivion, that gives Baker's writing its energy and its wit. But it also renders him incapable of considering what is worth saving and what is not. Oblivion sometimes has its uses. Given that libraries really do encounter more words and more paper than they can handle, this reluctance to make judgments of value is a serious lacuna for a library activist. Sometimes, one imagines and even hopes, ephemera are just ephemera.[29]

This weakness also seriously undermines the ability to use *Double Fold* in the debate about the future of the book, the library, archives, and the disciplines of librarians and archivists.

Perhaps one day, as some muse, the book we take to the beach or onto the airplane will be a thin electronic wafer. Perhaps. It is likely to happen, however, only when the electronic surrogate is as portable, useful, and friendly as the inexpensive paperback with its curled edges and worn spine, stretched and twisted from repeated readings. The true indicator of a transition may be when an electronic guru like Negroponte puts his words only into the bits and bytes of the computer. In the meantime, libraries will administer print book collections but, and here is where Baker fails again, these institutions also will have to cope with constantly changing electronic sources and ephemeral materials, making difficult decisions about what to make available to their constituents which are constantly transforming.

The problem in placing Baker's *Double Fold* into this debate about the future of the book and print is that Baker does not present a true vision or try to engage anyone in debate; instead, he simply indicts librarians and archivists in a manner that does not elevate discussion about how they are or should be preserving the materials in their care. Julian Dibbel, writing in the *Village Voice*, believes Nicholson Baker lost an opportunity to "speak more amply about its great subtextual theme, which is after all a key conundrum of the Information Age, postmodernity, or whatever else you want to call these data-daffy circum-millennial times: the fact that information itself is undivorceably both matter and abstraction, occupying not just the boundless head space of image and meaning, but the pricey real space of sagging shelves and bloated hard drives." Noting that Baker alludes to Vannevar Bush's 1945 essay, "As We May Think," Dibbel wonders why Baker does not discuss the implications of that essay—a "touchstone text of the information sciences" imagining an "office-of-the-future device called the Memex—a desk-size reader containing within it the microfilmed text of every document anyone could want to read, searchable so that the user could sail through the universe of texts as if through open seas"—for what modern era librarians seem to be doing. Dibbel thinks that

"Bush's fantasy is no crazier than Baker's. In essence, both of them dream of having access to all the information ever published, and it drives them nuts to see a single scrap of it fall through the cracks. But the world and all the order in it are always slipping through the cracks, and the failure to reconcile oneself to that is, among other things, as good a definition of obsessive compulsion as any."[30] These are excellent points, and they are what we can do in the classroom with a text like *Double Fold.*

When interviewed by the *Chronicle of Higher Education,* Baker was asked a question recalling Bush and the Memex machine, the interviewer pointed out that students on campus in the future might be able to "carry around entire archives in a small electronic device." Baker responded that while this seems exciting, when you go to a bookstore you find people interested in other things: "They're wandering around, looking way down near the floor or up near the ceiling, and all the books are different sizes, different colors." Baker muses: "There's some basic appeal of heterogeneity that books satisfy—that they all look different. And something about that is really pleasing to people. I mean I wouldn't want all my textbooks to be the exact same size and color and design. The design of things is so important."[31] And, here again, we find that Baker has confused the mission of libraries with museums or lost sight of the fact that an archival mission is not merely about touching old things. Besides not all books are beautifully designed or add to our sensory pleasures.

Pick up any book sitting in your house or office and ask if this object needs to be preserved in its original form. It is possible that I might answer yes, until I realize that my attitudes are based on personal convenience. The book is a wonder, a highly convenient information tool, especially if it possesses a good table of contents and index and if the author has managed to organize his thoughts and arguments in a logical fashion. This is a very different reaction, however, than that of dealing with the matter of preserving this book as an artifact and obligating some library or archives to assume such a responsibility. For most of the books we own and use, we can function just as well with a surrogate of some sort. Nicholson Baker's *Double Fold* would present a problem in formatting because of a small section of color plates that are crucial to his argument, but these could be easily dealt with in a color microfilm supplement or digitization. There is nothing intrinsically interesting about Baker's book that requires us to keep it in its original form. It is not a landmark publication form, issued in a limited run, or possessing any other attributes unique to its construction and manufacture. In my own office, residing just a few feet from *Double Fold,* are some books that necessitate different treatment. Edward Tufte's three books on information visualization sit proudly on my shelves, tomes that even I resist scribbling in (as I do for all of my other volumes).[32] Beautifully printed with many color illustrations, including some three-dimensional foldouts, the books are examples of publications needing to be kept in their original form. Tufte writes that one of his books "celebrates escapes from flatland, rendering several hundred superb displays of complex data."[33] Indeed, in his seminars on design, Tufte often talks about how he resorted to self-printing in order to obtain the quality of publication he needed to address adequately his topic. These are books that are artifacts in their own right, and it would be nonsense to toss them onto the scrap heap or to try to reduce them to a more sterile format like microfilm. But how many of the thousands of books published annually deserve such treatment?

In one of the stranger reviews of *Double Fold*, devoting as much attention to Baker's "nutty, Californian flavor" and "leftist political views," Stephen Schwartz does capture how so many are reacting to the book and the notion of librarianship represented in it. Schwartz agrees with Baker that "modern library policy gives the impression of a society rushing in the direction of the new and abandoning its past achievements." And Schwartz also agrees with Baker about the nature of graduate library science programs:

In addition, librarians have—via the godforsaken college-degree system known as "library science"—professionalized themselves into mandarins. The art of bibliography has grown pompous from the advanced degrees now required for even the lowliest job in a local library. Debates over paper and microfilm are merely a reflection of a much deeper crisis. This is a struggle over space—in our minds, hearts, souls, and identities—that the enemies of America hope to fill with lies.[34]

With such reviews as this (and the many others), America's librarians (and archivists) need to realize that they are under siege from many quarters because the public does not understand what they or their institutions really do. It is an attack started by Baker in the early 1990s when he noticed the destruction of the old library card catalogs.

NOTES

1. Michael Dirda, "*Double Fold: Libraries and the Assault on Paper*, by Nicholson Baker," *Washington Post*, April 15, 2001, available at *http://washingtonpost.com/wp-dyn/style/books/A11253-2001Apr12.html*, accessed April 18, 2001.

2. Michael Dirda, *Readings: Essays & Literary Entertainments* (Bloomington: Indiana University Press, 2000), p. 30.

3. Dirda, *Readings*, p. 215.

4. Luke Mitchell, "The Lessons of Shredded Paper," *The Standard*, April 6, 2001, available at *http://www.thestandard.com/article/0,1902,23440,00.html*.

5. Michiko Kakutani, "Microfilm Gets a Black Eye from a Friend of Paper," *New York Times*, April 10, 2001, p. B10.

6. Ed Vulliamy, "History in Peril from 'Slash and Burn' Librarians," *New York*

Observer, April 22, 2001, available at *http://www.guardian.co.uk/Archive/Article/ 0,4273,4173746,00.html*, accessed May 5, 2001.

7. Neil Postman, *The End of Education: Redefining the Value of School* (New York: Alfred A. Knopf, 1995).

8. Lionel Casson, *Libraries in the Ancient World* (New Haven, Conn.: Yale University Press, 2001), pp. 127–130.

9. Clifford Lynch, "The Battle to Define the Future of the Book in the Digital World," *First Monday* 6 (June 2001), available at *http://firstmonday.org/issues/issue66/lynch/*.

10. Henry Petroski, *The Book on the Bookshelf* (New York: Alfred A. Knopf, 1999), p. 9.

11. Nicholas Negroponte, *Being Digital* (New York: Alfred A. Knopf, 1995).

12. Barry Sanders, *A Is for Ox: Violence, Electronic Media, and the Silencing of the Written Word* (New York: Pantheon Books, 1994).

13. Negroponte, *Being Digital*, p. 6.

14. Negroponte, *Being Digital*, p. 8.

15. Negroponte, *Being Digital*, p. 13.

16. Negroponte, *Being Digital*, p. 164.

17. Sanders, *A Is for Ox*, p. xi. For an expansion of these ideas, see his *The Private Death of Public Discourse* (Boston: Beacon Press, 1998).

18. Sven Birkerts, *The Gutenberg Elegies: The Fate of Reading in an Electronic Age* (Boston: Faber and Faber, 1994).

19. Birkerts, *Gutenberg Elegies*, p. 133.

20. Birkerts, *Gutenberg Elegies*, p. 129.

21. Richard A. Lanham, *The Electronic Word: Democracy, Technology, and the Arts* (Chicago: University of Chicago Press, 1993).

22. Lanham, *The Electronic Word*, p. xiii.

23. Lanham, *The Electronic Word*, p. 3.

24. Postman, *The End of Education*, pp. 189, 191.

25. Peter N. Stearns, *Meaning Over Memory: Recasting the Teaching of Culture and History* (Chapel Hill: University of North Carolina Press, 1993).

26. Gerald Graff, *Beyond the Culture Wars: How Teaching the Conflicts Can Revitalize American Education* (New York: W.W. Norton and Co., 1992).

27. Graff, *Beyond the Culture Wars*, p. 7.

28. Mark C. Carnes, ed., *Novel History: Historians and Novelists Confront America's Past (and Each Other)* (New York: Simon and Schuster, 2001), p. 68.

29. Alexander Star, "The Paper Pusher," *The New Republic*, 4506 (May 28, 2001): 40, 41.

30. Julian Dibbel, "The Paper Chase," *Village Voice Literary Supplement*, April 2001, available at *http://www.villagevoice.com/vls/174/dibbell.shtml*, accessed May 5, 2001.

31. Jeffrey R. Young, "Logging in with . . . Nicholson Baker: Author Says Libraries Shouldn't Abandon Paper," *Chronicle of Higher Education*, May 10, 2001, available at *http://chroncile.com/free/2001/05/2001051003t.htm*, accessed May 10, 2001.

32. Edward R. Tufte, *The Visual Display of Quantitative Information* (Cheshire, Conn.: Graphics Press, 1983); *Envisioning Information* (Cheshire, Conn.: Graphics

Press, 1990); *Visual Explanations: Images and Quantities, Evidence and Narrative* (Cheshire, Conn.: Graphics Press, 1997).

   33. Tufte, *Envisioning Information*, p. 9.

   34. Stephen Schwartz, "Paper Chase: Nicholson Baker's Defense of the Printed Word," *The Weekly Standard*, May 21, 2001, pp. 39–40 (quotations, p. 40).

Chapter Seven

Burning Libraries, Discards, Card Catalogs, Nicholson Baker, and Library History

Nicholson Baker's _Double Fold_ has not arrived like a thunderbolt from the heavens, although the continuous stream of reviews in the first few months after its release might have suggested otherwise. A few years before, one of the more curious chapters in the history of American librarianship started. In 1994 writer Nicholson Baker published a provocative and controversial essay in _The New Yorker_ about the predilection of libraries to destroy old card catalogs after the establishment of online, automated catalogs.[1] Baker's essay stirred up a hornet's nest of debate and criticism in the library profession, with _The New Yorker_ itself publishing seven letters (three from librarians), _Library Journal_ publishing an interview with Baker in mid-1996, and numerous listservs on the Internet discussing the article and the issues seemingly raised by it. Institutions throw away old, outmoded stuff all the time; why should there be all the fuss about this case? Now we know better, of course, but this level of hype about something as routine as library card catalogs was certainly new for librarians in the early 1990s, although earlier transformations of library cataloging techniques had also been greeted with similar speculation, criticism, and soul-searching. The difference with Nicholson Baker and his first foray in library criticism is that it was the beginning of a sustained crusade about libraries, reaching its pinnacle with his book _Double Fold_, and with him showing no signs of losing interest.

What were Baker's gripes about modern library cataloging? Readers of Baker's _Double Fold_, who were not familiar with the author's earlier writings, will not be surprised about his views. Baker complains about weaknesses of online library catalogs, especially his sense of their facility in connecting information like author, subject, title, and other critical data, inconsistency in cataloging data, and weaknesses in guides to online users about how to utilize the catalogs. As any librarian or archivist will acknowledge, these problems have existed in *all* library cataloging, dating back hundreds of years. Nancy E. Douglas, a cataloguer at an academic library, provided the most substantial verification of the problems with Baker's perspective. Douglas contended that "most of our public card catalogs were not priceless archival treasures worthy of eternal preservation." Rather, "they were excellent, functional-but-flawed finding tools, crippled in achieving their purposes by budget constrictions, the limitations of the *Library of Congress Subject Headings* list (LCSH), the confusion of non-intuitive or knowledge-based filing rules, human error, and vandalism." Douglas also disputed Baker's argument about the card catalogs as artifacts: "He bemoans the loss of 'specific historical information' such as original price and so on, and blames the loss on the removal of the public card catalog. Most libraries did not even record this in the public catalog; if kept at all, it appeared on less-available files such as a serials Kardex or a shelflist, often located far from public access." Finally, Douglas believes Baker is no more than an alarmist about such matters: "Baker's lament did not tell librarians anything new about the ongoing need to clean and simplify online catalogs. Baker did libraries a disservice in alarming a literate public about a matter even he admits is being improved constantly. There is nothing demeaning in considering the catalog to be a 'mere' finding aid; that is, indeed, its reason for being."[2]

Nicholson Baker's real complaint with the *online* catalog relates to the demise of the *old* card catalogs, and with this we find a consistency between his earlier writings and *Double Fold*. The beginning of the article provides description after description of the destruction of old catalogs as libraries switched to automated systems, sometimes marked by celebration and fanfare. All of these descriptions lead to this:

One of the odder features of this national paroxysm of shortsightedness and anti-intellectualism ('in a class with the burning of the library at Alexandria,' Helen Rand Parish, a historian specializing in the sixteenth century, said to me) is that it isn't the result of wicked forces outside the library walls. We can't blame Saracen sackers, B-52s, anarchists, or thieves; nor can we blame propagandistic politicians intent on revising the past, moralistic book banners, or over-acidic formulations of paper. The villains, instead, are smart, well-meaning library administrators, quite certain that they are only doing what is right for their institutions.[3]

Here we see, of course, the same formula that he uses in *Double Fold*, the misguided work of library administrators against the common sense of maintaining what anybody can see is valuable.

Baker's quotation about the destruction of the library at Alexandria brings to mind the allusion of the destruction of the monasteries in sixteenth-century England, something that most reviewers picked up on, along with the idea that no matter how overstated his case, there is something going on in libraries and archives that defies common sense. Michiko Kakutani, in his review in the *New York Times*, writes: "Baker's passionate espousal of his convictions can lead him to indulge in hyperbole, not to mention vituperation directed at well-meaning if sometimes misguided people eager to save the information in supposedly deteriorating publications," then quoting the Baker comment about the monk harassing. Then, Kakutani writes: "Despite the more alarmist passages in this book, despite its often meandering and repetitive structure, Baker's core arguments possess a bedrock common sense."[4] As I have noted earlier, the willingness of these professional book reviewers to buy Baker's arguments hook, line, and sinker might seem to be more symptomatic of the weaknesses of such reviewing, but it is certainly something that Baker played on as well with his earliest anti-library essay.

Like the ways in which Baker chronicles the selling of newspapers to commercial ventures which then resell vintage newspapers as birthday presents, or the glee with which he discovers eBay and auction prices fetched for books deaccessioned by libraries, Baker also dotes in his earlier essay on what happens to the old card catalogs. Some cards are requested as "souvenirs," but most are destroyed.[5] Others are disassembled and used as "scrap paper."[6] How could libraries do this to objects that are "things of efficacy" and even "grandeur."[7] Baker grudgingly notes the advantages that online systems have, but even here we have a sense of wonder Baker believes we should recognize in the older catalogs: "Card catalogs attract vandals because they are expressive of needful social trust and communal achievement, as are other common targets, such as subway cars, railroad bridges, mailboxes, and traffic signs."[8] Then, again, Baker can build an effective argument, one that seems quite plausible, for accessing an individual's Rolodex as a "piece of literary history," being a "record of some of the more cherished connections you have formed with the world." In Baker's words, one can almost begin to believe that a Rolodex is a "form of autobiography."[9] Baker makes a simple step from this to calling the card catalog the "accreted autobiography of an institution" and the cataloguers as authors or like "medieval cathedral builders."[10]

Baker is nearly obsessed with the artifactual qualities of old card catalogs. He thinks these old catalogs, then being looked at by libraries as junk, might gain some "saving quaintness over the next fifty years."[11] Some of this seems to make sense, as when he writes:

If in seventy years a historian of science (say) wants to know whether some Nobel-laureate physics professor could possibly have seen and been influenced by a certain out-of-the-way Dutch mathematical monograph from the thirties that bears important similarities to the professor's work—whether, that is, it was part of the library's collection during the period when the professor was developing his ideas, or was acquired only after the professor's papers were published (perhaps acquired by the library as a gift from the professor's estate, because the professor was sent the monograph by the Dutchman himself, anxious to establish primacy)—the historian of science will have little chance of finding an answer to his question now, because the computer record will bear the (to him) meaningless date of the retrospective conversion of the card, i.e., sometime in the late eighties or early nineties, which has no relation to the time that the card was originally produced (and the book placed on the shelf), whereas the original card, even if it bore no direct date of creation, would have exhibited distinct features (typewriter style, format, cataloging conventions) that might have enabled a catalog-card paleographer to place it within a five-year period.[12]

The problem with this, of course, is even the presence of the old card or the book makes no guarantee or proof that the professor knew of this work. And the larger problem is how much such research would need to be done, and whether such potential research merits the saving of old card catalogs everywhere.

Baker hates the idea of anyone having to make judgments about what might or might not be saved, a problem I have commented on earlier and which only a few reviewers have picked up on. Grant Burns, in his review of *Double Fold*, was one of the few early reviewers to consider this matter, writing: "It may not be a good idea to invest the nation's resources in creating and maintaining a storage facility that does for published materials what my grandfather's basement did for the contents of the village junkyard." Rather, Burns notes that "refusal to judge is an abdication of one's fundamental human responsibility. Saving everything, simply because it exists, is such an abdication." He continues: "that is why responsible librarians don't save everything, and it is why pleas that the Library of Congress, or someone or something, hang onto everything published, everything recorded, just in case, have the ring of fear and neurosis. It is the fear of making choices, the fear of decisions, the fear of letting go, the neurotic need to cling to the past and its detritus."[13] Those old card catalog drawers will look good in the basement, and, in fact, the catalogs have appeared (original and in reproduction) in antique stores, flea markets, and specialty mail-order firms. And the old cards have been used in art works and for other purposes, providing an antiquarian sensibility of the value of these catalogs but hardly proving the larger scholarly values Baker assigns to them.

In an interesting divergence from his tirade about how the decision to destroy old books and newspapers was largely due to an obsession with space, Baker, in his earlier "Discards" essay, notes that libraries and librarians have always needed space and that a "library continues to buy books, and it selects what it throws out, on the basis of what it judges is of value to present and future uses of the library." Still, Baker has to over-state his case somewhere, and in the case of card catalogs, he contends that administrators want them out because *"they hate them."* Why? Here we gain more evidence about how much Baker dislikes librarians or, at the least, willingly makes them the scapegoat for his criticism:

The impulse to burn is there, it seems to me, because library administrators (more often male than female) want so keenly to distance themselves from the quasi-clerical associations that surround traditional librarianship—the filing, the typing, the shelving, the pasting, the labeling. Librarianship, they think (rightly), hasn't received the respect it deserves. The card catalog is to them a monument, not to intergenerational intellect, but to the idea of the lowly, meek-and-mild public li-brarian as she exists in the popular mind. The archetype, though they know it to be cheap and false, shames them; they believe that if they are disburdened of all that soiled cardboard, they will be able to define themselves as Brokers of Infor-mation and Off-Site Digital Retrievalists instead of as shy, bookish people with due-date stamps and wooden drawers to hold the nickel-and-dime overdue fines, with "Read to Your Child" posters over their heads and "February Is Black History Month" bookmarks at their fingertips.

In other words, Baker early on was depicting librarians as being insecure, as well as doing a sort of reversal of the gender issues often assigned to this profession. Baker also depicted librarians as deceitful:

When we redefine libraries as means rather than as places—as conduits of knowl-edge rather than as physical buildings filled with physical books—we may think that the new, more "visionary," more megatrendy definition embraces the old, but in fact it doesn't: the removal of the concrete word "books" from the library's statement of purpose is exactly the act that allows misguided administrators to work out their hostility toward printed history while the rest of us sleep.[14]

With this statement, we see Baker toying with the distrust many intellec-tuals and social critics assign to the technocracy of the modern Information Age. While there are many challenges associated with our modern era's reliance on information technology, Baker adopts a more extremist view as he implies sinister motives and other designs by a group that he thinks society usually viewed as meek and mild-mannered.

Three years after the first article, however, the debate about card catalogs was renewed as Ken Dowlin, head of the San Francisco Public Library and an advocate of the digital library, came under criticism, ultimately leading to his resignation for his failure to transform that venerable old public library system into his image of the modern information center. Baker him-self joined in a lawsuit against that public library (he described his com-plaints in a subsequent article in the October 14, 1996 *New Yorker*) and Dowlin, this time because of the alleged disposal of thousands of books supposedly to clear the way for an electronic library. The case, and Baker's participation, attracted national media attention. Baker, a novelist and essayist, had become a spokesperson for both old library catalogs and the mission of the traditional library. In this earlier controversy, we can see precursors of the later debate about newspapers and brittle books. When interviewed at his newspaper warehouse, for example, Nicholson Baker was reported to feel that the "information-services world is too willing to compromise its primary mission—the preservation of information, and therefore culture—for the sake of transient values like space, modernity, and supposed convenience" (as summarized by the reporter). In a direct quotation Baker says: "I'm not pretending that I'm an experienced archivist. I just know, in kind of a primitive way, that something is worth keeping."[15] These primitive feelings started when Baker discovered that libraries were destroying the paper card catalogs.

Librarians have not forgotten about Baker's earlier criticisms of their catalogs, even if *Double Fold* does not focus on this topic. As a result of Baker's intensifying criticism directed at libraries and librarians with his book, the author was the target of a hoax in early 2001. In March, reports appeared on a listserv (Publib) that Baker had formed the Ludd Library Foundation to build a library in San Francisco without any computers. A news release quoted Baker as saying: "Public libraries have emphasized gimmickry at the expense of books and reading," and that his library would have "real librarians" and a card catalog in a "quiet environment free of computers and computer games."[16] Baker was not amused, especially by the fabricated quotations. However, the hoax captured perfectly well what Baker wrote about in his various essays and *Double Fold*.

Others, reviewing Baker's *Double Fold*, also have not forgotten about the author's earlier forays into librarianship. In another of those exasperating reviews in which the reviewer buys Baker's arguments even when recognizing other perspectives brought to the table by this author, David Gates writes:

When Baker first began what looked like a second career as a "library activist"— a 1994 *New Yorker* piece about the iniquity of dumping card catalogs, a 1996 speech in the San Francisco Public Library's auditorium, after that institution had sent books to a landfill because there wasn't room to store them—I thought it a noble, quixotic and essentially bum idea. . . . Well, I thought, if that's how he wants to distract himself from his true calling, fine. We all have our little ways.

Then Gates adds this observation, just before launching into his agreement with Baker's assessment and his own outrage at what was going on in libraries: "Baker writes fiction much the way he does guerrilla librarianship: trying to cram into it, for safekeeping, everything he ever saw, heard, thought and read. Like Proust, Nabokov and any other thinking person who's racking up highway miles on the way to the grave, Baker's fixated on the subject of time: how much life a single instant contains, how many instants there are, how instantly they pass away forever."[17] This certainly provides an insight into why Baker has taken on librarians and their cataloging, collection development, and preservation activities, but it still does nothing to explain why Nicholson Baker should be taken seriously by anyone.

Like most controversies, the heat generated by this one has also caused it to miss some important issues, not the least of which is the neglected state of library archives (that is, the historical records documenting the libraries and library profession) in this nation. In that light, both Baker's extremely nostalgic sentiments about the old catalogs and the overly enthusiastic musings by advocates of electronic information technologies appear a bit misplaced. Even the popular press has displayed its predilection to focus on the sensational, or at the least to paint the debates in black-and-white terms. When the April 1997 issue of *The Atlantic Monthly*, in Anne Soukhanov's "Word Watch" column, picked up on the phrase "guerrilla librarianship"—the "use of surreptious measures by librarians determined to resist the large-scale 'deaccessioning' of rarely used books"[18]—it was easy to tell that we had really lost touch with the genuine issues facing librarianship in our so-called Information Age. Just the month before, Sallie Tisdale's critique of the evolving electronic library in *Harper's* reflected a popular uprising of sorts about the supposed role of the library in the modern Information Age.[19] Baker's book, *Double Fold*, seemed to be a major engagement in this revolution.

Because of the larger matters of library history, we must proceed with caution as we consider this recent controversy and reexamine it from the vantage of another threatened library catalog. The catalog described here, one at the Carnegie Library of Pittsburgh, is not endangered because of the wonders of new technologies or the visions of information professionals; it is in peril because American librarianship has rarely demonstrated a respect for the documents and artifacts of its past, and in this, Nicholson Baker has a point as he worries about how libraries are treating their book and newspaper collections (except that the degree of conspiracy Baker finds in all this is a bit strange). A century and a quarter of an organized library profession, powerful lobby groups supporting librarians in their quest against censorship and for broader access to information, and a remarkable transformation in information technologies have all rolled over the discipline with hardly an impact on the quest to preserve records, artifacts, and buildings associated with the history of librarianship. Old library catalogs, treated as interesting finds in a sort of archaeological triage of libraries as they evolve in the print to electronic era, will only be useful as an important professional issue to librarians if they enable librarians, and society, to comprehend the importance of preserving library archives as a means to understanding the success and failures, desired and hoped-for missions of the modern library. Meanwhile, another significant but neglected library catalog sits at the Carnegie in Pittsburgh, awaiting its fate without media attention or fanfare.

Nicholson Baker's "Discards" was an evocation of the muses protecting old libraries. Baker wrote about the problems with the online catalog and the cavalier way in which its precursor, the card catalog, was being tossed aside. Baker defended the old catalog as superior, detailing the sloppiness with which data is transferred from paper cards to the automated replacement. He also pointed to many of the online catalog's limitations, such as its failure to bring together material that is related by author, subject, title, or other features, the lack of consistency with catalog data for access points, and the lack of online references to guide users through a subject search. Baker also worried about the old card catalog as a historical record of what libraries and librarians had accomplished, or, at least, what they thought they had accomplished. These issues seem more serious, however, because of Baker's dramatic writing, very similar to what we have discovered in *Double Fold*. Destroying card catalogs is described as being the result of a "national shortsightedness and anti-intellectualism." He compares this to the "burning of the library at Alexandria."[20] While Baker fails to take into account the nuances of catalogs as records or the diversity of records supporting the public catalog (there are authority files, shelf lists, and even administrative records necessary for understanding the catalog the public uses), his essay does a good job in raising sensitivities about throwing off the old in the current technocratic age. His failure to see the entire spectrum of library records is similar to his failure to miss the other records of newspaper publishers or to adopt newspapers as the fundamental historical source. The bottom line is Baker's lack of understanding of libraries and archives.

Baker's laments about the passing of the card catalog are part of a long-lived genre of writing about the passing of eras in librarianship. Baker displays a fancy, an admiration, for the traditional catalog. This fascination with the catalog is hardly new. Over a century ago, in 1890, an article entitled "The Secrets of a Catalogue" appeared in the *Living Age*, discussing the manuscript catalog of the British Museum.[21] The essay was written midway through the publication of the catalog into book form, and the essay displays, similar to Baker's "Discards," warmth for the old "plain ledgers" in a plaintive fashion such as we see in Baker's writings:

The formidable series [manuscript copy of the British Museum's catalog] of plain ledgers does not look very entertaining, and most readers who prowl through the jungle of its contents are seriously hunting down their prey. But to the lover of books it is at least as interesting as the catalogue of a museum to the genuine antiquary; and even the unlearned in rambling through its pages may find some curious secrets hidden in its recesses. For the sphere of thought has its relics and [k]nicknacks as well as the material world; its vestiges of old myths and creeds, its fossil theories and dry bones of philosophy, its mummied worthies and stuffed characters, its ancient utensils of wisdom and ornaments of diction, its tomahawks of satire and war-clubs of debate, its freaks and marvels of the mind.[22]

Other essays about the printed British Museum catalog appeared in other popular and scholarly journals, mostly cheering on the publication making the catalog more widely accessible, such as Rudolph de Cordova's 1906 *Living Age* article describing the British Museum catalog as the "greatest gift which the last quarter of the nineteenth century bequeathed to the twentieth" and the "triumphant" activity of transforming the manuscript into a printed book.[23]

It was not unusual, in fact, for essays in early-twentieth-century popular journals to feature descriptions of printed book catalogs, reminding us that Baker's tirades against the loss of old catalogs is not an aberration or, for that matter, new (although perhaps Baker should be listed as the most effective critic of modern libraries, as he has grabbed not just public attention to what libraries are doing but even the attention of some library governing boards). The reviewer of *Double Fold* in my local newspaper criticized the book as being so detailed as to make it a "little tiresome" and as not adding up to a "balanced account." Yet, and this demonstrates the influence of Baker's writings, the reviewer concluded: "Let's hope this extended rant will give rise to much debate and policy change."[24]

Catalogs were also affectionately described as works of art. Baker, in his "Discards" article, showed such tendencies, writing of catalogers as "authors" of a "beloved manuscript" and the catalog as an "autobiography" and a "monument."[25] Articles in the popular press have long reflected such sentiments. Library catalogs are described as "creations" and the major intellectual achievements of librarians. An interest in cataloging rules, such as in an 1890 article in *The Nation* about the publication of the second edition of a cataloging manual, also indicates an abiding interest in the intellectual organizing of books and other publications.[26] As early as 1867 *Blackwoods Magazine* published an article suggesting how anyone could organize his book collection.[27] We can find the same kind of affection expressed by Baker for newspapers and books in his *Double Fold*, but what Nicholson Baker fails to recognize is that such expressions have been made for a long time, including by librarians. The building of libraries, library collections, and the tools providing access to the collections have all been recipients of descriptors suggesting pride in workmanship. An automated catalog can be a work of art as much as a paper one, although a critic like Baker does not seem willing to go that far (perhaps because he brings an antiquarian sensibility in the love of the old and the handmade, as much an obsession as those who relish the use above all else of the computer). The difference between Baker's earlier writings and his present crusade is that he has become more strident, perhaps out of frustration in dealing with librarians and archivists, although there is a consistency in his arguments that what is in a library should always stay there. In an online dialogue sponsored by *Slate*, Baker stated that "research libraries are communal assemblages of unknowables built by generations of intelligent librarians and that those librarianly decisions, fifty or a hundred years ago, as to what should become part of a great collection deserved respect." In other words, "libraries do have a responsibility to keep what they have on the shelf."[28] Likewise, Baker wants those old library card catalogs kept.

Library catalogs, as a democratic device providing access to all to great quantities of human knowledge, is another popular theme in the writing about these devices. Baker deals with such concerns by stressing the weaknesses of automated catalogs, ranging, in his opinion, from problems with authority control, irrelevant retrieval, failure to save a user's search strategy, lack of references for subject headings, and poor or sloppy entries in the online versions—all erecting barriers to the information people seek. These are not, of course, new concerns. In the mid- and late-nineteenth century, there were debates about different versions of catalogs, with the dictionary catalog (organized by alphabetical order) being hailed as the "democratic" approach to access over the classified catalog (organized by a classification scheme, representing knowledge by number and/or letter). The issue here is, of course, that any classification or access theme is imperfect because of the vast quantities of information involved. The other relevant matter is that librarians as well as archivists, working with manuscripts and organizational records instead of books, have been experimenting with retrieval systems for generations, recognizing along the way that there are always new problems and challenges on the horizon to be dealt with and resolved.

One such debate raged in 1877 in the pages of *The Nation* and *Library Journal*, responding to a letter from an H. A. Hagen who contended since any one who was learned would know the authors and titles in his own discipline that such cataloging schemes were unnecessary, relegating subject access to an unnecessary exercise and expense.[29] Despite such sentiments, by the end of the century, the notion of subject access seemed well established, as an 1898 essay in *The Athenaeum* stated that "It is now recognized on all sides that the reader who wishes to know books a library possesses on a given subject is quite as normal and as reasonable a person as the reader who wishes to know what books it possesses by a given author."[30] The concept of the scholar meandering through piles of documentary materials in search of the obscure fact or even in search of a subject is romantic—the stuff of Hollywood and literature, but it is not what most scholars wish to have to endure. Any researcher, and I write from personal experience as well, has been blessed from time to time by the serendipity involved in archival and library exploration, but we all prefer the means to work with more precision and efficiency.

Baker's criticism of online library catalogs may also be part of the genre of anti-technology writing that has been evident at crucial junctures in the past, and that has certainly become a staple of the past twenty years with the proliferation of computers from organizations to homes. Books by Neil Postman, Barry Sanders, Mark Slouka, and Clifford Stoll are just some of the recent writings questioning how technology is being used in our society,[31] some of which I discussed in the previous chapter. We can add Nicholson Baker to our list. In Baker's interview, published in the *Library Journal*, he stated that he thought of the card catalog as a "big, slow, beautiful thing, built over generations by many unthanked people." In fact, at other critical points in shifts in the technology of cataloging, there have been such sentimental writings about earlier technology.[32] Even as the Library of Congress began the printing and distributing of catalog cards in 1901, recognized as one of the most significant cooperative cataloging efforts in history, essays appeared lamenting the end of the printed book catalog. In 1914 E. L. Pearson published an essay in *The Nation* terming the card catalog as "preposterous and titantic," the latter a reference to something hailed as a technological breakthrough but destined to sink under its own claims.[33] In the same year in the *Library Journal*, Agnes Van Valkenburgh wrote that "it seems the fashion of late to say derogatory or mirth-provoking things of the catalog and cataloger," summarizing the growing frustration about how cataloging was done and perceived.[34]

The kind of technological threat chronicled by Baker is not new. In articles in journals like *Science Digest* (1944) and the *Atlantic Monthly* (1946), as the promises of the computer became evident and overreaching, the traditional library catalog was assailed, although quietly and politely with the promises of technological solutions to the control of library holdings.[35] By the 1960s, some essays began to appear heralding the transition from cards to computers that Nicholson Baker has attacked with a greater vehemence. An interview with the head of the New York Public Library's Research Division, published in the 1968 *New Yorker*, described that institution's card catalog as a device with "smudgy" cards and cards worn by the "thumbing of nearly sixty years."[36] A change was necessary. Baker's essay three decades later reflects the rising frustration by many with the advent of the electronic library and the disposal of those smudged, worn catalog cards.

Are there some old print or paper card catalogs needing to be preserved? Yes, with an emphasis on *some*. In the Carnegie Public Library of Pittsburgh, in its Science and Technology Department, sits an old card catalog that was active from 1909 until 1973. What makes this catalog interesting is that it is one of a half-dozen surviving classified catalogs left in the United

States. A classified catalog uses classification numbers for subject access instead of words or subject headings. These catalogs are ancient in origin, with evidence that libraries in Babylon and the famous library at Alexandria employed this type of control device.

The value of these classified catalogs rested in their enabling a more logical (and tighter) arrangement of subjects and book shelving, usually beginning with general material and proceeding to more specific materials, than the now more common dictionary catalogs which can physically and intellectually disperse books to a far greater extent. A user can move from general to specific subject areas and related areas without consulting a different part of the catalog, encapsulating an entire field of knowledge within one file and enabling an easier handling of terminological changes within a field, such as follows:

016.6	Bibliography of technology
016.62	Bibliography of engineering
016.6213	Bibliography of electrical engineering
016.62138	Bibliography of electronics engineering
016.621384	Bibliography of radio engineering
016.621384132	Bibliography of vacuum tubes

A subject structure, confusing to many users, is replaced by the classification approach. Books covering more than one topic can be given classification numbers for as many topics as necessary. Special libraries are also able to include a variety of materials—journal articles, reprints, patents, and microfilms in one file using a classified catalog.

Although an endangered species, there is no postage stamp commemorating this old catalog. At the end of the nineteenth century, classified catalogs were common and in the 1950s they even enjoyed more acclaim as some library cataloging specialists heralded the values of these catalogs. After the publication of Cutter's *Rules for a Dictionary Catalog* and Melvil Dewey's *A Classification and Subject Index*, both in 1876, and the adoption of these rules by the Library of Congress for its own catalog, the classified catalog rapidly moved toward extinction in the United States, outdone by the dictionary catalog arranged alphabetically and by subject. As libraries grew rapidly in this country and the social and educational backgrounds of library users broadened, librarians moved to more practical organizational schemes in order to help library users locate books and other materials. Standardization cost libraries and librarianship some of its colorfulness and character, but such standardization also led to improved means by which to assist researchers. It is, of course, a familiar story.

When the Carnegie opened its doors to the public in 1895, a published book catalog, using the Dewey classification scheme, was available for use. This published catalog was printed in the basement of the Carnegie using a linotype machine. Cards were printed for the local card catalog and the slugs were kept and filed alphabetically, the idea being to facilitate the printing of subsequent editions of the book catalog. Additional published catalogs were prepared and released by the Carnegie. In late 1900 it published a book catalog for the city schools. Two years later the Carnegie began serious discussion of printing a classified catalog of all the library's holdings for use in homes and offices and in order to do away with the increasing quantity of stored metal type used for printing the catalog cards. This classified catalog was published in 1907–1908, making use of the Dewey system for the classification and numbering schemes and totaling five volumes with information on 242,000 volumes. Supplements were printed until 1911, when it was determined that the compilation of the catalog was far too burdensome. In a standard work on library classification published in 1938, the Carnegie's published catalog was deemed to be one of the most notable, sharing the honor with the Boston Athenaeum, the Astor Library, the Peabody Institute of Baltimore, and the U.S. Surgeon's Library.

The origins of the Carnegie's science and technology catalog date to the Carnegie's discovery, early in its existence, that there was a demand for such literature and specialized reference. A staff member, with a background in chemistry and metallurgy, was hired in 1900. A Technology Division was established in 1901 as part of the Reference Department. Growing demand led to the creation of a separate department in 1902 and the start of a classified card catalog for its collections in 1907. The decision to use a classified catalog was based on the belief that specialized science researchers are accustomed to classified knowledge, reflected in that these kinds of catalogs were more common in science or technical libraries than in public or academic libraries.

The classified card catalog was opened for business in 1909 when the Technology Department received its new, separate room in the renovated Carnegie building. The 1909 Carnegie annual report suggested that the new catalog is "much more manageable" and "that for this special class of books, in which subjects continually change and expand, the arrangement offers many advantages." A few years later, the head of the department noted that it offered "its patrons exceptional advantages for self help by reason of the completeness and convenient arrangement of the catalogue." Using the Universal Decimal Classification system to fill in the inadequacies of the Dewey system, the technology staff also added information such as annotations on scope of subject, absorbing an ever-increasing amount of time. The end of the catalog came when the Carnegie made its switch in 1973 to the Library of Congress classification and started its use of the automated, online service OCLC.

The Carnegie's old classified catalog exists as a forlorn relic of older library practices and that of the Carnegie Library of Pittsburgh itself. A few other similar catalogs like it sit in a similar state in other American libraries. One, started about the same time as the Carnegie's and terminated (although available for consultation) in 1984, is at the John Crerar Library in Chicago. Another at Boston University was frozen in 1972 and discarded. Yet another was operative at the Engineering Societies Library of New York until 1995 when it was dismantled for conversion into an online catalog.

The Carnegie's classified catalog is a rare library artifact, a throwback to library practices that began to disappear a full century ago. Do we preserve this object, as Nicholson Baker would want us to do, as a reminder that electronic information technologies may not have made retrieval of information easier? Do we maintain this catalog as a crucial part of the library profession's archives? Do we abandon our electronic catalogs and return to the older card catalogs, classified and subject? Notice that such questions, while perhaps less aesthetically pleasing or romantic than those that Nicholson Baker asks, are more connected to the realities librarians and archivists face in servicing their patrons and meeting their missions. Baker drops in from the outside, a *deus ex machina*, bringing his wisdom and wit but in a sort of disconnected fashion.

We can quickly eliminate the need to consider a return to old library card catalogs and older information retrieval methods. A thirty-year investment in automation has paid off in that citizens of this country have greater access to greater quantities of information in a dazzling array of sources, from printed book and magazine to electronic books and newspapers, than ever before. While most do not believe traditional print sources will disappear, as Nicholson Baker worries, it is also true that the ability to find more quickly and cheaply larger amounts of relevant information will not be abandoned either. This brings us back to the original question posed by Baker in his first *New Yorker* essay, the destruction of old card catalogs. Baker desires them not to be discarded because he believes that they possess important information not captured in their electronic surrogates. This is a highly debatable point. What is not debatable, however, is that these catalogs are records or artifacts of past library practice. Discussion needs to reemerge about what should be done with these catalogs as evidence of library history, but this is a very different kind of discussion than that engaged in by Nicholson Baker.

Despite a steady stream of published studies on library history through the years, professional conferences devoted to the topic, and a few scholarly journals on the history of libraries and librarianship, American librarians have shown little respect·for the records and artifacts of their own past. In a 1991 article in *Libraries and Culture: A Journal of Library History*, I demonstrated how few libraries had made any provision for their archives. Virtually none of the major libraries supported in-house institutional archives, and only a slightly larger number had placed their older records in other archival repositories, such as historical societies or those at universities and colleges.[37] That the Carnegie supports a small archival program at the present for its library, natural history museum, art museum, and music hall units provides some hope that the old Science and Technology classified catalog will be preserved, both as a part of the Carnegie's own history and that of librarianship in general. But what about other surviving catalogs? What will be their fate? And notice here that I believe that some of these older catalogs should be preserved, but not because they are superior or because of some sort of nostalgia that causes us to believe that they are valuable because they are handiworks, a kind of library craft project. These older catalogs are worth preserving, as part of a process of careful deliberation, as documents of library history and American culture.

Given some of the ambitious recent efforts to document the development of the Internet and the World Wide Web, it seems logical that some resources should be devoted to ensuring the preservation of old manuscript catalogs, printed book catalogs, some card catalogs, and the evolution of automated, online catalogs. That so little attention has been given such issues by library professionals is disturbing, but not surprising, but not for *any* of the reasons pushed by Nicholson Baker.

There are at least several reasons why the development of library archives has faltered, at least in this country. First, librarians have been pressed to provide increasing services with limited, and even decreasing, resources. Baker would probably argue that at the heart of this is the library's fixation with modern technologies, but it is also true that many library users expect to avail themselves of such technologies at their local—and certainly their university—library. Second, there is the image of archives as old stuff, maintained for antiquarian and nostalgic purposes, but hardly crucial to current responsibilities, an image generally perpetuated by Baker. Archives, and records in general, need to be maintained for purposes of administrative continuity, compliance with external regulations, corporate memory, accountability, and a host of similar reasons. While the Carnegie's old classified catalog may not be of value for fiscal and administrative accountability, it is certainly crucial for understanding how cataloging and information retrieval purposes have changed. Who knows, it may be that the notion of a classified system will again become important for managing the ever-changing World Wide Web? Finally, librarians have demonstrated a lack of awareness of the reasons why records need to be maintained. Shirley Wiegand, in a book a few years ago, reported how ignorant librarians are of local, state, and federal laws and regulations dictating that they better manage the records of their own organizations.[38] It is not surprising, then, that old catalogs and related records are forgotten and, ultimately, destroyed or allowed to decay beyond the possibility of use.

We can forget about Baker's romantic notions of the card catalog. We should be thankful, however, for such writings that jolt the library profession out of its complacency about its own past and its own records and artifacts. The Carnegie Library of Pittsburgh's old classified catalog should not be a discard, and the Carnegie should recharge its support of an archives and records program as an example to other public libraries in the United States. The movement from card catalogs to online library catalogs has occurred for many reasons, especially for increasing access to the library collections and enhancing libraries' roles in the modern Information Age. Nicholson Baker acknowledges increased access with the online version of the library catalog, but he places far more emphasis on misguided decisions by library administrators, efforts to save space, and issues about the roles of librarians in society, while ignoring the historic fact that the old catalogs had many, many limitations (not unlike the errors Baker carefully documents with the online catalogs in "Discards").

Baker also discusses technology with the online catalogs as a *new* problem, also ignoring that the printed book catalogs and card catalogs were also the result of the use of new (for their day) technologies; in other words, librarians (even before their organization as a profession) were always seeking to adopt the newest technologies that made their collections accessible. Baker's weakness here is the same one he displays in *Double Fold* when he writes about microfilming and digitization as if it must be *instant* perfection or that it should operate on some kind of learning curve (learning from mistakes, trial and error, and unanticipated positive and negative results from new systems and applications). Baker is not a Luddite, but he does harbor some inherent negative suspicions about technology and technologists (especially the latter if they are library technologists), an issue explored in more detail in the next chapter.

NOTES

This chapter is based on my article coauthored with Jane Greenberg and Cynthia Porter. "Access Denied: The Discarding of Library History," *American Libraries* 29 (April 1998): 57–61. Jane Greenberg also allowed me to draw upon her unpublished "On Nicholson Baker's 'Discards' and the Library Catalog Genre in the Popular Press."

1. Nicholson Baker, "Discards," *New Yorker* 70 (April 4, 1994): 64–86. My citations are to the version of this essay published in Baker's *The Size of Thoughts: Essays and Other Lumber* (New York: Vintage Books, 1997), pp. 125–181.

2. Nancy E. Douglas, "Debating 'Discards': A Response to Nicholson Baker," *Rare Book and Manuscripts Librarianship* 9: 1 (1994): 41–47 (quotations, pp. 41, 46, 47).

3. Baker, *The Size of Thoughts*, p. 128.

4. Michiko Kakutani, "Double Fold: The Printed Word in All Its Glory," available at *http://www.annistonstar.com/books/books200104263184.html*, accessed June 3, 2001.

5. Baker, *The Size of Thoughts*, pp. 133–134.

6. Baker, *The Size of Thoughts*, p. 138.
7. Baker, *The Size of Thoughts*, p. 134.
8. Baker, *The Size of Thoughts*, pp. 135–136.
9. Baker, *The Size of Thoughts*, p. 140.
10. Baker, *The Size of Thoughts*, pp. 140–141.
11. Baker, *The Size of Thoughts*, p. 176.
12. Baker, *The Size of Thoughts*, p. 156.
13. Grant Burns, "To Breathe Is To Judge: An Attempt to Think Calmly about Nicholson Baker's Book, *Double Fold*," *NewPages.com*, available at *http://www.newpages.com/unclefrank/Number02.htm*, accessed June 3, 2001.
14. Baker, *The Size of Thoughts*, pp. 157–158.
15. Doug Hubley, "Old News: Fighting to Save a Historic Newspaper Collection, Author Nicholson Baker Makes His Stand on the Banks of the Salmon Falls River," *The Portland Phoenix*, November 9–16, 2000, available at *http://www.portlandphoenix.com/archive/features/00/11/10/PAPER.html*, accessed April 18, 2001.
16. "Nicholson Baker Returns in Prose and Prank," *American Libraries* 32 (April 2001): 28–29.
17. David Gates, "Paper Chase," *New York Times Book Review*, April 15, 2001, pp. 9–10 (quotations, p. 10).
18. Anne H. Soukhanov, "Word Watch," *Atlantic Monthly* 279 (April 1997), available at *http://www.theatlantic.com/issues/97apr/watch.htm*, accessed May 30, 2001.
19. Sallie Tisdale, "Silence, Please: The Public Library as Entertainment Center," *Harper's* 294 (March 1997): 65–72.
20. Baker, *The Size of Thoughts*, p. 128.
21. "Secrets of a Catalogue," *Living Age* 184 (February 8, 1890): 380–384.
22. "Secrets of a Catalogue," p. 380.
23. Rudolph de Cordova, "The Catalogue of the Library of the British Museum," *Living Age* 248 (January 27, 1906): 221–228.
24. John Schulman, "Author Takes Preservation of Printed Works into His Own Hands," *Pittsburgh Post-Gazette*, May 20, 2001, p. 9.
25. Baker, *The Size of Thoughts*, pp. 140–141.
26. Review of Cutter's *Rules for A Dictionary Catalog*, 2nd ed., *The Nation* 50 (March 27, 1890): 261.
27. "How to Make A Catalogue of Books," *Blackwoods* 101 (May 1867): 606–624.
28. The discussion is available at *http://slate.msn.com/code/BookClub/BookClub.asp?Sh . . . /2001&idMessages 527&iBio 5* accessed April 26, 2001. The discussion ran April 19, 2001.
29. H. A. Hagen, "The Librarian's Work" *The Nation* 24 (January 18, 1877): 40–41; *Library Journal* (1877): 1: 4–5, p. 191.
30. Review of James D. Brown's *Manual of Library Classification and Shelf Arrangement*, "Bibliographical Literature" *The Athenaeum* 2 (September 17, 1898): 364–365.
31. I have discussed the nature of these writings in "Drawing Sea Serpents: The Publishing Wars on Personal Computing and the Information Age," *First Monday*

(May 1998), available at *http://www.firstmonday.dk/issues/issue2_8/cox/index. html.*

32. David Dodd, "Requiem for the Discarded," *Library Journal* (May 15, 1996): 31–32 (quotation, p. 31).

33. E. L. Pearson, "The Pestilent Catalogue," *The Nation* 99 (July 1914): 130–131.

34. Agnes Van Valkenburgh, "A Plea for the Cataloger," *Library Journal* (September 1914): 679–681.

35. Fremont Rider, "Tomorrow's Books—100 to the Inch," *Science Digest* 16 (December 1944): 57, 62–63; Vannevar Bush, "As We May Think," available at *http://www.isg.sfu.ca/duchier/misc/vbush/*; also available in the *Atlantic Monthly* (July 1944).

36. "Nine Million Cards," *New Yorker* (June 22, 1968): 21–22.

37. Richard J. Cox, "Library History and Library Archives," *Libraries & Culture* 26 (Fall 1991): 569–593.

38. Shirley A. Wiegand, *Library Records: A Retention and Confidentiality Guide* (Westport, Conn.: Greenwood Press, 1994).

Chapter Eight

Persistent Images

Nicholson Baker is a hard man to pin down. Some of his views seem to reflect that of the stereotypical antiquarian or bibliophile, but he does not appear to be a hater of technology as is often the case with those enamored of print (even those who recognize that print is a technological product). Yet, Baker's hope that libraries and archives retain one of everything puts him in the company of people who have written critically, sometimes hysterically, about the impact of technologies on society. I am quite skeptical myself about technology and its implications, and I love printed books and the general utility of print, but I certainly come no where close to agreeing with Nicholson Baker about technology and its use in libraries or archives. As I have tried to demonstrate in this volume, I believe my differences come from having a very different understanding of what libraries and archives are about.

In all of his writings, Nicholson Baker provides ample evidence that he is not a technophobe. In his 1994 article, "Discards," Baker acknowledged that "without online catalogs, and the circulation and acquisition modules of software with which online catalogs are linked, libraries would simply not have been able to process all the books and journals that were arriving on their loading docks."[1] Baker describes his own use of online catalogs for his research for the "Discards" article, noting that they are "extremely convenient."[2] And regarding the development of OCLC, Baker describes it as a "handy, unilateral way of delivering the Library of Congress MARC files to member libraries turned into a highly democratic, omnidirectional collaboration among hundreds of thousands of once-isolated documental-

ists."[3] While Baker argues about quality control and other particulars in
the use of automation, the author never indicates a general aversion to
technology, but sees new challenges posed by the emerging technological
environment: "But in my experience, five minutes with any online catalog
is sufficient time to uncover states of disorder that simply would not have
arisen in what library administrators call a 'paper environment.' "[4] Baker
launches into a diatribe about the costs of these new technologies—what
he terms a "kind of self-inflicted online hell"[5] (a theme that becomes the
cornerstone of his crusade). But, again, Baker never lambasts the idea or
principles behind the goals of these online catalogs.

One of Baker's concerns with online catalogs is how they must be used
by patrons. Baker describes the ease of using the old cards, and then, in
his usual highly sarcastic phrasing, describes what the typical patron must
go through in using the online catalog: "It's as if you walked up to a card
catalog you hadn't used in a while and weren't sure whether, in order to
open a drawer, you were supposed to pull on the drawer handle, push on
the drawer handle, twirl the brass end of the holding rod, or fart twice and
sing 'God Bless America' in a hoarse falsetto."[6] Later, Baker adds: "card
catalogs are 'precoordinated,' whereas online catalogs are still almost entirely 'postcoordinated,' which means that the burden of figuring out how
the universe of subjects ought to be organized has been shifted away from
the cards and onto you, the user, who must now master Boolean 'AND
NOT' filters and keyword trickery and crabwise movement by adjacent call
numbers merely in order to block avalanches of irrelevancies."[7] Again, here
there is nothing inherently anti-technological, although such passages ignore the fact that manuscript and printed card catalogs often posed challenges for the uninitiated user, which is why libraries have reference
librarians and archives have reference archivists to help. Still, with all this,
Baker is optimistic about online catalogs. He writes: "I have no doubt that
it will all get better. That's the wonderful thing about software: it gets
better."[8] Baker then goes on, describing the future in online searching and
the power and convenience it will bring, although his waxing eloquently
may simply be the denouement for his final pleas for saving the old card
catalogs.

At the heart of Baker's concern is the fact that some book (some object)
will need to be used at some point in the future and we can never know
just what or when that use will happen. Baker believes that the "function
of a great library is to sort and store obscure books." He continues:

A book whose presence you think you will need throughout life, you buy. Libraries
are repositories for the out of print and the less desired, and we value them ines-
timably for that. The fact that most library books seldom circulate is part of the
mystery and power of libraries. The books are there, waiting from age to age until
their moment comes. And in the case of any given book, its moment may never

come—but we have no way of predicting that, since we are unable to know now what a future time will find of interest.[9]

Baker wants *every* "book to continue to exist somewhere, not to go extinct, because in some later ecosystem of knowledge it may be put to some surprising use—a cautionary use, a comic use, a cultural-historical use."[10] The value of old card catalogs for Baker, then, is that they seem valuable to this kind of potential use by researchers, although the author never scales this up for its implications for all libraries, not just the major research libraries (or even how we define something as a major research library).

Baker's *Double Fold* is not a rant about technology, something he also avoids in his earlier writings about libraries, although it is easy to interpret it in this fashion. Baker notes that in the library world he has become known as a "critic," "crank," and a "Luddite."[11] Those who criticize him as being anti-technology are missing the nuances of his writings, especially this controversial book, although Baker makes it easy to do so (and this is one of the immense frustrations of his writings) because of his style of writing and his reading of deeper, more sinister meaning into the work and motives of librarians and archivists. It is one thing when you write fiction to allow readers to read meaning into the words, the stories, and the narrative, but this certainly detracts from a work intended to be nonfiction. Nicholson Baker's constant reinterpretations of *Double Fold*, referred to throughout this book, are reminiscent of reading interpretation after interpretation of Melville's *Moby Dick*, after a while, you have no idea what the author may have intended when he originally wrote the book. In this case, however, Baker seems to be doing the reinterpretation himself (although I am sure he will see my commentary as going far beyond anything he tried to convey).

Baker's views about technology and its use in libraries or archives (although, again, archives are never really addressed directly) is a bit more muddled, at least defying the ability to characterize them easily. Throughout *Double Fold*, Baker likes to make sarcastic comments about technology in libraries. For example, Baker takes a swipe at the use of microfilm: "There are nice things about microfilm, too—the congenial clicks of your neighbor's forward button; the way the chosen image fuzzes and bows modestly offscreen as you press PRINT, as if it must retire to another room to change; the warbly whine of the reel's motor when the glass plate lifts to let the film rewind at straightaway speed . . ." poking fun it seems about the use of the old technology until he adds his assessment that librarians have been "lying" about the "extent of paper's fragility," forcing researchers to use the film and the clumsy readers.[12] Sarcasm aside, Baker likes to portray librarians as obsessed with technology. Verner V. Clapp, a leader in preservation, is described in substantial detail as being fixated on gadgets, leading other sheep-like librarians astray.[13] "Why couldn't he [Clapp] have left library administrators alone, rather than forever distracting them from their primary task as paper-keepers by dangling the lure of convulsive change before them, long before the change was practical, and long before it had revealed its many risks?"[14] The answer to this question is, of course, that keeping paper is not librarians' primary task; their primary task is meeting the *information* needs of their clientele, requiring them to experiment in technologies and even to take risks. Likewise, archivists are not merely paper keepers either, but they are mainly involved in maintaining records that can be used for an array of informational and evidential needs. Baker seems to resort to the stereotypical view of librarians and archivists as clerks.

For Baker, technology is not inherently evil, but it is easily distracting and it often represents other presumptions that Baker obviously dislikes. This is obvious in his discussion of JSTOR (Journal STORage), the digital copies of scholarly journals available over the World Wide Web. Baker likes its convenience, but he is concerned because it has led to the destruction of originals of the journals, the "central-plannerly view" of its advocates, and problems with its accuracy (which appear to be excessively exaggerated).[15] It is not particularly clear why originals of these journals are always needed, but it is certainly the case that Baker's perspective is not merely that of a technophobe.

Indeed, the essence of Baker's seemingly Luddite tendencies, or at least how easily it can be misconstrued that he has such tendencies, stems more from his view of librarians and his storyteller's interest in spinning a good yarn. Technology is not bad, but librarians can be odd and are easily duped. Baker relishes his discussion of Fremont Rider's 1944 book, *The Scholar and the Future of the Research Library*, arguing that books were growing exponentially and libraries had to adopt microfilming in order to deal with this growth. Baker glories in discussing Rider's quirky background and argues that library leaders were "hypnotized" by the book and its arguments.[16] More telling, and more indicative of Baker's approach, is how he revels in making connections between library leaders and the CIA, spinning a web of deceit, trickery, and certainly giving the impression of conspiracy (even if he does not use the word) looming in the library world. Librarians are not only easily duped, but some of them are involved in suspicious, clandestine activities that we, today, should recognize as the explanations for why they advocated the use of technology and the destruction of paper. Clapp had been a consultant to the CIA and was obviously unduly influenced by whatever the CIA was up to.[17] Baker's description of the quest to develop mass deacidification approaches, experimenting with dangerous chemicals emanating from the weapons industry, is another example of Baker's approach. He dismisses mass deacidification approaches (efforts which could save the original books) as a quest from some sort of "magical" approach, while relishing the odder aspects of librarians' adoption of what seem like Department of Defense approaches.[18] It is Baker's salacious telling of such connections, or even his descriptions of some of the library leaders (Clapp was a "polymathic, bow-tie-wearing career librarian"[19]) that makes you realize that Baker becomes so absorbed in the delicacies of the story that he loses his way in distinguishing between the important and unimportant. This is less nonfiction than a David Lodge serio-comic novel of academic life. This is less a jeremiad and more a John Le Carre spy thriller.

The honest truth is that there are better ways to approach technology and its use in libraries or archives. A problem with Baker is that he seems to adopt a McLuhanesque view of technology, in which a new technology replaces or destroys an earlier one. Baker assumes, rather revels, in the idea that librarians have picked microfilm or digitization (although he only hints at the latter) as a replacement for paper. Some of this is because of insidious motives by library administrators (it is just a space saving approach), but the bottom line is that the tension between paper and other information technologies or between print as information source and its tactile pleasures of the artifact just makes for a better story than the actual complexities that librarians and archivists face in meeting constituents' information needs or the monumental challenges of preservation and the resources required for this role (issues that I will discuss in the next chapter). The fact that traditional books and manuscripts hold continuing images in the imaginations of even the leading technocrats can be seen by examining the trendiest of the digital era publications, *Wired*. Yet, these images seem to be used in a healthier fashion than is evident by Nicholson Baker in his writings.

Not too many years ago, in 1993 to be exact, *Wired* magazine made its much-heralded debut as a trendy arbiter of the digerati. While we now know that seven years in computer years are like dog years, *Wired* continues to provide a pervasive and biting social commentary on information technology, the politics of cyber-culture, and the power claims of information. Glossy, eye appealing, and oversized, the issues of this magazine take up enormous space in the average office in a deliberate fashion. The bright lime cover of the folio-sized January 2001 issue plays with its theme, design, with provocative teasers (like those trying to get us to watch the evening news) such as "Touch Me All Over" and three declarative statements about articles found inside—"Flash Forward!"; "Zip Drive!"; and "Border War!" After twenty or so pages of glossy and mostly visual advertisements, the reader finds the table of contents with article titles such as "The New ID," "Power Players," "The Good, The Bad, and The Ugly," and "RAW Essence." Each article is heavily illustrated, mixed amongst a myriad of advertisements and brief articles that are often indistinguishable from the advertisements. There is little question that the intention of this design is as much about catching attention, and whether this is a reflection of our society's shortening attention span or a purposeful byproduct of magazines like *Wired* is another topic.

The monthly magazine was and is intended to be a talisman of those on the cutting edge of information technology. The articles are hip, as are the advertisements. Often, it is difficult to discern where the articles end and the ads begin, and vice versa, prompting one individual to see this magazine as the embodiment of McLuhan's ideas with "word-play" and "typographical tricks."[20] *Wired* is a part of (or a maker of) popular culture, and it aims to be a mark of distinction for those who are *really* with the emergent new high-tech society. Implicit in its ads, its articles, and the many editorials—arranged like a scrapbook or parodying a Web site—is the idea that we are not just on the brink of a new era but well into one promising new kinds of information, information sources, and information purveyors, all coming together to represent a new society. Yet, embedded in *Wired*'s many messages seem to be the suggestion of the persistence of *traditional* libraries and archives along with the artifacts of these traditional repositories, printed books and paper documents—something very different than the fears expressed by Nicholson Baker in his writings. Whether the editors and writers are parodying these places and objects or not, it is not hard to imagine that they must hope that their trendy magazine will be securely snuggled in with the other physical artifacts of its era for future generations to puzzle over. And, given its glitzy colors, there is a need to preserve the original print version *along with* its Web site, a dual issue reflecting that librarians and archivists have a complicated challenge in dealing with both print and electronic versions of one source. If we really want to understand *Wired*, we will also need to have archivists identify, select, and care for the business records of the organization supporting the publication of the magazine and the other ventures of this company. So much for reflecting on simple approaches.

Reflecting on how *Wired* depicts libraries and archives is both instructive, enabling us to be more critical of the many voices either promising a new age or longing for an older and calmer era, and entertaining, providing a colorful and dynamic reflection of old and comfortable things (books and manuscripts) and places (libraries, archival repositories, historical societies, and museums). Given the purpose of this magazine, one would expect to find traditional print books or paper documents to be objects labeled as distinctively passé (after all, this magazine is written and published by individuals with an even greater love of technology than the ones described by Nicholson Baker). If the magazine is truly McLuhanesque, then it will be depicting the passing of one information form as another comes into favor. But something else may be going on. *Wired*'s publishers and editors describe the magazine as the "journal of record for the future. It's daring. Compelling. Innovative. Courageous. Insightful. It speaks not just to high-tech professionals and the business savvy, but also to the forward-looking, the culturally astute, and the simply curious." The magazine promises each month to report on the "people, companies, and ideas that are transforming the way we live. It delivers incisive analysis and resonant storytelling from some of the world's most provocative writers." *Wired* brings "competitive, intelligent journalism. . . . On the front lines of the 21st century."[21]

Traditional objects, certainly one means by which to consider libraries and archives, would seem to be targets for a magazine such as this. The sociologist Edward Shils indicates that tradition, in its "barest, most elementary sense" means a *"traditum*: it is anything which is transmitted or handed down from the past to the present." Tradition includes "material objects, beliefs about all sorts of things, images of persons and events, practices and institutions. It includes buildings, monuments, landscapes, sculptures, paintings, books, tools, machines." Since traditions, according to Shils, change as a "consequence of demographic, political, military, or economic changes,"[22] one might expect to find in *Wired* the death knell of books and manuscripts as well as their keepers, librarians and archivists. McLuhan would be proud. What emerges, however, is a very different perspective. McLuhan may be an image, a façade, a symbol for the magazine's claim to have its finger on the pulse of those wired into the new age; in 1996 the magazine even conducted an e-mail interview with someone who had been posting messages under McLuhan's name, convincing the interviewer "that if the poster was not McLuhan himself, it was a bot programmed with an eerie command of McLuhan's life and inimitable perspective."[23] Whatever one might think of journalists interviewing individuals who are posing as now-dead authorities, it is obvious that *Wired* needs to tie itself to savvy futurists like McLuhan and ask questions about topics like whether the book is dead ("The book is not dead. When the book is finally freed from its aura of authority and its 'soulfulness,' it will return as a convenient interface. Just as the advent of printing created a market for medieval culture, the advent of the Net will build an audience for book authors.")

From the start *Wired* was hip, but it always struggled with being a profitable venture (although partly because of its connections to other more risky online and publishing ventures).[24] Being on the edge was difficult to maintain, and it constantly found itself in the position of reinventing itself because of the competition from imitators. Within three years of starting, *Wired* was being described as having been caught up with and, in the effort to stay on the edge (of something, anything), it was noted that "*Wired*'s subject matter has moved somewhat away from pure technology and toward social and cultural trend forecasting."[25] Five years after its creation, Wired Ventures sold the paper magazine and became an Internet company. As one report suggests: "One thing that appears certain is that Wired founder Louis Rossetto's vision of creating a multimedia octopus with tentacles in magazine, book, TV, and Internet publishing will never materialize."[26]

Ironies abound, of course, with this publication venture, as I am sure that they do with all cultural icons (think of Madonna). Not long after the magazine started publication, people noticed that the individuals behind the venture "take their roles as chroniclers of life on the information highway very seriously." *Wired* "has no stationery, won't buy employees pencils and pens, and prefers vendors who communicate with the company by electronic mail." In its view, paper was useful only for publishing magazines. The first editor of *Wired*, Louis Rossetto, early on mused that "A magazine is the right medium for high thought content and beautiful graphics. . . . We don't sell information; we sell point of view. That's much more valuable."[27] At times, it seemed, the magazine parodied itself.

The magazine's struggles with its financial status pale in comparison to its rank as one of the publications with that proverbial finger on the pulse of society. Its importance is even recognized by its detractors. John Dvorak, lamenting its "sickening hero-worshipping and pathetic blathering," still admits that *Wired* is a "cultural icon," although one in ruins. "Many may consider Louis Rossetto the biggest jerk in the world, but he is *Wired*, and they shoved him out because he was doing his job as editor too well. He's known for defending writers' rights and spotting cultural changes better than anyone. Furthermore, my complaints about puffery and self-conscious writing are far overshadowed by the incredible articles the magazine has printed over the years."[28] One might say, I surmise, the same about Nicholson Baker. Another commentator, considering that even its name is obsolete as the world moves "toward the wireless, the embedded, and the ubiquitous," describes *Wired*'s ads as the "middens, the discards of an earlier digital civilization, the silicon and plastic potshards that future archaeologists will analyze as artifacts of our (approximate) era." In this reflection, Reva Basch continues: "It's easy to pick on a device-driven publication. *Wired*, with its self-conscious cool, its technolust and hardware fetishism, is almost too obvious a target. The cognitive whiplash from a 5-year-old issue of *Wired* isn't as jolting as from a 1950s-era *Popular Science* with its personal jet-packs and self-cleaning houses. But give *Wired* another 30 years. It's a fundamental rule of the universe: Quaint happens."[29] These archaeological allusions are precisely the kind of thing that appeals to Nicholson Baker, and I can envision him arguing for the library community's preservation of the old printed versions of this magazine, and it is a wonder Baker does not publish in that venue as well.

Such reflections on *Wired* are commonplace. Jediadiah Purdy's analysis of the magazine, while full of frustrations with the writers' and editors' perspectives about a "new brand of libertarianism" where government exists "only to iron out a few inconveniences" or, at its worst, where it looks like the "adolescent effusion of overgrown boys with too much money," nonetheless believes that the magazine is a "gauge of the digital age":

Wired is the lifestyle magazine par excellence—the chapbook of tastes, taboos, and aspirations—for the shock troops of the information economy. More than 300,000 readers earn their average annual income of over $80,000 designing, selling, and hacking the computing systems that increasingly shape everyone's workplace, home, and civic life. More than any other group's, their job description includes designing the future. *Wired* outfits that future, announcing which ideas and products are "wired" and which "tired"; keeping up a "jargon watch" so that readers will know to say "lifestyle reboot," not "power cocooning"; pointing out the goods and manner that bring "street cred," as in credibility; and holding forth on "fetishes," the "super-goods of the super-wired."[30]

All of this lends credence to the notion that this magazine ought to be saved as a source on the late-twentieth-century's self-absorption with information, both on the shelves of libraries and with all the assorted business and other records, somewhere in an archive (although there are many other magazines competing with *Wired* needing to be analyzed and sorted out as well). Again, librarians and archivists face choices, ones needing to be made based on critical, intelligent assessment but also mindful of financial and other constraints or competing interests.

It actually makes little difference about the successes, pretensions, and failures of *Wired*. We merely need to recognize that the magazine continues to play an important role among the leaders of the Information Age. Decades from now we will examine it, despite how much longer it lasts, simply because the magazine suggests how many aspects of late-twentieth and early-twenty-first century culture were treated in some quarters of that society. David Brooks, a commentator on this culture while in its midst, argues that magazines like *Wired* may be, in fact, other than they appear: "This is how the culture war ends," Brooks writes. "The institutions that once challenged the moral order don't disappear. In fact, they grow more popular. But their meanings change. They get digested by the mainstream bourgeois order, and all the cultural weapons that once were used to undermine middle-class morality, however disgusting, are drained of their subversive content." Brooks believes the

[C]ounterculturalists have invaded the business world and brought their countercultural frameworks with them. . . ." So the radicals have transformed even corporate America. But they themselves have also been transformed. They have embraced worldly ambition. They accept and even lionize the judgments of the marketplace. They celebrate work, profit, and capital gains. There has never been a time in American history when business people had such prestige, when so few Americans saw themselves as mortal enemies of capitalism.

Brooks places *Wired* into this context: "Magazines like *Wired, Fast Company*, and *Red Herring* may have countercultural trappings, but ultimately they are business magazines. They celebrate the business person's virtues, and these virtues now set the tone for American life."[31] Be that as it may, *Wired* enables us to crawl under the skins of capitalists, counterculturalists, and the digerati and see a bit more clearly what is going on. Fifty years from now, we might have forgotten about David Brooks, but it is likely that that lime-green cover of *Wired* will stare back at some scholar studying the culture of the self-obsessed digerati of the early twentieth century. Whether the scholar will use the magazine in a library or archives or some other repository or while sitting at home browsing the digital archive of the Web may make little difference except in attesting to *Wired*'s own presuppositions about print and paper.

Whatever might be the changing purposes of *Wired*, it is a magazine featuring depictions of traditional libraries, books, archives, and records. Some of this is added by advertisers. An advertisement for 3Com U.S. Robotics shows the photograph of an old library, lined with old books and Renaissance-era shelves. The ad reads, in part, "Wander the world's great libraries with the new U.S. Robotics V.90 56K standard modem."[32] In an advertisement for digital marketing, Amazon.com and Oracle shows a book being fanned open on a library table. The beginning of the ad reads, "Becoming Earth's Biggest Bookstore was Easy. Doing It Over the Internet was the Cool Part."[33] An advertisement for Sony QTR-1SL backup tape shows a picture of Abraham Lincoln with his handwriting bled into the background. This advertisement starts out: "His most enduring work is only 274 words long and took less than 3 minutes to read. Big ideas aren't necessarily large."[34] An advertisement for Kodak plays on the idea of records: "Think of this as a time capsule. A document. A postcard from the first stop on a trip across Country. These are images of America. We are the future that *Wired* talked about five years ago. Let's see what we look like." The advertisement then opens up to reveal an array of images from Levittown, New York on October 18, 1997, describing how you can scan and e-mail the images.[35]

Books, manuscripts, photographs, and libraries are all part of the language by which the present age must be discussed, but this kind of discussion is occurring in a very different way than as practiced by Nicholson Baker. Baker romanticizes and elevates the *object*, while what we find in publications like *Wired* is something different—a more balanced notion that these older texts and objects have symbolic and other values making them worth keeping along with other information sources. Baker gives us only an either-or scenario.

The use of images of old books, libraries, and manuscripts fits in the capitalistic venture that has been, if not unique to, at least exemplified by, *Wired*. It also suggests, however, that these items continue to possess a lingering, symbolic appeal to even the digerati. This is evident in other ways. We stumble across a late-nineteenth-century photograph superimposed by old-fashioned script with a short article entitled "Killing Words" describing Stuart Shapiro's Killer Fonts: "Teamed with fontographer Ted Ollier, Shapiro culled letters, manuscripts, and books for handwriting samples from various murderous sorts."[36] *Wired* also appropriates images of traditional sources such as books and manuscripts because it recognizes the symbolic power of them, especially when juxtaposed with other symbols. This may not be that different from the manner in which Baker appropriates the symbolism of print and artifact to compose his indictment of librarians and archivists. In a swipe at the continuing efforts of the federal government to regulate cyberspace, there is an image of the original manuscript of the Constitution with a seal stamped over the upper left-hand corner, reading "APPROVED FOR USE IN CYBERSPACE, UNITED STATES SUPREME COURT, June 20, 1997."[37] A beautiful image from Robert Hooke's 1665 print masterpiece, *Micrographia*, is used to capture the essence of a one-paragraph story about how Adobe Systems CEO John Warnock has founded Octavo to digitize old rare volumes: "The hi-res CD-ROMs capture water stains, paper grain, and other details. But Octavo sells more than pretty pictures—a layer of hypertext and PostScript type behind the image makes most books fully searchable and connects to translations and related Web resources."[38] Could it be that such books and manuscripts are graphically appealing to the designers of the magazine, contributing to its flashy visual appeal?

That traditional books and manuscripts have a continuing appeal to the cyber-elite is documented in some of the articles published in *Wired*. In a brief article entitled "Bookie," there is a description of the work of rare books and manuscripts dealer Kenneth Rendell for clients in building collections of books and manuscripts, especially for the cyber-elite:

Rendell says he was caught off guard by one thing once he began offering his skills to the geek class. "The stereotypes aren't true," he says. "They read and collect great literature as well as rare scientific works. The world of technology is filled with discerning people who know what they want to collect. . . ." For junior titans, Rendell recommends saving your own computer ephemera: "All the packaging that comes with whatever you buy. Operating manuals, things like that. No one ever keeps them, and there are very few left from the early computer age. Anyone who has such a collection could probably set his own price."[39]

I suspect that Rendell might recommend saving all those back issues of *Wired* as well.

Another source for *Wired*'s interests in traditional documents stems from its recognition of the ways the notion of "document" was changing. One of *Wired*'s regular feature writers, David Weinberger, contributed a short meditation on this topic:

Have you noticed that the word *document* doesn't mean much these days? It covers everything from a text-only word processing file to a spreadsheet to a Java-soaked interactive Web page. It didn't used to be like this. A document was a piece of paper—such as a will or passport—with an official role in our legal system. But when the makers of word processors looked for something to call their special kind of files, they imported *document*. As multimedia entered what used to be text-only files, the word stretched to the point of meaninglessness. Just try to make sense of the file types Windows 95 puts into the Document menu entry. The fact that we can't even say what a document is anymore indicates the profundity of the change we are undergoing in how we interact with information and, ultimately, our world.[40]

Such concerns were mimicked in an array of articles on this topic in the magazine, ranging from the digital book and digital libraries to far-reaching consequences regarding such activities as reading and work. Such writings, no matter their brevity, suggest sophistication absent in Baker's *Double Fold*, as he merely indicts using very static notions of printed books and newspapers.

Wired's approach to the digital or e-book and the future of the printed book has been fairly evenhanded. Some of the articles have been straightforward reports regarding new technologies, such as an article about Joe Jacobson's efforts to create a paper that would support digital printing directly to it, each page having its own microprocessor—so you have intelligent paper.[41] This magazine has featured a number of essays about the new books and their impact on reading. Steve Silberman, senior culture writer at Wired News, described various commercial efforts to create e-books—the "SoftBook," "RocketBook," and "Everybook." Silberman considers the concept of a book: "The book made of paper, bound in sturdy vellum covers, is an icon of permanence, of thoughts deemed worthy enough to be fixed in a form designed to endure. In the digital era, however, we've come to think of texts as fluid resources, circulating through the watercourse of the Net and pouring themselves into convenient forms in our browsers." Silberman believes the digital book is an "empty vessel"— "A text inhabits the book for as long as you care to store it, before reading and deleting it to make room for more texts, or offloading it to an online 'bookshelf' for later." And he thinks we will have to design books that also become parts of our lives like the printed book: "This generation of digital reading machines abandons the protocol that has defined the age of computing—scrolling—in favor of presenting text like a bound book; that is, as a codex, or sequence of pages."[42] David Weinberger recognized a shift from reading to referencing, noting that the "first books moving online are reference manuals. We want random and instant access to the information we need. And so, increasingly, online reference works are being designed as software applications rather than as online books." Reading will be, Weinberger believes, a term "to describe engaging printed matter where sequence *does* count, where the order of the presentation is an important part of its value—novels, essays, poems. Reading will become a time of continuity in a fragmented world."[43]

Resounding throughout *Wired* are affirmations of the future of the printed book. An interview with Umberto Eco contains lots of references to books and their future. Eco argues about the limitations of the Internet and that the book has a future despite the power of this new technology. Eco indicates that the predictions of the demise of the book are limited: "It's a bad habit that people will probably never shake. It's like the old cliche about the end of a century being a time of decadence and the beginning signaling a rebirth. It's just a way of organizing history to fit a story we want to tell."[44] Eco was interviewed because he is a popular and oft-cited author among the cyber-elite, not because of his views about print. The Information Age curmudgeon, Nicholas Negroponte, is, however, a regular columnist for the magazine, and he used his column to comment on the future of the book, answering the question he had repeatedly been asked after publishing his technophillic testament *Being Digital*—if digital was so great why did he write a print-based book? "The existence of books is solace to those who think the world is turning into a digital dump," muses Negroponte. "The act of writing a book is evidence, you see, that all is not lost for those who read Shakespeare, go to church, play baseball, enjoy ballet, or like a good long walk in the woods." Negroponte argues that writing books is different than printing them, and he thinks printing books will stop by the year 2020, if for no other reason than the cost of paper. Negroponte acknowledges that he wrote a print book because it is the medium of today and not a bad one, being easy to use among other things.[45] While *Wired* features such debates about topics like the future of print in order to live up to its own purpose of being a trend indicator, it also may be that *Wired*'s consistent emphasis on books and libraries stems from its predictions about just how long it will take to digitize existing print books.[46] While Nicholson Baker believes that librarians and archivists are destroying the documentary heritage, the authors in and publishers of *Wired* present a more complex combination of technological, societal, and economic factors.

One of the strongest contributions of *Wired* has been its ability to pull together and comment on a wide variety of developments in information technology, with prognostications about cultural and societal implications including those affecting the role of libraries and archives. Stuart Moulthrop reflected on Neal Stephenson's novel, *The Diamond Age*, in the context of a discussion about technophilia and technophobia. Stephenson's book is an

ecologically updated version of a book—not a static object, but an active interface to a global information network. It may look "exactly like a book," but it is actually a nanotechnological parallel computer linked to a biomechanical processing collective. What does this incredibly complex machine do? It brings people together and helps them share stories, much as books have always done and as the best parts of the Internet do today. . . . To be sure, Stephenson's novel also contains some heavy technological anxiety. Revolution is a scary proposition, and Stephenson lets us know it. But in its vision of a reinvented book, *The Diamond Age* offers a useful parable for the contemporary silicon decades. Print may pass away but words and stories survive; a good story is worth a dozen jeremiads any day.[47]

Wired seems to be about storytelling more than delivering jeremiads, although it does a good bit of the latter. At the least, what Nicholson Baker fails to understand is that librarians and archivists will also be responsible for these electronic alternatives to the printed book and newspaper.

Given *Wired*'s readership and intended coverage, it is natural that the magazine followed the increasing work in library and archival digitization. And in covering this beat, *Wired* also discovered the wonders and riches of historical manuscripts and rare books and society's continuing interest in them. Some of the articles are naturals, such as the lengthy discourse on the Church of Jesus Christ of Latter-Day Saints digitization of its extensive microfilm holdings, a noteworthy business venture.[48] *Wired*'s coverage of the high profile Library of Congress American Memory project is also not a surprise given the media attention about this project, but its poetic depiction of the original manuscripts seems to go beyond reporting. The article on the project mentions Jefferson's four-page JPEG rough draft of the Declaration of Independence with cross-outs, erasures, and scrawled changes from Adams and Franklin—a "spellcheckerless editing nightmare."

Print, for example, your own copy of Walt Whitman's earliest notebooks, wherein the poet writes with a tattered and ugly scrawl—in prose not so nearly as momentous and liberating as his great verse—musing about death, souls, and corpses. Peruse Teddy Roosevelt's presidential papers, which include six action-packed pages (filled with florid, anally retentive penmanship) about traveling by sleigh in a snowstorm to see first wife Alice Lee in 1880.[49]

One senses an almost romantic longing or sentimentality to touch these firsthand and original reports about the past, not unlike what we sense in reading Nicholson Baker.

One also finds in *Wired*'s discussions a sense of the serendipitous discoveries and pleasures one has in using archival records and the resources of rare books and special collections. In an article about an online Civil War archive, the first page of the article is a black-and-white photograph of the web site's designer standing in a field, posed in the fashion of a Civil War era photograph. The article is an interview with the site's creator, and the interviewer/author is a senior editor at *Smart-Money* magazine. His online archive is The Valley. Questioned as to the impact of television on his way of thinking, the web designer responds that "Ironically, people think of television as a step toward digital information, but in terms of narrative it may be even more linear than print. With a television screen, you feel the need to tell a story." When asked, then, if there was no narrative to his archive, he notes there is a story.

But you can also make your own story through the process of triangulation—comparing fragments from a diary to an article in the newspaper and then connecting that to the Census. While, alone, those might just be inert information, combining them somehow electrifies all three. And it may be a story that you are the very first person to have seen. . . . The Valley is trying to give you enough ordinates to get your bearings in this place we call the past.

An archives is mentioned, a real archives, when the interviewer asks him if something is lost when history can be rewritten via the computer:

Life is short. People are curious about the past, but there's a finite amount of time they'll spend living in the past unless they have a passion for it, like I do. In *Promise*, there's a moment when a boy listens to a lynching on the first Edison talking machine. I still recall finding that story: sitting in the Georgia Department of Archives and History at a formica table, flipping through someone's old typewritten memoir, "Memories of a Presbyterian Picnic," or something like that, and all of a sudden saying, "Whoa, look at that!" I still get chills up my spine.

Edward Ayers argues that the purpose of The Valley is to help people recreate this. "The main thing is to see the past through your own eyes and not have to take someone else's word for it." Ayers worries about the "almost superstitious belief in evidence. I have faith that the historical record is capacious enough that no single argument, of whatever sort, can withstand the weight of overwhelming evidence."[50] And the evidence suggests that books and manuscripts, even in a magazine like *Wired*, deliberately trying to be connected to cutting edge uses of information technology, continue to possess symbolic value.

Wired's interest in covering any commercial applications of digital objects provides a rich array of stories and images about archives and books, documents and libraries. In one article we find modern libraries linked to medieval monasteries and the copying of texts, of course in the modern version with a twist. The article describes a group of monasteries in the United States converting old library catalog cards into MARC records for use in online catalogs. "More than a millennium ago, robed monks laboriously copied the works of the classical world onto parchment, preserving them for modern eyes. Today, *copying* is not so critical. After all, we have OCR scanners that do that flawlessly. In the age of information overload, modern monks and nuns are building something that will be much more important: markers, road maps, the links to the files in the cabinets and the books in the libraries." The article describes the creation of this network through Edward Leonard and the Electronic Scriptorium, Ltd., dating back to 1990, a development that brought in much needed money to the monasteries. "Monastics have everything needed for Scriptorium work: education, judgment, and, above all, precision and patience," the article concludes, providing a partial image of the contemporary librarian.[51] Of course, for Baker, the modern librarian is harassing monks, not emulating them or continuing their mission to preserve our documentary heritage.

In fact, the fate of librarians is not overlooked by the magazine. An article about changing the curriculum of the University of California Berkeley's School of Information Management and Systems features an interview with Dean Hal Varian who says that librarians associated themselves too closely to a social institution (the library), partially accounting for the closing of fifteen library schools since 1976 and a drop in the number of library degrees granted. Varian notes changes in other schools, like Michigan, and the brief article's author suggests, "But along the way, these schools have also shifted from an emphasis on training librarians and archivists to serve the public to a profession more oriented toward managing the information needs of business and government."[52] However hip and trendy *Wired* may seek to be, it is still connected with very old professional debates more likely to be played out in the pages of mainstream professional journals like *American Libraries* or *Library Journal*.

One might not be so optimistic about bookstores and booksellers. As electronic commerce is a large topic for *Wired*, there is ample coverage of online bookstores and sales. A long article on Jeff Bezos, founder and CEO of Amazon.com featured promises of a new America. Bezos believes that the "bifurcation of shopping and consumer desire into shoptainment and just-in-time components" will transform urban America, eliminating strip malls, and that "The new merchant . . . is a community builder, a facilitator, a networker."[53]

Somehow, the idea of community bookstores, long before established as community centers, was left out of this notion. Such a challenge materialized a few months later with an article about Barnes and Noble's moving to a new digital venue. "Because Amazon, the dread enemy, is expanding to sell everything from flowers to pharmaceuticals, some think a narrow concentration on the evolution of the book will be the brothers' salvation," the article reported. Steve and Len Riggio, the masterminds behind the book superstore, were now concentrating on problems such as the distribution of printed copies and keeping stock. "Instead of being printed on milled pulp and trucked to stores, the works of everyone from John Milton to Michael Crichton will be stored digitally, and as likely downloaded from the Internet onto personal computers from electronic books, or dashed off on home printers, in small, highly efficient print runs by high-speed presses, or on-demand right in the bookstore."[54] *Wired* likes to be ahead of the curve, and with such articles as these it seems to be looking into the not too distant future because of the present technological means to make this a reality. Whether this will happen or not depends just as much on cultural, economic, and other factors—but this can be the topic of future *Wired* articles.

Wired has become a leading advocate for complete freedom of expression on the Internet, and it has regularly published essays challenging traditional notions of copyright and related concepts. The magazine sees the Internet as the new "public square" that will transform concepts like copyright.[55] Partially, as a result, records as a source of accountability is a regular aspect of articles being published in the magazine. The magazine reports on the uses of the Web as a political advocacy tool to increase accountability of government to its citizens.[56] *Wired* also consistently reports on how the government refuses to use the World Wide Web to make records and other information sources more widely available to the public. Malcolm Howard contrasts how the "capabilities and efficiency of information technology— often touted as the harbingers of democratic enlightenment—are ironically being used to justify an even greater clampdown on public access to government records," because of fears about personal privacy or government security. Howard cautions that "If these questions aren't addressed, court decisions . . . will be framed by the parameters of outdated programming; poorly reasoned tenets of law will become encoded in the software running tomorrow's democracy; there will be no money to facilitate the distribution of information fairly to all; and the average bloke will still have no protection from Big Brother."[57]

Wired also features articles on one of the hottest, most controversial, and problematic modern record-keeping issues, the use and management of electronic mail.[58] Such issues, complex and contradictory and constantly shifting, are mostly absent from Nicholson Baker's writings. We live in a world of gray, but Baker has given us only contrasting images of black and white.

Wired does not seem to be communicating to the world that books and manuscripts or libraries and archives are outmoded or even dying, and certainly not that they are endangered in any substantial fashion. Certainly, the *Wired* writers are suggesting that these traditional objects and places are changing, but this reporting (along with the magazine's stunning visuals and image-loaded advertisements) is framed within the context of the physical allure of real places, books, and documents. This is not intended to be comforting for librarians and archivists and their friends and supporters, but it is merely intended to be an observation. Shils notes that traditions reside within a "social structure," and they change or are transformed as the structure changes: "Human beings have to adhere to some beliefs," the sociologist argues. "They must believe something about the world in which they live. . . . They renounce one tradition in order to accept a variant of that tradition or quit another tradition. They do not accept or reject at random. They have reasons . . . for their assimilation and divestiture of

traditions."[59] The pages of *Wired* seem to suggest that the notions of books
and manuscripts as artifacts and libraries and archives as places are part
of an enduring societal mentality. Indeed, the continued publication of
Wired as a glossy print magazine, one that could comfortably sit on the
shelves alongside the *National Geographic* or *Martha Stewart's Living*,
seems to be an affirmation of such a tradition.

The physical artifact that is *Wired*, the print magazine, also seems to call
out for some sense of the traditional function of libraries and archives. The
experience of using the actual artifact versus the electronic version available
on the Web is one that is completely different. Using the magazine via the
Web (*http://www.wired.com/wired/*) provides extremely good access to the
words found in the publication. However, the advertisements and illustrations (including all those nice reproductions of books and manuscripts) are
absent and the symbolic power of these traditional information sources is
nearly lost, just as Nicholson Baker argues about what happens with the
digital version of newspapers. It is as if the *Wired* editors and writers are
hoping that these traditional repositories will persist and save the artifacts.
Indeed, if I had tried to understand the *Wired* perspective by just relying
on the electronic archive, I would have concluded something very different—an interest in the debates about the printed book and the handwritten
document but not the enduring graphically symbolic significance of these
artifacts. Just as some commentators are now arguing that the high-tech
economy and society is returning value to such cherished concepts as place
and geography,[60] what we learn by holding and reading a print and using
an electronic version of the same journal may return us to the ability to be
able to comprehend the value of traditional information sources. The modern Information Age may refresh our sense of the need for archives and
libraries, although we need still to learn how to refrain from sentimentality
or romanticized notions of what these repositories of societal memory represent. Nonetheless, *Wired* is an unusually important magazine of its era,
one that should be selected for preservation in its artifactual (printed)
form. We cannot really argue this for every publication, despite Nicholson
Baker's arguments.

Some of the issues Baker takes up, as essential to his crusade, defy com-
monsense views of the world and relate to our imagery of books, newspapers, and manuscripts. The Dutch biologist Midas Dekkers, in his
intriguing and moving book *The Way of All Flesh: The Romance of Ruins*,
provides ample examples. Much of his book is about resisting the inevitable, death and decay. He argues, for example, that we can't keep everything: "You can't keep everything; you'd expire under the weight of your
own possessions. That's how curators and archivists see it too. Their main
tasks aren't to save and store but to discard and destroy."[61] Such a senti-
ment flies directly in the face of what Baker desires; he wants it all and he
thinks libraries are like archives or museums. Dekkers, who perceives that

both librarians and museum directors see the long-term futility in their own work, provides a graphic account of the constantly deteriorating nature of paper, noting that insects turn "what we see as a library" into a "restaurant." But it is not just the little nibblers. Dekkers describes how "our information carriers are becoming increasingly transitory" because of the inherent vices of their own construction. He has a particular view on newspapers: "Given the impermanence of both their medium and their message, newspapers are a symbol of transitoriness. A mayfly made of paper. What you eagerly reach for one day is only good enough—so the cliché goes— to wrap fish in the next. . . . Decay is as inherent to newsprint as the food in your shopping bag is populated by an army of micro-organisms that fancy themselves in heaven."[62] Then there is the losing battle of archivists and museum curators:

Without a collective memory, humanity is irredeemably lost. Unlike animal society, human society needs more than genes for passing on information from one generation to the next. We also like to pass on what was learned in the course of our lifetime and from previous generations. Museums and archives help us do that. Their thick walls and imposing facades form a heavily reinforced brainpan designed to keep time's destruction at bay, even though museum directors, more than anyone else know what a futile attempt this is.[63]

Baker displays arrogance, ignorance, and naivete with his simplistic arguments about books and newspapers. The work of librarians and archivists, mistakes and all, has been intended to deal with immense odds. Baker discounts all that, finding conspiracy and stupidity instead.

The flickering images of books and manuscripts, libraries and archives in the pages of *Wired* reveal the complexity of humanity's struggle with its memory, meaning, and mortality. That the most notoriously technocratic among us would find some meaning in these images is testimony to human nature's will to survive. Nicholson Baker would have us believe that library and archives professionals have betrayed such human impulses. Writers like Dekkers, as opposed to writers like Baker, see the inherent ironies that these professionals have to struggle with, namely that most things are not built to last and even those things that are, are not eternal. Once when asked in class about my definition of the time scale of archival value, as used by microfilm and other reformatting standards specialists, I quipped that it encompassed from now until the initial microsecond after my death. I was not trying, with this answer, to avoid defining the concept, but I was trying to indicate that the archival value of books, newspapers, manuscripts, and other documentary sources is part of a long, complicated process involving technology, human ingenuity, and many generations of reformatting and decision making. As Stewart Brand argues, we always need to keep the long-term view in mind (in increments of ten thousand years) but this will always involve elaborate, risky, and flawed (because it is human) decision making appealing to the human instincts reflected in the images of documentary sources in *Wired* and in Baker's *Double Fold*. Brand notes that

digital storage is easy; digital preservation is hard. Preservation means keeping the stored information catalogued, accessible, and usable on current media, which requires constant effort and expense. . . . Furthermore, though contemporary information has economic value and pays its way, there is no business case for archives, so the creators or original collectors of digital information rarely have the incentive—or skills or continuity—to preserve their material. It's a task for long-lived nonprofit organizations such as libraries, universities, and government agencies, who may or may not have the mandate or funding to do the job.[64]

It is these kinds of mundane matters (costs and responsibilities) that Nicholson Baker ignores in his writings about libraries and archives and the preservation of the documentary heritage. The result is a stilted view of what libraries and archives are all about.

NOTES

1. Nicholson Baker, *The Size of Thoughts* (New York: Vintage Books, 1997), p. 134.
2. Baker, *The Size of Thoughts*, p. 136.
3. Baker, *The Size of Thoughts*, p. 147.
4. Baker, *The Size of Thoughts*, p. 152.
5. Baker, *The Size of Thoughts*, p. 154 (as an example).
6. Baker, *The Size of Thoughts*, p. 163.
7. Baker, *The Size of Thoughts*, p. 165.
8. Baker, *The Size of Thoughts*, p. 165.
9. Baker, *The Size of Thoughts*, p. 159.
10. Baker, *The Size of Thoughts*, p. 160.
11. Nicholson Baker, *Double Fold: Libraries and the Assault on Paper* (New York: Random House, 2001), p. vii.
12. Baker, *Double Fold*, pp. 40–41.
13. Baker, *Double Fold*, pp. 82, 85, 88, 93.
14. Baker, *Double Fold*, p. 94.
15. Baker, *Double Fold*, pp. 68–72.
16. Baker, *Double Fold*, pp. 74–81.
17. Baker, *Double Fold*, pp. 29, 30, 85, 91.
18. Baker, *Double Fold*, pp. 111–135.
19. Baker, *Double Fold*, p. 28.
20. George McMurdo, "Getting 'Wired' for McLuhan's Cyberculture," *Journal of Information Science* 21: 5 (1995): 371–381 (quotation, p. 372).
21. This is the description found in the "About Us" section of the magazine's Web site, *http://www.wired.com/wired/about/*, accessed December 22, 2000.

22. Edward Shils, *Tradition* (Chicago: University of Chicago Press, 1981), pp. 12, 240.

23. Gary Wolf, "Channeling McLuhan," *Wired* 4 (January 1996), available at *http://www.wired.com/wired/archive/4.01/channeling.html*.

24. Janice Maloney, "Why *Wired* Misfired," *Columbia Journalism Review* 36 (March-April 1998): 10–11.

25. "Has the World Caught Up to *Wired*," *Mediaweek* 6 (April 1, 1996): 32.

26. Susan Moran, "Wired Looks for Niche in a World It Once Defined," *Internet World* 4 (May 18, 1998): 19.

27. Christopher Palmeri, "No Paper Trail," *Forbes* 154 (July 18, 1994): 18.

28. John C. Dvorak, "Wired or Tired?," *PC/Computing* 11 (May 1998): 83.

29. Reva Basch, "Back to the Future," *Online* 23 (January-February 1999): 96.

30. Jediadiah S. Purdy, "The God of the Digerati," *American Prospect* 37 (March-April 1998): 86–90.

31. David Brooks, "The New Upper Class: How Conservatives Won the Culture War, and Lost the Peace," *The Weekly Standard* (May 8, 2000): 21–26 (quotations, pp. 22, 24, 25). This article is adapted from the author's book, *BOBOS in Paradise: The New Upper Class and How They Got There.*

32. *Wired* 6 (June 1998): 193.

33. *Wired* 6 (January 1998): 151.

34. *Wired* 4 (December 1996): 298.

35. *Wired* 6 (January 1998): insert after p. 152.

36. Dave Cravotta, "Killing Words," *Wired* 5 (July 1997): 46, available at *http://www.wired.com/wired/archive/5.07/eword.html?pg*.

37. *Wired* 5 (September 1997): 41.

38. Jennifer Hillner, "Postscript," *Wired* 7 (April 1999): 44–45 (quotation, p. 45). The text, minus the beautiful reproduction, is available at *http://www.wired.com/wired/archive/7.04/eword.html?pg*.

39. "Bookie," *Wired* 7 (May 1999): 84.

40. David Weinberger, "What's a Document?" *Wired* 4 (August 1996): 112, available at *http://www.wired.com/wired/archive/4.08/document.html*.

41. Charles Platt, "Digital Ink," *Wired* 5 (May 1997): 162–166, 208–209, 211, available at *http://www.wired.com/wired/archive/5.05/ff_digitalink.html*.

42. Steve Silberman, "Ex Libris: The Joys of Curling Up With a Good Digital Reading Device," *Wired* 6 (July 1998): 98, 100–102, 104 (quotations, pp. 100, 102), available at *http://www.wired.com/wired/archive/6.07/es_ebooks.html*.

43. David Weinberger, "The Balm of Reading," *Wired* 4 (January 1996): 117, available at *http://www.wired.com/wired/archive/4.01/weinberger.if.html*.

44. Lee Marshall, "The World According to Eco," *Wired* 5 (March 1997): 145–148, 194, 196, 198 (quotation, p. 198), available at *http://www.wired.com/wired/archive/5.03/ff_eco.html*.

45. Nicholas Negroponte, "The Future of the Book," *Wired* 4 (February 1996): 188, available at *http://www.wired.com/wired/archive/4.02/negroponte.html*.

46. In "The Future of Libraries," *Wired* 3 (December 1995): 68, interviews with five experts (Ken Dowlin, Hector Garcia-Molina, Clifford Lynch, Ellen Poisson, and Bob Zich) about whether and how fast libraries will be digitized and the impact on the future of real libraries. The predictions for having half of the Library of Congress digitized ranged from the year 2020 to 2065. Predictions of first virtual

large library range from being "unlikely" to the year 2030. Predictions about free net access in public libraries range from "unlikely" to the year 2005. Predictions about virtual reality in libraries range from 1997 to 2020. The text is available at *http://www.wired.com/wired/archive/3.12/realitycheck.html.*

47. Stuart Moulthrop, "Very Like a Book," *Wired* 3 (November 1995): 136, 138, also available at *http://www.wired.com/wired/archive/3.11/moulthrop.if.html.*

48. Erik Davis, "Databases of the Dead," *Wired* 7 (July 1999): 134–141, 180, 183, available at *http://www.wired.com/wired/archive/7.07/mormons.html.*

49. Harold Goldberg, "One Nation's Treasure," *Wired* 5 (September 1997): 167.

50. Amy Virshup, "Pixeling Dixie: Edward Ayers Isn't Just Bringing the Civil War to the Web; His Online Archive is Changing History," *Wired* 6 (May 1998): 138–139, available at *http://www.wired.com/wired/archive/6.05/ayers.html.*

51. Heather Millar, "The Electronic Scriptorium," *Wired* 4 (August 1996): 94, 96, 98, 100, 102, 104 (quotations, pp. 94, 100), available at *http://www.wired.com/wired/archive/4.08/es.cybermonks.html.*

52. Brian Caulfield, "Morphing the Librarians: Fighting Off Extinction in the Information Age," *Wired* 5 (August 1997): 64, available at *http://www.wired.com/wired/archive/5.08/scans.html?pg.*

53. Chip Bayers, "The Inner Bezos: Amazon.com's Founder Figured Out How to Sell Books on the Web, and Now He Wants to Sell You Everything Else. Simple, Right? So Why is He So Far Ahead of the Pack?" *Wired* 7 (March 1999): 115–120 (quotations, pp. 116, 118), available at *http://www.wired.com/wired/archive/7.03/bezos.html.*

54. Warren St. John, "Barnes & Noble's Epiphany: The brick-and-mortar giant burned through $100 million online to get smacked by Amazon.com. So what does it do? Go public. And oh, yeah—reinvent the book," *Wired* 7 (June 1999): 132, 134, 136, 138, 140, 142, 144 (quotation, p. 134), available at *http://www.wired.com/wired/archive/7.06/barnes.html.*

55. See "Internet v. United States Department of Justice, Janet Reno, et al.," *Wired* 4 (May 1996): 84, 86, 88–91; Peter Tupper, "Information Activism," *Wired* 4 (April 1996): 102, available at *http://www.wired.com/wired/archive/4.04/infoact.html*; William Bennett Turner, "What Part of 'No Law' Don't You Understand?," *Wired* 4 (March 1996): 104, 106, 108, 110, 112, available at *http://www.wired.com/wired/archive/4.03/no.law.html*; and, especially, Pamela Samuelson, "The Copyright Grab," *Wired* 4 (January 1996): 134–138, 188, 190–191, a lengthy commentary on Bruce Lehman's white paper *Intellectual Property and the National Information Infrastructure*, available at *http://www.wired.com/wired/archive/5.03/netizen.html.*

56. Brian Caulfield, "Private Eyes, Public Records," *Wired* 5 (May 1997): 39, available at *http://www.wired.com/wired/archive/5.05/eword.html?pg*, reports on Kim Alexander, head of the California Voter Foundation, lobbying to have California political candidates file electronic lists of campaign contributions that could be posted online. While legislators killed the effort, Alexander posted a list of the biggest contributors herself.

57. Malcolm Howard, "No Freedom of Information," *Wired* 5 (April 1997):

90, 92, 94, 96 (quotations, pp. 90, 96), available at *http://www.wired.com/wired/archive/5.04/es_freedom.html*.

58. David S. Bennahum, "Daemon Seed: Old Email Never Dies," *Wired* 7 (May 1999): 100, 102, 104, 106–108, 111, available at *http://www.wired.com/wired/archive/7.05/email.html*.

59. Shils, *Tradition*, pp. 262–263.

60. See, for example, Joel Kotkin, *The New Geography: How the Digital Revolution is Reshaping the American Landscape* (New York: Random House, 2000).

61. Midas Dekkers, *The Way of All Flesh: The Romance of Ruins*, trans. Sherry Marx-Macdonald (New York: Farrar, Straus and Giroux, 2000), p. 62.

62. Dekkers, *The Way of All Flesh*, pp. 75–77.

63. Dekkers, *The Way of All Flesh*, p. 205.

64. Stewart Brand, *The Clock of the Long Now: Time and Responsibility* (New York: Basic Books, 1999), p. 88.

Chapter Nine

Mundane Matters

Nicholson Baker likes numbers, and he likes the minutiae of methods. Perhaps he thinks they add credibility to his arguments, but more often than not his statistics and descriptions of library and archival methodologies do the opposite—they undermine the force of his good points (when he makes them) because they seem simplistic or misapplied (even if powerful to those outside of the archives and library community). Baker also likes to deal with minute technical details of a function like preservation, but again, his treatment of the details often pull him far from his main issues, unless we assume that his purpose is to poke fun at how librarians and archivists approach their responsibilities. My intention in this chapter is to discuss these issues, in a general way, since I am neither a library economist/statistician nor conservation/preservation expert. These matters, however mundane they may seem, need to be addressed more systematically by the library and archives communities, and I am sure they will be (and I am sure they will lead to debate and differences of opinion as well). My purpose here is to merely touch upon the issues raised by Nicholson Baker and to express my concerns about the general weaknesses of his arguments, in the context of my longer response to his book. Indeed, the themes of this brief chapter could be the themes of lengthy essays by experts in library history, conservation, library economics, and other fields.

Part of the problem with Nicholson Baker's discussion of money and his statistics may raise from the tone of his comments, a problem I have mentioned in a number of places and certainly not a problem isolated to his use of numbers. Baker comes across as an antiestablishment social commentator, or, at the least, he likes to play on potential public paranoia about misguided big government programs or the fears about capitalistic ventures becoming monopolies over our historical sources. When he describes the U.S. Newspaper Program, Baker states that libraries were given forty-five million dollars in "so-called preservation money" and "zero dollars for storage space." Supported by the National Endowment for the Humanities, the effect of this program, according to Baker, has been to serve as a justification and incentive for libraries to solve their space problems.[1] As I have mentioned, not all of the monies assigned to this program have been earmarked for microfilming, since one of the primary achievements of the program has been an intensive effort to gain bibliographic control over American newspapers. And while there may have been some people who grabbed onto the U.S. Newspaper Program as only a means to saving space, the purposes of the program were to inventory and preserve the content of the newspapers in a means that would enhance access to the newspapers. His fears about Bell & Howell gaining control of the newspaper archives (by which Baker means only the printed newspapers themselves, but which rightly should be expanded to include other records created by newspaper publishers) because of its vast holdings of microfilm for commercial purposes are meant to add another sinister note to the decisions that libraries have made to replace their originals with these copies.[2] Issues of costs, access, and preservation are not factored into such an assessment, but they do not need to be according to Baker.

Nicholson Baker, especially in the case of the newspapers, may use numbers, but they are carefully or sloppily (depending on how cynical one might wish to be regarding Baker's motives) chosen statistics. Mike Crump of the British Library provided these figures for the scale of the newspaper challenge: "The current collection of newspapers is 32 kms. of shelf-length in size for hard copy with an additional 13kms. of microfilm. It grows at the rate of over a third of a kilometer a year." And, again:

At the Newspaper Library, we currently possess some 32 kilometers of newspaper titles in hard copy. We acquire 338 meters of UK newspapers on paper per year. Because no collection exists in isolation, we acquire in addition 35 meters of foreign newspapers, and many more titles on microfilm, each year at a cost of £91k to complement the UK collection. These are significant growth-rates and the Library calculates that the Colindale (both the Library site itself and the additional storage facility at 120 Colindale Avenue) will be full in 2003.[3]

These are daunting figures, and they provide more of the context for the kinds of statements Nicholson Baker makes about the preservation and management of newspapers. The space needs are enormous, and they require some sort of process by which the newspaper collections can be managed and in a way that enables scholars and the public to gain access to them. All of this might be irrelevant for Baker, since he believes that all the British Library was interested in when it deaccessioned and put the newspapers up for sale was money.[4]

The British Library or Library of Congress, and their quest for space or money, are not isolated or aberrant case studies in the library or archives world. In fact, this is a general theme of Baker's book. He writes extensively about how it was all about money and space, about marketing and public relations.[5] The campaign using words like "brittle," "dust," and "crisis" were all lies, led by strong-willed crusaders like Patricia Battin of the Commission on Preservation and Access. It was not the deterioration of paper that was the culprit, but "savage, ungovernable space yearnings in concert with an ill-conceived long-term plan to stock the sparkling digital pond with film-hatchery trout."[6] All I ask is if *anything* said by individuals like Battin is any more excessive than statements like this by Nicholson Baker?

Nicholson Baker has not been challenged as often as he should have been about his numbers, especially given that he has been throwing them around for nearly a decade. Responding to Baker's first salvo as a library activist, Brian Helstein discussed a number of problems in the author's assessment of library cataloging, applying simple common sense that the old catalogs were as full of errors (perhaps more) than the newer online versions, but making a better point when he wrote: "Collection access, collection money and collection preservation are the issues that Nicholson Baker should have addressed."[7] In other words, Baker missed the big picture in examining the card catalogs, perhaps thinking that he was correcting this problem with his *Double Fold* book. In his campaign against the San Francisco Public Library, Baker claimed that the new library building had less space for book storage than the old building, and the public library administrators retorted:

Nicholson Baker has done a great disservice to the San Francisco Public Library and the people of San Francisco. He has insisted that the new library is smaller than the old one. To prove his point, he and others broke into the old Main Library to measure the shelves and subsequently published their erroneous results on the front page of the San Francisco daily newspaper. In fact, the new Main Library has over nine miles more shelf space than the old building. Only when the library extended an invitation to the local press to measure the shelves for themselves did Baker admit that his figures were wrong (they were off by 25 miles).[8]

But, ultimately, it looks like it is the public library administrators who lost the battle, if not the war, no matter who is right or wrong about the issue of available space for book storage. Molz and Dain, in their study of modern public libraries, describe the saga of San Francisco's new public library building and the controversy surrounding it (including one Nicholson Baker) as an "interesting, and probably cautionary, case in point of

the use of Friends and foundations and the pitfalls of public-private col-
laborations." As they describe this controversy:

> The San Francisco situation can be seen as a conjuncture of feisty Bay Area politics,
> inadequate damage control by the library administration, and general trends in
> librarianship—automation, private fundraising, attention to multiculturalism and
> current community interests, and the construction of monumental new buildings
> equipped with the latest information technologies. Some of the criticisms suggest a
> certain nostalgia for an irretrievable past of politics, economics, and technology
> different from today's, and others reflect internal library conflicts and management-
> union relations in San Francisco. But serious ethical concerns not unique to San
> Francisco were raised, and the intense public discussion displayed a community
> interest in the library and its mission from which those worrying about the insti-
> tution's marginality or imminent demise might take heart.[9]

Their statement, "an irretrievable past of politics, economics, and technology different from today's," seems particularly relevant as one reads
Baker's library crusade writings.

I might add that perhaps all librarians and archivists (including one Richard Cox) might take heart that the public furor about library and archive
preservation generated by Nicholson Baker might actually breathe some
new life into what many might perceive from the inside as tired old debates.
Libraries and archives are not marginal nor face imminent demise *if* a book
like *Double Fold* attracts such wide interest, even *if* the interest might have
more to do with the public stereotypes perpetuated by Baker in its pages.
But for this book to serve such a purpose, it requires librarians and archivists to speak up and round out the dialogue. Librarians and archivists
need to admit their mistakes, while trying to make the public and policymakers understand *why* these mistakes may have been made as well as
their overall mission regarding the documentary heritage. The quest for
preservation solutions like mass deacidification, for example, have as much
to do with the reality of financial limitations as with spending real dollars.

Baker dotes on the high costs of all library and archives preservation
activities. Typical of his assessments is this statement: "Compared to storing the originals in some big building, microfilming is (like digitization)
wildly expensive, even in high-contrast black and white—it costs over a
hundred and fifty dollars per volume to film a typical newspaper collection,
versus less than five dollars a volume to build outlying storage for it and
have a person truck to-and-fro whatever people want to see."[10] There are
many problems with this kind of statement. Isn't all preservation expensive?
It is. Are Baker's warehouses archival facilities? They can't be, at the consistently low prices he seems to allude to in his statements. Is the person
retrieving the volume a professional or just a clerk? The person must be a
clerk. Has the costs of cataloging the newspapers been factored in? Baker's

cost estimate would suggest that it has not. Is the facility really convenient to researchers (does it matter what the cost is to the researcher to get access to the sources)? Given the location of Baker's own newspaper repository, this does not seem to matter.

For Baker such criticisms must seem truly like quibbles, and perhaps not even close to the interesting issues. Throughout *Double Fold* Baker loves to dote on the outrageous (according to him) costs associated with microfilming and other technology. Baker notes how Verner Clapp's directorship of the new and "very flush" Council on Library Resources led to spending "hundreds of thousands of Ford Foundation dollars on technologies of image shrinkage."[11] He cites a 1962 report on automation at the Library of Congress that recommended that the Library shell out fifty to eighty million dollars for such technologies, three times its annual budget.[12] All he is trying to demonstrate, of course, is that the money has been misapplied. If it had been used for simple storage, given that all of the claims about the physical deterioration of paper are either false or exaggerated, we would not be facing the problems in the care of books and newspapers we do today. After all, Baker's book is about an "assault" by libraries and librarians on paper.

In an effort to be honest, it is important to indicate that in certain aspects of preservation work librarians and archivists do not know the costs. In a study by Michèle Cloonan and Shelby Sanett on preservation costs for electronic records (meaning records that were born digitally), the investigators concluded:

In essence, we were asking, what is it going to cost the institution to preserve, maintain, and provide access to electronic records? We thought this was an important question because for many institutions and projects, knowing what the bottom line is, is THE major factor which influences decision-making, and determines goals and objectives, as well as the strategies to meet them. The majority of the managers we interviewed are gathering financial data now and plan to report costs as part of their projects' results. Only a few projects are far enough along to have developed cost figures. The interviewees ranged from large national archives, to projects developing testbeds. The range of the costs for electronic record preservation is from \$10,000–\$2.6 million per year. Cost categories include staff, consultants, facilities, equipment, storage system monitoring, staff access and research and development.[13]

Perhaps it might be just to be critical that the library and archives professions have not worked out these figures long before now, but it is worth noting two matters raised by the assessment of these researchers in the context of our Baker discussion. First, the rapidly changing technologies make the cost figures a chimera. Second, the recognized complexities of considering the multiple factors of staff, facilities, equipment, and on the list continues is far more realistic, if depressing, than Baker's easy depiction of cheap warehouses, shelving, and clerks.

As the reader can tell from my own comments in this book, Nicholson Baker's appropriation of warehouse imagery distracts me. As one colleague listening to a presentation I made about Baker's book reminded me, it was the library community, most notably the Association of Research Libraries, that used this imagery in order to make a case for cheap storage and expansion of academic libraries. Sigh. I just can't even force myself to search the origins of the idea of libraries and archives as warehouses, although I am sure that this is probably true. For one thing, the imagery persists. Despite my complaints about Nicholson Baker's consistent allusions to libraries and archives as warehouses, there is a kind of new warehousing going on among some libraries and archival institutions. Among academic libraries, off-site and often cooperative depository libraries have been created to move low-use items into stable environmental spaces at very modest per item costs.[14] For another, archivists and librarians have often resorted to catch phrases and popular concepts that can capture public and government support. The challenge may be sorting out these allusions and terms in a meaningful way, a task especially more difficult by one who is outside the profession. If Baker can not see that the distinctions between *preservation* and *conservation* are not intended to obscure or obfuscate, it is hard to see how he can be sensitive to efforts made by librarians and archivists to transcend their own professional jargon and to discuss book and archival storage as warehousing.[15]

Looking more closely at how Baker discusses such matters as warehousing leads one to identify mind-boggling inconsistencies in his own arguments. Baker does at one point focus on access, arguing that the Brittle Books program certainly has not improved access because it has often made decisions to remove and destroy (as they are being reformatted) books from potential access by local scholars: "The ability to summon words from distant, normally unreachable sources, which can be a fine thing for scholarship, is being linked to the compulsory removal of local physical access, which is a terrible thing for scholarship."[16] Baker never describes how his decision to create his newspaper archive addressed such matters. Nor does Baker look at what seems to happen as books in research libraries are moved off site. The study of the Amherst Library off-site storage facility reveals that even after faculty protest about removal of materials and the creation of user-friendly and convenient facilities that collection use is low. Out of 90,000 items stored there, an average of two items per week circulated: "The demand for the materials was extremely modest. On-site use was surprisingly minimal as well. Since its opening, only one or two faculty per year visited the depository to consult library materials stored there."[17] The point in all of this is that access must be weighed against actual or potential use along with other factors such as funding and space issues.

Current discussions about digitization now focus more on efforts to enhance access and to advance scholarship than on preservation.[18]

One of the more revealing aspects of his attitude about libraries and
archives is his treatment of the sales value of the discarded books and
newspapers. On the one side he describes how the commercial enterprise
Historic Newspaper Archive acquires old original newspaper runs from
libraries and archives and then sells individual issues as keepsakes:

In the company's twenty-five thousand square feet of warehouse space in Rahway,
New Jersey, innumerable partially gutted volumes wait in lugubrious disorder on
tall industrial shelves and stacked in four-foot piles and on pallets. I paid a visit
one winter afternoon. The Christmas rush was over, and the place was very quiet.
Torn sheets, sticking out from damaged volumes overhead, slapped and fluttered
in a warm breeze that came from refrigerator-sized heaters mounted on the ceiling.
When an order came in for a particular date, a worker would pull out a volume
of the Lewistown *Evening Journal*, say (once of Bowdoin College), slice out the
issue, neaten the rough edges using a large electric machine called a guillotine
(adorned on one side with photos of swimsuit models), and slip it in a clear vinyl
sleeve for shipping. Every order comes with a 'certificate of authenticity' printed in
floral script.[19]

While Baker criticizes what is happening with the selling of these newspapers as personal collectibles, he also uses the market values of discarded
books as an indicator of the value of the collections that librarians and
archivists are abusing. He calculates, based on a "replacement value of
forty dollars apiece" that the Library of Congress Preservation Microfilming Office "threw out more than ten million dollars' worth of public
property between 1968 and 1984."[20] Baker lists a number of financially-
valuable books with Library of Congress markings as "surplus" or "du-
plicate" that commanded high prices from dealers or at auctions, noting
that a "great research library must keep its duplicates, even its triplicates,
for a number of reasons, the most basic ones being that books become
worn with use, lost, stolen, or misshelved."[21] I have already commented
that the marketplace is not rational nor the best means of determining
value. Just as importantly, there is a kind of disconnect or inconsistency
here between his criticism of the selling of newspapers as keepsakes and
the valuing of books or newspapers through the marketplace. Obviously,
the intent here is for *shock* value. How could librarians and archivists be
doing their jobs if they discard such financially valuable materials?

There is another way of evaluating library and archival collections than
either the aesthetic criteria or financial value Baker most often seems to
use. Some preservation administrators have advocated the adoption of a
business risk management model, arguing:

The model is not based on the monetary value of library holdings. Instead, it focuses on business risk and proposes a framework of controls to minimize the risks that threaten the viability of those assets. This perspective views libraries as businesses and their collections as integral to achieving business objectives. With this model, managers can identify priorities for institutional investments in collections and make more compelling budget justifications for necessary resources, because the relationship between assets (collections) and the library's mission work is made explicit to financial decision makers.

As institutionalized at the Library of Congress, risk management tells us something very different than Baker's argument for salvaging one copy of everything. As applied the model suggests:

The assessments would be done in the divisions where collections of differing formats were either permanently stored or temporarily handled as they arrived, or where they were serviced in some manner within the Library. That way, staff could assess the risk to items over the course of their life cycle—from acquisition to cataloging and from service to storage. Staff could also distinguish between the risks to different types of material. For example, the risks to a recent monograph on the Japanese economy, printed on acid-free paper and of little artifactual value, would be different from the risks to a Hollywood feature film from 1956 or to the 1991 *Sports Illustrated* swimsuit issue. Each item has its own risks, based on physical features of the recording medium and perceived value, and in each case, the risks are dynamic and change over time. A judicious choice of formats and genres produces a risk assessment that allows extrapolation from these data to similar types of collection items.

Here we discern the complexity of interplay between format, use, institutional mission, societal value, scholarly use, and a host of other factors. A variety of potential risks are identified, including bibliographic (not accessible by title, author, or subject), inventory (lack of record of the item), preservation (item may be too fragile), and physical (the item is subject to loss or theft).[22] However, if librarians and archivists are being criticized for their adoption of warehousing and other imagery to describe their needs, one can only imagine what will happen to their use of business concepts such as risk management. That they have to resort to such methods and means suggest the realities that librarians and archivists work within and, at times, against (as opposed to the sort of free-agent imagery that abounds in *Double Fold*).

If Baker's numbers are suspect, even more problematic is his view of how library and archives preservation has been carried out. Previously I have alluded to his less than careful sense of the historical development of preservation principles or methods. Nicholson Baker treats library and archives preservation as one large grab bag of things to be pulled out and examined, and the result is his scathing denunciation of how librarians and archivists have approached preservation. Baker lacks any sense of the dependence of an idea or method on the emergence of subsequent approaches. He criticizes the Library of Congress for destroying "rag-paper" editions of major newspapers even though the quality of the paper was superb.[23] Baker is right to criticize but he is wrong to lump together older decisions that probably would not be made today or to describe them as if they are part of present policy and practice. As I have tried to suggest, faulty ideas and applications were often necessary in order to make advances, and in this, I believe, we see nothing more than something that is very basic to all disciplines and inherent in the human condition. Jason Epstein, in predicting a wide-scale shift to printing books on demand, provides an appropriate example of this:

But there is no wizard to create with a wave of the hand this digital future. There are only mortals finding their way, by the slow, indirect, and uncertain means by which human beings have exploited previous paradigm shifts. To expect a practical business plan for unmediated electronic publishing to arise full blown from the existing industry would be to disregard the waywardness of human endeavor, the complexity of the emerging digital future, and the understandable, if quixotic, wish of today's publishers to enter the digital future in approximately their present form.[24]

We see a similar problem in how Baker seems to suggest that librarians and archivists ought to have solved the preservation challenge or simply accepted that paper is the only viable means. He forgets librarians and archivists are mere mortals. Librarians and archivists deserve to be criticized, perhaps, when they give up their more conservative tendencies to proceed with caution, but the rapidly changing information technologies, shrinking budgets, escalating demands, and other factors have often conspired to force them to experiment and take risks as they endeavor to keep the larger picture in view of preserving the documentary heritage.

Nevertheless, Nicholson Baker's treatment of preservation reads well, replete with many excellent points and citations to a wide range of literature, but his perspective on preservation may have more to do with his assumptions about what libraries and archives are all about. Abby Smith, discussing the function of preservation in American research libraries (the purported focus of Baker's tome), starts this way:

Since the invention of movable type five-and-a-half centuries ago, there has been an explosion of recorded information following each technological innovation in recording media, from the manufacture of cheap paper in the 1840s to the pressing of compact discs in the 1980s. Libraries must now manage stores of information proliferating so rapidly that they threaten to overwhelm anyone's capacity to use them efficiently and intelligently. Based on our knowledge of the past, two things can be said definitively about future library collections: not all recorded information will survive, and we will never be able to predict accurately which information will be in demand by scholars in the future. Librarians routinely make conscious and active interventions to collect and preserve things, even if they cannot now know what the researchers of the future will need. They work in a variety of ways with the research community to identify which resources are and will be in demand by users of their collections and, taking into consideration the collecting practices of other research institutions, to develop policies for acquiring and building the collections.

Baker seems to buy into little of this—he quibbles with the fragility of the recording media, he seems oblivious to the volume of information being managed by such libraries, and even his agreement that we cannot predict future use leads to a mind-boggling conclusion that all must be saved (just in case).[25]

Baker also loves to challenge the opinions of preservation experts about the durability of paper. He acknowledges that all media, paper and electronic, deteriorate if "left in the sun," but he wonders about the sanity of such concerns, and Baker especially chaffs at the notion of how soon such deterioration will occur.[26] Baker discounts many such concerns since many things are fragile but still deserve to be preserved, and he believes that all of the "agitation" over acidity in paper is unwarranted since acidic pages can still be read and used.[27] Baker tosses out most scientific or any analysis of the aging of paper.[28] Baker discounts the importance of all the efforts to find a stable base for microfilm, obviously intent on discrediting such reformatting and intent on revealing the weaknesses of such media. He focuses on all the problems and notes, even with all the standards and care, "serious mistakes still occur."[29] And the critical point in the book is Baker's development of his own test, the "Turn Endurance Test," to replace the ill-fated double fold test. Baker's test simply determines how many times you can read a book before it needs some sort of conservation treatment, and in reading it I was reminded of a parody by one of Baker's literary heroes, John Updike, on golf instruction manuals.[30] There are times when I find it hard to distinguish between when Baker may be serious and when he is just playing with us.

We need to be realistic. Many of the problems librarians and archivists face in managing even printed paper or manuscript on paper collections stem from mistakes in manufacture by the paper industry, inferior technologies in binding and printing, and a host of other problems residing far outside the authority of librarians and archivists. And, as I have stated elsewhere, the newer standards in paper manufacturing and bookbinding, promising greater stability, have more to do with the energetic and sometimes experimental, risk-taking ventures of librarians and archivists. What Baker dwells on in *Double Fold* are worse case scenarios or the eccentric or quirky decisions made by some librarians and archivists.

A recent review of scientific studies of preservation/conservation issues revealed how complex and challenging it is to study, predict, evaluate, and generally deal with the kinds of documentary sources libraries and archives assume responsibility for. Baker argues against, for example, accelerated aging tests. In this report there seems to be vindication of what Baker is contending. The report suggests "There is a fundamental problem in the use of accelerated aging," since the "complex properties of paper that are often registered in accelerated aging (e.g., folding endurance, tear resistance, and paper discoloration) cannot be simply and unambiguously related to its chemical composition." The report summarizes that "A complicating factor is the way in which the paper is exposed to the aging conditions. . . . Some of these studies have shown that under both accelerated and natural aging conditions, the center of a stack of paper undergoes greater deterioration than do the regions located near the outside." And the report goes on to relate different ways that aging studies can be improved or complemented: "Further research is needed on the applicability of accelerated aging and into the standardization of aging tests. Whereas accelerated-aging tests are often carried out to make prognoses, e.g., to calculate life expectancy or quantify the effects of conservation treatments, the predictive value of these tests is still seriously questioned."[31]

Many of Baker's concerns about such tests are reflected reasonably well, then, by others and add to his assertions that all he is doing in *Double Fold* is to report back what he has been told. In describing a forty-year-old study about saving a copy of every book in environmentally stable warehouses, Baker still criticizes the idea because the study revealed that the "condition of a given book 'varied greatly' from library to library: an important observation, since it implied that book longevity depends on local variables (humidity and temperature, rough treatment, styles of rebinding) as much as it does on the innate chemical properties—the 'inherent vice'—of the paper."[32]

A recent summary of scientific research on paper likewise notes:

An interesting line of research in this context is the comparison of identical copies of books that, as part of separate library collections, have been stored under different conditions and show different stages of deterioration. Besides offering insight into the effects of environment on the rate of the natural aging of paper, the results of these studies may also indicate which environmental factors are responsible for the observed differences in aging, and thus in the rate of decay. Such comparative investigations can be of indirect value in developing reliable accelerated-aging methods.[33]

I leave it to the reader as to what the differences in emphasis or intent might be between the two.

Where we are getting better (meaning more reliable) costs figures, we can also see the weaknesses of Baker's approach. In considering digitization projects, Steven Puglia, National Archives and Records Administration, indicates that a third of the cost is for digital conversion (32 percent overall); another third of the cost is in metadata creation, including cataloging, description, and indexing (29 percent overall); and another third is for administration and quality control (39 percent overall).[34] Indeed, not only is this more complicated than the simpler counting of Baker, but it is very difficult to boil things down to a page per cost schema since the nature of the materials housed in libraries and archives varies so much (but, and in this we agree with Baker, it is expensive). In a project to digitize the 55,000 glass plate negatives of the *Chicago Daily News*, the project staff reported that they were "creating scans at about $2.11 per glass plate, with 29% of that comprising equipment costs and 71% going to staff salaries." They continued:

But this is just stage one of the project. Stage two, creating intellectual control over the collection, will significantly increase our costs. The creation of full MARC catalog records on a one-to-one basis is time-consuming and expensive. We have just recently begun this stage of the project and expect that it will take about two years. We will shift the scanning staff into support roles for the catalogers as the scanning nears completion so that they can conduct additional research on an as-need basis, thus allowing the catalogers to concentrate on production. The savings in real over projected costs in scanning will enable us to enhance the quality of the cataloging and indexing of the negatives, improving searchability of the materials and hence their value to researchers.[35]

In discussing complex preservation matters, Bakers does, at times, make good points. Noting that digitally reproducing newspapers would be very expensive today, Baker also adds that when the technology improves and the costs go down that the major problem may be the lack of originals to digitize.[36] It is a compelling point, or so it seems. Baker's argument still begs the fact about whether *every* newspaper would need to be digitized, and it ignores the fact that maybe the technology will improve to the point where it can accommodate the reproduction of a poor microfilm into a digital format. Again, while I have argued for the careful selection of newspapers and books that need to be preserved in their original format, it makes sense also to think that some sort of selection process must be at work even in larger digitization schemes. It is no more utopian, I guess, to think that every original ought to be preserved as it is to assume that every information text will be digitized and made available for use.

Nicholson Baker's use of financial figures and preservation techniques is all wrapped up in the quirky personalities he discovers along the way. Libraries and archives have, for sure, their share of such individuals, just as much as any profession in society. Baker cites a dissertation done by a library director urging the digitization of all books and their discarding to save money. I suppose it is relevant that the author of this study has a "push-broom mustache and a cheerfully bald forehead," is a "robe-wearing member of a Catholic order," and, based on a telephone conversation, is a "gentle, genial man,"[37] because it reflects that hidden under the mild exteriors of librarians everywhere are strange and insidious threats to our print culture. There is no discussion of the impact of the dissertation, the author's influence, or any other matter that would suggest that this study is in the forefront of thinking by library science theorists or practitioners. Baker does indicate that he learned of this dissertation from Michael Lesk of the National Science Foundation who agrees with it, that "in order for libraries to provide the best service to the most people for the least money, they ought to begin large-scale scanning projects right now, and simultaneously divest themselves of their originals."[38] On the surface this sounds terrible, but there is no indication that Lesk is arguing to get rid of all the books or about what selection process he would use. In fact, Baker quotes Lesk as saying that in the case of a book bound by a "famous bookbinder," he would not want to destroy the original, but that in the case of the "majority" of nineteenth-century publications "you would be better off with one digital copy and one carefully watched paper copy, than you are with relying on eight different or ten different decaying paper copies and no digital access." This sounds very different than Baker's characterization of it. Moreover, Baker is worried about the loss of *any* book: "Why can't we have the benefits of the new and extravagantly expensive digital copy *and* keep the convenience and beauty and historical testimony of the original books resting on the shelves, where they've always been, thanks to the sweat equity of our prescient predecessors?"[39] How "fabulously expensive" might it be if we just keep everything? Baker merely characterizes such individuals as Battin and Lesk as "resolute anti-artifactualists."[40]

The frustration one has with Baker is that although he lambastes another quirky figure like Fremont Rider and the influence of Rider's hypothesis of libraries' doubling their book size every sixteen years as being wrong, Baker himself throws around equally suspect hypotheses about costs, preservation techniques, and other similar matters that could do as much damage to the future of libraries as Baker contends Rider did in the past. Baker writes: "Rider was wrong," but "no matter—Rider believed his figures to be true, or at least he hoped they were more or less true (he liked and wrote science fiction), and books do undeniably pile up fast."[41] Should we surmise that Baker's figures and critiques might be so far off because he writes fiction? In a similar fashion Baker suggests that Clapp conducted a microfilming costs assessment until he got the figures he wanted to support his position that it was inexpensive, even profitable for libraries to replace originals with microfilm. But now the culprit was not a love of science fiction but "operations-research analysis."[42]

He does this again, I believe, when he goes after William J. Barrow and Barrow's work on paper aging and the use of lamination.[43] Baker quotes from others about how Barrow was an "aggressive promoter" and appealing to librarians because he offered simple solutions. Yes, librarians would only be interested in simple ideas and it's unthinkable that one in their midst should be aggressive. I find it interesting that Baker cites Thomas Conroy's estimation of Barrow's appeal to librarians, being that "he proposed simple solutions to extremely complex and unfashionable problems,"[44] a way that we could perhaps describe some of Baker's own ideas. Baker does link Barrow's work to what has occurred in recent years in libraries and archives, especially the use of tests like the double fold test and other statistically-generating preservation approaches; Baker believes that librarians have been limited in their preservation approaches by continuing to be in the era of "Barrow-inspired statistical-deterioration survey" work.[45] Barrow's inspiration has led to a focus on the wrong issues, and again Baker pounds on preservation experts: "Many of the books may be gone, but their quotably quantified test results live on in the hearts and bibliographies of preservation managers, who by the late seventies began to have fantasies of sampling the paper in their own collections, in order to see how catastrophically degraded and grant-getably reformattable it was."[46]

There are other low (perhaps the better term here is distracting) points in Baker's discussion about preservation techniques. His long description of the use of potentially dangerous materials to develop mass deacidification techniques takes the reader far afield from Baker's main aims in urging the library profession to rethink how it treats original printed materials.[47] Baker glories in the story of the use of these materials, mainly diethyl zinc (DEZ), obviously in an effort only to demonstrate how silly librarians and archivists can be or how easily duped they can be. It is a reminder that Baker is a storyteller and suggests why so many reviewers warmly responded to the emotional and compelling stories presented in *Double Fold*. The recounting of such efforts misses the point that librarians and other custodians of our documentary heritage were so dedicated to their mission to preserve as much as they could and to stretch their resources as far as they would go that they tried anything with the slightest promise of accomplishing the job. Were mistakes made? Certainly. Did the Library of Congress make blunders? Definitely. Does the library and archives preservation community deserve the treatment they receive in this portion of *Double Fold?* No. Even in the Librarian of Congress's decision to stop the use of DEZ, Baker has to toy with us that the leader of this institution (James Billington) likes "spending lots of money on machinery," and now he was merely more fascinated with "mass digitization" than mass deacidification. The shift to what became the American Memory project is not seen as an effort to bring historic collections to the public or as part of a response to the intense pressure of the present era to open up collections far beyond the scope of scholars, rather it is all reduced to a grown man playing with toys.

As with so much of the book, it is the twist Baker gives to the telling that leaves the reader wondering what really is going on within our libraries and archives. As for mass deacidification, Baker laments it and he notes that "some conservators believe that all mass deacidification is a mistake: given the near infinitude of recipes for paper, new and old, and the impossibility complex reactions that ensue over time, the alkaline buffer may do bad things to fibers, and to inks and dyes and bindings, that we cannot foresee."[48] Who can refute this? Clearly there is dissent in the ranks (although Baker gives the impression that there was little debate about such efforts during their experimental phases),[49] but Baker, remember, argues that paper is not deteriorating as quickly as claimed and that it only needs to be warehoused. Are such recommendations any more irresponsible than those he so graphically attacks in *Double Fold?* Baker clearly is tilting at windmills here. The recent report on preservation science I mentioned earlier in this chapter concluded its international survey by stating that "Preservation science is moving steadily away from the investigation of individual artifacts and individual conservation problems." The report suggests a shift away from the individual artifact (the focus of Baker's book and indicative of the fact that it is part of a backlash away from such efforts):

More and more, the scientific research is tuned to large-scale, national, or international preservation activities. At the same time, preservation managers are becoming more interested in passive measures than in active conservation and are often limiting real treatment and restoration to a very small part of their collections. Consequently, current preservation science concentrates more on damage prevention (e.g., storage conditions) than on the development of new or improved conservation techniques. . . . Parallel to the trend toward passive conservation, financial constraints limit research that is aimed primarily at individual items or small parts of a collection. Recent funding for research has favored large-scale activities that are intended to prevent damage to the original (this includes digitization and microfilming, which can limit use of, and therefore damage to, the original). The trend toward passive conservation is bolstered by reactions to "mistakes" in previously performed treatments.[50]

Baker forces the reader's attention to consider reasons for what he considers to be the abandonment of paper and printed artifacts. All of the Library of Congress's efforts to lead in preservation experimentation, Baker reduces to misguided "ideology" because instead of building or renting storage facilities it was wasting money on mass deacidification and other such efforts. "The bones of the collection were deformed in a deliberate squeeze," Baker writes.[51] Other mass reformatting efforts, such as the study of the use of optical disk technology, are simply characterized as one more "gaping preservational cash pit."[52] Damn those stupid librarians, Baker tells the reader (over and over again), especially those who have access to federal government dollars (we know how wasteful that can be) or connections to the fatted foundations that can fund their childish delusions. Meanwhile, preservation specialists around the world search for ways of stabilizing historical collections in all media, not only paper.

Nicholson Baker does grasp that there is immense debate and disagreement *within* the library and archives communities, but he does not understand the meaning of such professional discourse. It appears that Baker has written *Double Fold* because he wants to draw public attention to the next threat to books and newspapers and other paper artifacts: "The second major wave of book wastage and mutilation, comparable to the microfilm wave but potentiality much more extensive, is just beginning."[53] But it is not happening without professional debate, controversy, reflection, research, and experimentation. Librarians and archivists will always search for new and better solutions to preserving our documentary heritage. Along the way we will certainly see mistakes, colorful personalities, weird ideas, and all the other stuff that makes the information community interesting and provides it some hope for finding solutions.

NOTES

1. Nicholson Baker, *Double Fold: Libraries and the Assault on Paper* (New York: Random House, 2001), pp. 15–16.

2. Baker, *Double Fold*, pp. 18–19.

3. Mike Crump, "The British Library's Policy with regard to Newspaper Disposal," paper presented at the University of London conference, March 2001, available at *http://www.sas.ac.uk/Ies/RCHB/News%20Crump.htm*.

4. Baker, *Double Fold*, p. 24.

5. Baker, *Double Fold*, pp. 168–222 is a good portion to read for this purpose.

6. Baker, *Double Fold*, p. 183.

7. Brian A. Helstien, "Libraries: Once and Future," *The Electronic Library* 13 (June 1995): 203–207 (quotation, p. 206).

8. Quoted in Michael Schuyler, "SFPL, Viewed from the Top Left Corner," *Computers in Libraries* 17 (April 1997): 32–34 (quotation, p. 34).

9. Redmond Kathleen Molz and Phyllis Dain, *Civic Space/Cyberspace: The American Public Library in the Information Age* (Cambridge: MIT Press, 1999), pp. 74, 76.

10. Baker, *Double Fold*, p. 26.

11. Baker, *Double Fold*, p. 29.

12. Baker, *Double Fold*, p. 87.

13. Michèle V. Cloonan and Shelby Sanett, "Comparing Preservation Strategies and Practices for Electronic Records," paper presented at a preservation conference in York, England, December 8, 2000, available at *http://www.rlg.org/events/pres-2000/cloonan.html*.

14. Willis E. Bridegam, *A Collaborative Approach to Collection Storage: The Five-College Library Depository* (Washington, D.C.: Council on Library and Information Resources, June 2001), available at *http://www.clir.org/pubs/reports/pub97/contents.html*.

15. Baker, *Double Fold*, pp. 107–108.

16. Baker, *Double Fold*, p. 257.

17. Bridegam, *A Collaborative Approach to Collection Storage*.

18. See, especially, Abby Smith, *Why Digitize?* (Washington, D.C.: Council on Library and Information Resources, February 1999), available at *http://www.clir.org/pubs/abstract/pub80.html*.

19. Baker, *Double Fold*, p. 19.

20. Baker, *Double Fold*, p. 99.

21. Baker, *Double Fold*, pp. 102–103.

22. Laura Price and Abby Smith, *Managing Cultural Assets from a Business Perspective* (Washington, D.C.: Council on Library and Information Resources, March 2000), available at *http://www.clir.org/pubs/reports/pub90/contents.html*.

23. Baker, *Double Fold*, p. 35.

24. Jason Epstein, "Reading: The Digital Future," *The New York Review of Books* 48 (July 5, 2001): 46–48 (quotation, p. 46).

25. Abby Smith, *The Future of the Past: Preservation in American Research Libraries* (Washington, D.C.: Council on Library and Information Resources, April 1999), available at *http://www.clir.org/pubs/reports/pub82/pub82text.html*.

26. Baker, *Double Fold*, pp. 5–6.

27. Baker, *Double Fold*, p. 7.

28. Baker, *Double Fold*, p. 8.

29. Baker, *Double Fold*, pp. 41–46 (quotation, p. 45).

30. Baker, *Double Fold*, pp. 158–161. For the Updike parody, see John Updike, *Golf Dreams: Writings on Golf* (New York: Alfred A. Knopf, 1966), pp. 6–12.

31. Henk J. Porck and René Teygeler, *Preservation Science Survey: An Overview of Recent Developments in Research on the Conservation of Selected Analog Library and Archival Materials* (Washington, D.C.: Council on Library and Information Resources, December 2000), available at *http://www.clir.org/pubs/reports/pub95/contents.html*.

32. Baker, *Double Fold*, p. 98.

33. Porck and Teygeler, *Preservation Science Survey*.

34. Steven Puglia, "The Cost of Digital Imaging Projects," *RLGDigiNews* 3 (October 15, 1999), available at *http://www.rlg.org/preserv/diginews/diginews3-5.html#feature*.

35. Matthew Cook, "Economies of Scale: Digitizing the *Chicago Daily News*," *RLG DigiNews* 4 (February 15, 2000), available at *http://www.rlg.org/preserv/diginews/diginews4-1.html feature2*.

36. Baker, *Double Fold*, p. 16.

37. Baker, *Double Fold*, pp. 54–55.

38. Baker, *Double Fold*, p. 66.

39. Baker, *Double Fold*, p. 67.

40. Baker, *Double Fold*, p. 241.

41. Baker, *Double Fold*, p. 77.

42. Baker, *Double Fold*, pp. 94–95.

43. Baker, *Double Fold*, pp. 141–157.
44. Baker, *Double Fold*, p. 146.
45. Baker, *Double Fold*, p. 162.
46. Baker, *Double Fold*, p. 155.
47. Baker, *Double Fold*, pp. 111–135.
48. Baker, *Double Fold*, p. 134.
49. As it happens, there was spirited debate and criticism about all of the aspects detailed by Baker as efforts to develop mass deacidification approaches proceeded, not the sheepish following by the library and archives community implied in *Double Fold*. See, for example, writings such as these: Richard D. Smith, "Deacidifying Library Collections: Myths and Realities," *Restaurator* 8: 2/3 (1987): 69–93; William J. Welsh, "In Defence of DEZ: LC's Perspective," *Library Journal* 112 (January 1987): 62–63; Karl Nyren, "The DEZ Process and the Library of Congress," *Library Journal* 111 (September 15, 1986): 33–35; Jack C. Thompson and George Cunha, "Mass Deacidification: Thoughts on the Cunha Report," *Restaurator* 9: 3 (1988): 147–162.
50. Porck and Teygeler, *Preservation Science Survey*.
51. Baker, *Double Fold*, p. 140.
52. Baker, *Double Fold*, pp. 136–140.
53. Baker, *Double Fold*, p. 249.

Chapter Ten

Mom, I Harass Monks (Too)

After my debate with Nicholson Baker at Simmons Graduate School of Library and Information Science (part of Simmons College) in Boston in May 2001, a number of longtime colleagues in attendance had some funny things to say to me (fortunately they reserved these comments for private asides and not as part of the public question and answer session). One quipped that she generally never agreed with me, but that she did in this (one) instance. Another colleague asked if I felt funny, since they sensed that I was speaking to a group who was more in tune with my viewpoints than that of Nicholson Baker and that this must have been an unusual experience for me. Finally, another, laughing, asked how I thought about being the new poster boy for the library and archives professions.

These comments represent for me one of the two most awkward aspects that I had to overcome in writing this book. For most of my career I have been an outspoken critic _within_ the archival profession. Suddenly I find myself defending it, while expanding my perspective to include the _archival_ responsibilities of the library discipline. A closely related second aspect is my uneasy feeling that I have developed an obsession with Nicholson Baker, much like he describes his own fixation with John Updike in one of his earlier books. Just as Baker displays his envy, at that earlier point in his career, about Updike's popularity, I suspect there is a sense of my envy at the public attention given Baker's _Double Fold_. It is precisely why I originally wanted to title this book _Him and Me_, a play on Baker's book about Updike entitled _U and I_.[1] In this closing chapter I try to express my own presumptions as an archivist so that readers have the opportunity to understand how and why I argue what I do in this volume.

The year 2000 marked some personal milestones for me. Early in the year I celebrated my fiftieth birthday, one of those sobering events in which one begins to reflect more on the end of careers and lives than in considering their promise and potential. I was promoted to full professor in my school, and I saw the release of two books on archives and records topics, one on historical reflections and the other on policy issues, summing up much of my last decade of thinking, debating with others, and writing,[2] an effort that started with my first major book in 1990.[3] All of these events, but especially the publication of the books, caused me to consider whether I had uttered my last thoughts—at least my final important ones—on the importance of records in society, the role of archivists and records managers, and the future of both records and the professionals who care for them. There was no need to worry, however, as Nicholson Baker was about to enter the scene with his book and provide me plenty to think and write about in regards to the care of our documentary heritage.

In many ways my own career, spanning almost thirty years, reflects the major events and debates characterizing the North American archival community. However, I can't really say that I am always moving with the field in the same general direction, a statement I would not have made a decade ago. Some of this is the result of a changing archival profession, but more of this is the outcome of my own personal transformation, especially in this last decade. While some might look for unifying themes in my writings since the early 1970s, I prefer to see my writings reflecting my own changing viewpoints. I am not a systematic theologian in the records professions—writing a creed or confession for archivists or records managers; in fact I would argue that there never should be such rigid views. Rather, my writings, conference presentations, and teaching have followed my perceptions of the changing parameters of the archival profession since 1970.

My career has been divided between work as a manuscripts curator, primarily responsible for personal, family, and small business and organizational records; a government archivist and records manager; and educator of future archivists and records managers. Becoming an educator transformed my self-identity as an archivist or records professional in a number of ways, leading me to discuss, regularly and without the use of professional jargon, the nature of records work with those outside of the field. Becoming a professor of archives and records management, working within a school training individuals to be information professionals, also caused me to relate records work and values to a new group of scholars and professionals, ranging from librarians to information scientists, knowledge managers, information policy specialists, and others. Finally, becoming an archival educator put me within a small group of other educators, as graduate education in my field has been transformed within North America in the past two decades. Not all of this has been easy, but it has been more than a little interesting. Obviously, Nicholson Baker believes the professional education of librarians and archivists has led to an abandonment of their historic missions, although he tends only to make passing and not very informative comments about the substance of his argument (suggesting a plea to the popular mistrust of what is going on in higher education these days). While I see education as central to the success of work like archival administration, Baker sees it at the core of the demise of such disciplines.

Reflecting on just thirty years of archives and records management work may seem to be ludicrous, given the age of the field. The discipline of archives and records management is old, dating back to the most ancient societies. The making and maintaining of records was considered a mark of civilization and individuals holding posts comparable to modern records professionals were accorded a status sometimes nearing the privileges of priests and rulers. Many of the core principles were formed during the Renaissance, in response to a transition from orality to writing, the prevalence of forgeries, and new forms of research and scholarship utilizing records. The *modern* archives profession is, however, only a century old, another manifestation of the specialization and professionalism earmarking all of society in the late nineteenth and early twentieth centuries.

The first professional associations in Europe were formed in the 1890s, the time period when the first manuals and theoretical treatises were published.[4] In the United States, the modern archives profession is generally dated from the 1930s when the National Archives and the Society of American Archivists were established. Thus my career, abbreviated as it may seem in terms of the millennia of efforts to create and administer records, nevertheless spans nearly a third of the modern profession and parallels the field's concern with electronic records. My career also coincides with the period when the field began to develop its own, serious scholarship (although the main development of this scholarship lies ahead). That Nicholson Baker does not seem to recognize the distinctions between librarians and archivists or fully comprehend the *archival* aspect of the mission of librarianship may be partly due to the lower profile of such scholarship (although Baker makes exemplary use of the library and preservation literature with an occasional reference to articles in archival science venues). Baker also is one of many modern commentators who disparage the emergence of professions, while I believe professionalism to be critical to how specialists like archivists will work and how successful they will be in meeting societal needs.

The scholarship emanating from the North American archives profession has been radically transformed in the past three decades. Prior to 1970, there was one main professional journal (the *American Archivist*), publications from the National Archives, and a few manuals combining theory and practice. When I entered the field, this was all there was to

guide one's initiation into archival work, meaning it was reasonably easy
to absorb it all and fueling the idea that archival work was something only
learned about through practice rather than study. Sitting down and reading
through the *American Archivist* was as good an approach as any. Over the
past thirty years, however, we have seen the emergence of stronger graduate
education programs, a rebirth of interest in theoretical concerns, a stronger
emphasis on research (especially with the creation of doctoral programs),
and an entirely new focus on records and record-keeping systems because
of rapidly changing technologies. All of this has breached the walls protecting cherished principles, leading to new methods and theories. Accompanying this has been a massive pouring out of *basic* manuals and
textbooks, written in reaction to a growing sense of the complexities of
records, record-keeping systems, and records work. While we do not yet
have archives and records management for dummies, parodying that popular series of manuals on computers and other practical topics, we do have
some that come close to it.[5] This is one reason why, I believe, Nicholson
Baker has given us a kind of truncated view of library and archival preservation; while he makes references to events or attitudes at particular time
periods, Baker often seems to blend them all into one porridge and lacks
any sense of change, past and in progress. Baker switches back and forth
between practices ranging over a half century without considering the nature of progress within fields such as archives, librarianship, and preservation. It is a fatal error, minimizing the validity of his ideas and concerns.

From my own perspective, I think I have made my most important contributions to the archival profession since becoming an educator of archivists in 1988, but this may be more the result of a widening gap between
myself as an educator and most practitioners, reflecting the old popular
notion that one learns more from teaching than doing (although there continues to be a tension in professions like archives between educators and
practitioners, something I think Baker recognizes). In the years following I
have been involved more deeply in research and theory, having published
six books with several more presently underway. I also headed a major
research project in electronic records management, resulting in work supporting two doctoral dissertations[6] and a number of articles and products
that have been frequently cited and used worldwide by archivists and records managers.[7] For an academic, identity generally derives from two
sources—research and publication and the teaching of students, a very
different notion of practice from others in the profession who are concerned
with the daily challenges of managing and preserving records. It is why I
tend to look at the broader issues—self-defined professional mission, societal mandates, and organizational differences—rather than the minutiae
being dealt with by Nicholson Baker.

My conviction is that most professional archivists (those with a substantial professional orientation and purpose, not just everyone hanging out a

shingle as an archivist because they like old documents) ought to be constantly wrestling with research and writing about archives and records management as part of a symbiotic process with their work as records professionals. This is really what my career has been about, and I think it is not merely a career for an academic (that is, I started regularly writing about archives fifteen years *before* becoming a faculty member). Admittedly, we have many in the field writing finding aids, exhibition catalogs, and in other such venues. I applaud their efforts. But we need more people in the discipline contending with critical issues, questioning assumptions, writing about archives in other disciplines, and producing understandable writings about archives and records for policymakers and citizens alike. I have been influenced by people like Terry Cook and Margaret Hedstrom, who have had careers as both practitioners and academics, for their abilities to ask the right questions and to speak to the right people. And I have been encouraged that others are coming along, perhaps including some of my former students. It is another reason why I took the trouble to write this lengthy response to Nicholson Baker, somewhat fearful that we won't have sufficient replies from within the fields responsible for the documentary heritage and even more concerned that Nicholson Baker's emotional, sentimental, and not always well-informed perspective will shape our dialogue with the public in the future. Given the nature of our field, I fully expect that some (perhaps many) will disagree with me, but I hope that my words will aid individuals to shape their own views.

Through my more than a quarter of a century in the archives and records management field, I have written steadily on a wide variety of archival and records management topics. Some of these publications generated from work responsibilities or professional association committee and task force activities, but many also were the result of my developing interests in the history of the profession, research and development needs, and other areas such as training and education. More recently, I have tried to make some inroads into publishing in more popular journals or journals in disciplines outside of the archives and records management field to reach a broader audience about the importance of records, especially those possessing archival value. I have published in a wide array of disciplines, reflecting both the multidisciplinary nature of archives and records management as well as my own approach to research in this field, including archives, history, records management, library science, information science, museum, and genealogical journals, and in journals in North America as well as in Australia, England, Ireland, Italy, and Spain. My research writings draw on qualitative and quantitative methods, are frequently cited, and are often the subject of debate within the field. My work on archival appraisal, electronic records management, professionalism, archival history, and archival theory is drawn upon by others, represents my main continuing interests, and probably most important, shaped my convictions reflected in my response to Nicholson Baker.

Because of my research concerning the archives and records management field, I have been involved in a number of efforts to evaluate the existing professional literature and to develop new research agendas.[8] My career has long been associated with articulating research agendas, as others have noted.[9] All of my writings of this sort have stressed the need for more systematic research in every facet of the profession, both applied and theoretical, especially the preparation of case studies. While the professional literature continues to expand, the portion of it relating to research needs or being genuinely research-oriented remains small. In this sense, some of Nicholson Baker's complaints about lack of rigor in research or in publicizing rationales for library and archives preservation are compatible with my own concerns. Baker is right in that archivists and librarians have not sufficiently explained themselves or provided adequate reasons for some of their preservation activities. Perhaps it will take such a rant from outside of our community to wake us up about what and how we need to communicate.

Much of my research and writing has put me squarely into the midst of professional debates about whether theory or practice is the fundamental manner in which the field generates its knowledge. My view is that *knowledge* of records, generated by both formal theory development and direct work with records systems, is a fundamental component of what constitutes *any* part of the records profession. Those critical of the theory approach tend to view my work critically.[10] My research (and teaching) is based on the concept that principles derive from both practice and testing theory, and that these principles can be generalized into archival theory that is crucial to teaching and explaining archives but that also supports practice and research. Controversial or not, my writings have tended to identify me with a core group of archival thinkers and theorists, although only one of many such groups, in the past two decades.[11] My problem with Baker's conclusions is that he often makes them from no real understanding about books, print, newspapers, media, information, or other related topics, and he argues instead that he is merely reporting what other experts have told him. Given the theme and tone of *Double Fold* I am not sure this is good enough. How or why he chooses what experts he does is often not explained.

An interest in the history of the archives field has marked my entire career as an archivist, first as a working archivist and then as an educator of archivists. My earliest interest was in the development of archives and historical manuscripts in a single state, partly because of my early career in that state and as part of an effort to understand the nature of archives there.[12] In those days of minimal basic manuals and few courses on archival work, I resorted to studying the historical evolution of particular programs and record genres in order to comprehend what they represented and how they needed to be managed at a particular point in time. For example, when I became the head of the Baltimore City Archives I immersed myself into that program's own archives as a means of understanding why it had developed in the form that it had, answering questions about apparent problems that were unresolved after a quarter of a century of existence. Because of this early work, I developed a strong sense of the value of historical knowledge of the field for its use in current work and future planning.[13] This has led to efforts to understand the general state of historical scholarship about both archives and record-keeping systems.[14] The research in this area has taken two approaches, one involving research in primary records and the other focusing on critiquing historical studies concerning the development of archives and records management. My emphasis on the history of records, archives, archives programs, and the archival profession has been recognized by others in the field.[15] Baker's weakness in the history of librarianship and archival work is telling, I think, leading him to make false starts and draw incomplete or inaccurate conclusions. Reaction to my archival history research has been interesting. Despite whatever criticisms are offered by such authors in regard to my historical work, the bigger issue may be why so little of this kind of research is going on in the archival field, a topic I explored in an essay on archival history for a special issue of *Libraries & Culture*.[16] Perhaps Baker's *Double Fold* will prompt some to look more carefully at the history of library and archival preservation, since his critique frames many questions deserving careful and more systematic replies than he offers.

The paucity of writing on American archival history is why I brought together, in a heavily revised fashion, a book reevaluating the history of archives and records management, the first such volume intended for a professional audience.[17] The book considers the "mythic" origins of modern records management, an examination of archives and records management from the ancient era to the present, the reasons for the lack of a national system of records administration, changing concepts of archival appraisal, the role of archives and records in public memory, changing views of the education of records professionals, the ongoing debate about documentary editing, and the archival mission in cyber-culture. This book and my other writings attest to my sense that all scholarship in the archives and records management field must, by necessity, have a heavy historical orientation, or, as Neil Postman argues, history is a "meta-subject. . . . No one can claim adequate knowledge of a subject unless one knows how such knowledge came to be."[18] And this is exactly a portion of my problem with *Double Fold*.

My interest in the history of the archival field continues to be unabated, but this does not appear to be the case with the profession overall. I revised my much earlier essays on the development of archives in Maryland as a case study in archival history, partly as an effort to stimulate new work in this area (but also reflecting the fact that these essays remain current because of so little other work on archival history from any perspective). This interest stems from recent work in examining the general nature of historical research in this field, helping me to recognize that the revision of my fuller study on a single state's archival development is both relevant and important. I also am beginning work on a study of the presidential library system (a topic also possessing considerable implications in the policy of access, privacy, and ownership in government record-keeping). Studies about state archival histories and the presidential library system are nonexistent,[19] a surprising occurrence given the immense interest in public memory leading to examination of institutions and movements closely related to archives (such as historic preservation and museums).[20] What may be ironic is that my own views about the presidential library system may be as controversial to some as Nicholson Baker's views about library and archival preservation are to me (and others). There is much, I suspect, that we have in common, especially in trying to influence change within the fields responsible for managing our documentary heritage. The primary difference, I think, is that I work from within and with a greater knowledge of and sensitivity to the nuances of the issues than what Mr. Baker possesses. The chief value of Baker's *Double Fold* may be that it serves as a warning to individuals like me that we cannot take for granted that we or our discipline will be understood or appreciated by external observers.

Another major aspect of my research and writing has concerned the education of archivists and records managers. This has been a major theme in my books, in which I have devoted considerable space to considering the historical evolution of education in the records professions.[21] I have also chaired professional conference programs related to this issue, resulting in published proceedings,[22] encouraged students at both masters and doctoral levels to explore professional concerns such as education in preparing papers for publication,[23] and applied my ideas to drafting new graduate education standards or trying to influence such standards.[24] Some of this writing, indeed the primary reason why I was chairing committees dealing with education *before* becoming an educator, had to do with earlier work on the nature of the archival profession mandating some consideration of education.[25] It is in the last decade, however, as I have had more time to think about and practice as an educator, that my more important writings have been done on this topic. Prior to becoming an educator, most of my writings were case studies or heavily dependent on the institutions where I worked, while since becoming an educator I have had the advantage of being able to look at issues in and challenges to the records professions from a broader perspective. I now can view education and training *both* as a practitioner and an educator, a perspective provided to only a small number of individuals in North America, and one that confirms that practice will always be an important part of the field's basic knowledge as well as its education. However, one without the other severely weakens both and, of course, the profession and its societal mandate. It is why I am exasperated with Baker that he blames much of what he sees as failures in library and archives preservation on the education of a new generation of better-equipped preservation administrators and conservators. These individuals are not being brainwashed into using the dreaded double fold test or in turning aside from the artifactual values of print and manuscript objects. Quite to the contrary, these individuals are oriented to the problems and weaknesses and gaps in previous approaches and previous generations—and, in fact, many educators like myself will use *Double Fold* in our classrooms.

Since becoming an educator, my interests have focused on research relating to critical issues affecting the archival profession's mission, especially the education of its practitioners but also encompassing other topics such as the image of the archivist and archival profession. I have examined, in particular, curricular issues,[26] how continuing education relates to graduate education and how it supports the field,[27] the nature of archives as a specialization within library and information science education,[28] and the trends in employment requirements for entry-level archivists.[29] The societal image is a critical issue because it impacts on the profession's ability to advocate on behalf of its mission or to lobby for such critical functions as the creation or strengthening of graduate programs, although some records professionals see the fascination with this topic as relating to societal status and other matters that only could be characterized as professional angst. In this area I have investigated how children's literature reflects or does not reflect archival records,[30] how archives and archivists have been treated in the recent scholarship on public memory,[31] how national newspapers have treated archives and records,[32] and how popular management books reflect archives and records issues.[33] All of these topics are part of the larger societal context of archives and records management work. Baker's writings, it seems, poke and prod at the stereotypical notions of librarians especially (archivists seem invisible), and I think it is deliberate and unfortunate but an attack that no one should be particularly surprised about.

Archivists, as is the case with other professionals, are always concerned about their image, although rarely have they tried to study this issue in order to understand the societal elements contributing to their image and to strengthen their roles within their employing organizations and the larger society. Careful study generally reveals that archival images stem as much from what archivists do and say as from other societal features. In other words, archivists often create their own image, especially by how they view and treat their own professional education, credentials, and professionalism.[34] My writings assert what I believe to be a fundamental truth, that efforts to strengthen education and to build a substantial professional knowledge are not part of some conspiracy to develop an antiegalitarian discipline that excludes certain individuals but that these efforts are part of an ongoing challenge to manage records and record-keeping systems for the benefit of organizations, society, and posterity. Baker, in his writings, appeals to such sentiments, it seems. As a result of my strong views, as well as the changing nature of the archival profession, my writings are often cited by those critical of stronger standards for such matters as education and credentials. In one essay, critical of the trend toward incorporating graduate archival education in library and information science, my writings were cited eleven times in fifty-three notes as representative or leading examples of the *other* perspective.[35] It will be interesting to see how others with different perspectives than mine within the profession respond to Baker's writings, especially as archival education has continued to grow.[36] More, better-focused, and rigorous educational programs are needed, not less as Nicholson Baker seems to suggest.

My interest in the appraisal of records possessing archival or continuing value originated in my professional career as I had responsibilities for collecting in a manuscript repository and then records management and archives responsibilities in government. Stemming from this experience, and because of work with other colleagues interested in such issues, the 1980s, prior to my coming to the university, was a time when I formulated some initial ideas about archival appraisal[37] *and* became involved in a major research and development project examining the then newly formulated idea of archival documentation strategies.[38] From this work and my later teaching on the topic, I have attempted to develop some statements summarizing the principles of archival appraisal, especially since archivists assume that there are standards guiding this function but generally perform this work on an ad hoc basis.[39] It is interesting to me that efforts to summarize principles for such functions as appraisal are rare or, even worse, often ignored completely. At a conference on architectural records appraisal in the early 1990s, practitioners managing such records reacted harshly to conceptual statements about appraisal, including even suggestions that they might codify their practical knowledge in a manner that others could use.[40] Because of such attitudes, professional knowledge is often retarded, case studies neglected, and the potential of the World Wide Web for sharing such information lost (such as easily making available case studies, policies, and other materials). It may be that the suspicions held by Baker about selection and his case for saving every original document result from basic human impulses and the lack of higher profile discussions of how and why library and archival collections are formed. Baker's lack of selectivity and my sense of the need for more aggressive appraisal may be the points where the two of us are farthest apart. It may also be the realm where some archivists and librarians might gravitate to Baker's camp, recognizing the difficulty in making decisions that lead to neglect or destruction of certain kinds of documentary materials. Baker is certainly most annoyed that in our present era preservation involves destruction.

My writings on archival appraisal are often not used as intended—to develop new or improved appraisal methodologies. Change in institutional practices is difficult to make, although the future of the archival mission and the management of records depends on such change taking place. Nevertheless, I continue to be asked to contribute essays to publications reevaluating the fundamentals of archival work and the knowledge supporting this work,[41] suggesting that there are some unsettling notions about what archivists are doing when they appraise. At the least there is a misinterpretation of what the advocates of the documentation strategy were proposing, not the rejecting of earlier approaches but their amplification. Such uncertainties and confusion became even more pronounced with electronic records management, revealing the complex challenges of media that Nicholson Baker often seems to ignore.

My plans for future research in the archival appraisal function fall mostly within the realm of interdisciplinary study, as archivists need far more critical evaluation about how well this aspect of archival and records management work has gone. I hope to try to do some cross-disciplinary writing, evaluating how selection approaches in library science, museum studies, historic preservation, and other fields relates to or are different from what passes for archival appraisal. I have become extremely interested in the notion of collective or public memory and the place of archives in it. I have a plan for examining the idea of how public memory is constructed by evaluating how libraries, museums, archives, historic sites, and other cultural organizations engage in selection for preservation, exhibition, and interpretation. I have tried to explore some of these issues in some conference proceedings.[42] Some of my earlier writings also reflect such themes.[43] It is fair to say that Baker's *Double Fold* is a kind of contribution to the field of public memory, not as a study of it but as a primary text reflecting increasing concerns about the loss of such memory in the face of rapid technological and other changes. We obviously have very different views about what is happening.

I became involved with electronic records management issues because of my need to integrate this area into my teaching and also because of the emergence of major research and application needs within the field. Obviously, students needed to be oriented to electronic records management because more and more organizations were depending on electronic systems to create and maintain their records. Partly because of my position as an educator, but more directly because of my advocacy for research and stronger professional qualifications, I became involved in a number of profession-wide initiatives to redress the matter of electronic records management. The prime stimulant for this work was my participation in a government archivists and records management institute held at my school from 1989 to 1994.[44] I was also involved in developing a profession-wide research agenda, curriculum elements for teaching in this area,[45] and other professional conferences considering the impact of electronic records and information technology on archival and records management work. As a result of the research, I have also written a number of broader statements calling for the archives and records management professions to rethink how they approach electronic records concerns. These include a reevaluation of the notion of custody as an archival principle,[46] the manner in which records managers view electronic records issues,[47] the notion of computer literacy for records professionals,[48] and the relevancy of technology convergence for the records professions.[49] My most significant research came as part of a major effort to develop functional requirements for record-keeping that could be used in electronic systems. Some of this led to the normal issuance of research reports.[50] The research also led me to write essays reflecting more broadly on the nature and importance of records.[51] The functional requirements project has become the basis for significant research by archivists and others in North America, Europe, and Australia. This work has also become part of a continuing profession-wide controversy about how best to approach electronic records management. Perhaps most telling is that in a critical reaction to the school of thought on electronic records management, my work reflects that I am identified as one of the leading articulators (of a group of five) representing a "new paradigm for electronic records."[52] It is obvious to me that all of my subsequent research on archives and records management matters will not stray far from electronic records management issues. Suffice it to say that *any* research in the archives and records management field will have to address the electronic records management realm. An example of a recent research paper on this topic is my study on what North American archivists cite for authority when writing about electronic records management.[53] While I have made efforts to incorporate a broader view of records, extending across an array of media, Nicholson Baker has developed a more restricted perspective of archivists and librarians as paper keepers. Such a narrow view weakens his case because it is impossible to ignore the societal and institutional contexts in which librarians and archivists must function.

Over the past decade or so, one of my interests has increasingly been advocating for the importance of records and archives and the professions supporting their management. Within the records professions, I have written about such matters and many of the previously cited publications reflect this.[54] I have also tried to write about such matters outside of the archives and records management fields, either by commenting on critical and highly visible records topics or by writing about records and archives in journals in other professional disciplines. I have used some of the electronic journals for commentaries on current affairs, writing about the controversies surrounding documentary editing,[55] the conflicting literature about the promises and perils of the Information Age,[56] and the contradictions of lavishing great attention on the preservation of the original manuscript of the Declaration of Independence in the Information Age.[57] I have also published in some more popular and widely read journals about the difficulty of selecting historical records in the midst of an era characterized by culture wars and postmodernist philosophies,[58] the preservation of library records in a technocratic age,[59] and ethical matters.[60] My writings about Nicholson Baker's library crusade, including this book, certainly fit into this category.

Such writing reflects, of course, a move beyond only theoretical or conceptual ideas to the practical concerns reflected in a profession such as the archives and records field. Blending (or relating) theory or knowledge to practical issues can be seen in my continuing efforts to demonstrate why records and archives play an important role in many aspects of society. I finished, about the same time as this book, another book with David Wallace, a former doctoral student of mine now on the faculty of the University of Michigan School of Information, on records and accountability. The volume includes essays on a wide range of topics, including the Swiss banks and Nazi gold, investigations into alleged Nazi war criminals, the tobacco litigation, the Internal Revenue Service records management controversy, various human rights cases and record-keeping issues in Latin America and Africa, forgery, recent controversies about the ownership of looted art during the Second World War, custody of the Martin Luther King, Jr. papers, the documentary editing of the United States Foreign Relations records, record-keeping and the Iran-Contra affair, and the Enola Gay exhibit debate—all cases that have been making headlines in recent years. In the meantime, I continue to reexplore some of the most cherished aspects of archival work as a means of throwing light on the most important issues facing archivists and all records professionals. Refurbishing the exhibition showing the original Declaration of Independence does, for example, bring up some very basic issues about how archivists and society need to view the increasing dependence on electronic record-keeping systems. Such unholy (for some) thoughts come from teaching, where it is my responsibility to dissect and reform basic archival principles and methodologies and to motivate students to think and challenge assumptions about these principles and methodologies. This is why Nicholson Baker's writings, from an educational point of view, have been welcome. Baker's essays and *Double Fold* provide persuasive and graphic testimony to popular misperceptions of both librarians and archivists. Baker's focus on the printed book and newspaper as artifacts provide wonderful opportunities for students to reflect on the nature and role of information in our society.

Classroom responsibilities both reflect and nurture research, and, regardless, teaching is a fundamental mark of an academic's work quality. In all my teaching I have been involved in a variety of educational approaches. Most of my teaching has relied on traditional lecture and seminar methods, required by the term-long courses and short-term institutes and workshops. My teaching objective is to ground students preparing for careers in archives and records management in the theories, methodologies, and practices of this field. In pursuing this objective, I am in harmony with educational purposes advocated by a small group of educators in the archives and records management field.[61] There is a broader mandate I impose upon myself as well. I view my role as a change agent in the field (probably not all that different from how Baker views his own crusade), primarily by assisting future practitioners to be able to evaluate critically the current challenges facing the profession and to develop solutions to these challenges, another reason why I certainly have and will continue to use Nicholson Baker's writings in the classroom. This is why I distinguish what I do as education not training, the difference between short-term and long-term preparation. It is also why I emphasize, at both the masters and doctoral levels, research about professional issues. With this larger perspective on what I am doing as an educator, I also see a strongly symbiotic relationship between my own research, writing, and teaching. Often my choices about what I conduct research on are made by needs to explore new topics or to challenge old ones in my teaching. Just as often some of my research and writing is stimulated by questions and issues raised by students.[62] In some cases, I have drawn on research conducted for other reasons, and used it to write in a manner that could be used effectively within the classroom.[63]

I employ a variety of methods by which to meet these objectives in teaching. I immerse the students in reading in order to gain a thorough comprehension of professional knowledge and the professional literature. Students are required to become familiar with the classic or landmark writings, the current standards, and the wide range of opinions and debates characterizing contemporary records work. I purposefully assign writings debating crucial issues and writings presenting widely conflicting views about professional missions, methods, and practices. Baker's controversial ideas, along with his ample use of or commentary on important writings in librarianship and to a lesser degree in archival studies, prompt considerable discussion among students (as well as in the field at large). Although Baker often tends to portray librarians as a nonthinking species and their education backgrounds as more indoctrination than education, his writings can be very useful to stimulate healthy discussion within the classroom.

I also attempt to build contextual frames in both lecture and seminar approaches, interpreting each method, theory, or element of practice as a product of its time. Students are made to consider the historical development of every aspect of the profession, partly so as to comprehend the present issues and challenges in a longer view (and, in time, to understand that contemporary issues often are not new at all). It is the lack of such contextual frames that makes *Double Fold* so difficult to read. I emphasize the history and changing nature of record-keeping, believing that it is essential that individuals preparing for careers in records management, information resources management, and archival administration understand what a record or document is, how the concept of a record has changed or remained the same, and how systems governing the creation and use of records have changed and are changing. As Neil Postman writes: "A book is all history. Everything about it takes one back in time—from the way it is produced to its linear mode of exposition to the fact that the past tense is its most comfortable form of address."[64] Archivists and records managers must understand that a record is all history as well. Books, records, libraries, and archives are all challenged as reputable forms of information and evidence since the advent of the Internet and the World Wide Web. Paul Duguid, in a recent essay, writes that "accepted by many as an 'agent of change' in the Gutenberg revolution, the book is easily cast as a force of reaction in the information age."[65] Some consider the record as even more reactionary. It might seem that Baker would agree with such notions, but he actually never explains his view of the book (and newspaper) other than as objects adding beauty and charm to our lives. While this might be important, it is not reflective of the growing scholarship on the history and nature of print.

Much of what I teach, whether theoretical or conceptual, is related to current practice, encompassing practical exercises along with research intended to enable students to delve into some aspect of the discipline in greater detail and relate archives and records management to the broader information professions, especially the changing uses of information technologies.[66] I see my courses as supporting the development of a broad and fundamental knowledge, while I view the research paper as a means for having the student examine more deeply at least one aspect of this knowledge.[67] These papers also serve other purposes, such as helping the students to think critically, to apply their developing knowledge in particular ways, and to make contributions to the existing professional knowledge through the submission of the better papers to journals in the field. I also emphasize the possibility of having students build from their own professional interests and experiences. Many of the students who enter our school to study archives and records management either are currently employed in records work or have had experience in particular archives and records management settings. Some students, because of their educational backgrounds (which are diverse), have also developed particular career objectives and interests, bringing a broad range of knowledge and experience that Nicholson Baker clearly does not understand exists in such schools or maybe in the library and archives discipline in general.

The reasons why I teach in the manner I do has much to do with the nature of archival education and my own previous experience as an archivist, as well as with my continuing observations about the nature of ar-

chives and records management work. My views on the field were molded
by my experiences, including a realization of my own inadequate education
prior to assuming some of the responsibilities I held. My preparation con-
sisted of a combination of scattered graduate courses, workshops and institutes, and on-the-job training. None of this was, in my opinion, as
effective as it should have been in preparing me for a career. Much of what
I teach, how I teach, and what I have students do is to enable them *not* to
have to suffer through what I did in my early career.

My previous career (previous to becoming an educator) also gave me
some unique opportunities to delve into the nature of archival education
and work. I was involved in analyzing statewide archival and historical
records planning efforts from a national perspective,[68] in authoring a major
statewide plan for Alabama,[69] and in developing a self-study guide for historical records repositories.[70] All of these opportunities helped me to develop a more critical, knowledgeable view about the education of archivists
and records managers that has served me well in developing and offering
graduate courses in this field and that has fostered a critical spirit about
the profession. These activities also brought me into contact with individuals who also were questioning many of the most cherished assumptions
held by the profession. Baker seems also to be attacking cherished assumptions about library and archival preservation, but the tone of his critiques
leads not to reform or rethinking but to cynicism and anti-professionalism.

Graduate archival education has undergone a remarkable transformation
in the past decade. Up through the 1980s, most entered the field with a
modicum of formal education, mostly a cobbling together of workshops
and institutes and, perhaps, one or two introductory graduate courses
(much as I had received in the early 1970s).[71] Since then, there has been a
resurgence of development in graduate archival education programs, including separate masters degrees and multiple faculty specialists at a core
group of schools. There remains a legacy of problems because of this relatively recent development. There is tension between educators and practitioners, misunderstanding about the need for research and the nature of
theory, and confusion about the differences and purposes of education and
training. I orient students to these continuing issues and tensions, while
helping them to understand how to overcome them and build viable archives and records programs (and careers). In other words, my courses are
deliberately designed to push students *beyond* the current level of expectations for graduate archival education so that they are prepared not only
for careers but to be leaders in the profession. At the same time, I am
constantly examining the broader professional issues facing archival and
records management education, such as curricular issues,[72] the nature of
research in the field,[73] continuing education and its relationship to graduate
education,[74] and professional advocacy and its relationship to the archival
field.[75]

It is not in my nature to *not* have something to say. But what I am not certain about is where I will be writing and for what audiences. My interest is in working to help society to comprehend the importance of records, and this may or may not include a role for the current generation of archivists and records managers (although I believe it is certainly up to these records professionals to determine the nature of their roles and contributions by what they choose to do or not to do). The book represented here, responding to Baker's *Double Fold*, is, in fact, intended for a wider audience, those individuals who have read and been influenced by that tome. While I know archivists and librarians have read and are reading *Double Fold*, it is also obvious that Baker's book has gained considerably more attention outside of the library and archives professions. Not too many years ago, at a conference in Australia on the public image of archivists, I stated the following:

I have been writing about archival issues for archivists from nearly the day I started working as an archivist. I have been recently thinking that perhaps it is time to make a change. . . . Now I wonder if what I, and others, should have been doing is writing about archives for other professionals and for a wider public audience. This is the direction that I am seriously toiling with. . . . We need to get society worrying about the demise of the archival record as it now seems to be worried about the demise of the printed book. We need to stop being afraid of being advocates for our mission. Archivists need to be inspired and to inspire. And, we all need to have fun in doing this.[76]

Nicholson Baker has provided me the impetus to try to do such things, and for that I am grateful. I hope my book has inspired some to rethink the issues Baker raises and to reconsider the nature of archives and libraries.

NOTES

1. Nicholson Baker, *U and I: A True Story* (New York: Vintage Books, 1991).
2. These books were *Closing An Era: Historical Reflections on Archives and Records* (Westport, Conn.: Greenwood Press, 2000) and *Managing Records As Evidence and Information* (Westport, Conn.: Quorum Books, 2001).
3. *American Archival Analysis: The Recent Development of the Archival Profession in the United States* (Metuchen, N.J.: Scarecrow Press, 1990).
4. Compare Terry Cook, "What is Past is Prologue: A History of Archival Ideas Since 1898, and the Future Paradigm Shift," *Archivaria* 43 (Spring 1997) with Luciana Duranti, *Diplomatics: New Uses for an Old Science* (Lanham, Md.: Society of American Archivists and Association of Canadian Archivists in association with Scarecrow Press, 1998). Cook reflects a much more fluid generation of archival theory and practices.
5. Gregory Hunter, *Developing and Maintaining Practical Archives* (New York: Neal-Schuman, 1996). This publisher specializes in publishing "how-to-do-it" manuals.
6. Wendy Duff, "The Influence of Warrant on the Acceptance and Credibility

of the Functional Requirements for Recordkeeping," Ph.D. dissertation, University of Pittsburgh, 1996; and David A. Wallace, "The Public's Use of Federal Record-keeping Statutes to Shape Federal Information Policy: A Study of the PROFS Case," Ph.D. dissertation, University of Pittsburgh, 1997.

7. Examples of these publications can be found at *http://www.lis.pitt.edu/ nhprc/bibl-do.html*.

8. "American Archival Literature: Expanding Horizons and Continuing Needs, 1901–1987," *American Archivist* 50 (Summer 1987): 306–323; with Helen W. Samuels, "The Archivist's 'First Responsibility': A Research Agenda for the Identification and Selection of Records of Enduring Value," *American Archivist* 51 (Winter/Spring 1988): 28–42; "An Analysis of Archival Research, 1970–1992, and the Role and Function of the *American Archivist*," *American Archivist* 57 (Spring 1994): 278–288.

9. Mary Sue Stephenson, "The Function and Content of Research Methods in Graduate Archival Studies Education," *Archivaria* 35 (Spring 1993): 192–195.

10. For example, John W. Roberts, "Practice Makes Perfect, Theory Makes Theorists," *Archivaria* 37 (Spring 1994): 111–121.

11. Jean-Pierre Wallot, "Archival Oneness in the Midst of Diversity: A Personal Perspective," *American Archivist* 59 (Winter 1996): 18 fn 17.

12. These essays include "A History of the Calvert Papers, MS. 174," *Maryland Historical Magazine* 68 (Fall 1973): 309–322; "Public Records in Colonial Maryland," *American Archivist* 37 (April 1974): 263–275; "The Historical Development of the Manuscripts Division of the Maryland Historical Society," *Maryland Historical Magazine* 69 (Winter 1974): 409–417; "The Creation and Maintenance of Baltimore's Passenger Ship Lists by the Municipal Government, 1833–1866," *Maryland Genealogical Society Bulletin* 22 (Winter 1981): 2–9; "A Century of Frustration: The Movement for the Founding of the State Archives in Maryland, 1811–1935," *Maryland Historical Magazine* 78 (Summer 1983): 106–117; "The Need for Comprehensive Records Programs in Local Government: Learning by Mistakes in Baltimore, 1947–82," *Provenance* 1 (Fall 1983): 14–34; and "The Origins of American Religious Archives: Ethan Allen, Pioneer Church Historian and Archivist of Maryland," *Journal of the Canadian Church Historical Society* 29 (October 1987): 48–63.

13. The best example of this is my "Alabama's Archival Heritage, 1850–1985," *Alabama Review* 40 (October 1987): 284–307, part of an intensive two-year effort to develop a statewide plan for archives and historical records programs; the full plan was published as *Assessing Alabama's Archives: A Plan for the Preservation of the State's Historical Records* (Montgomery: Alabama Historical Records Advisory Board, 1985).

14. "American Archival History: Its Development, Needs, and Opportunities," *American Archivist* 46 (Winter 1983): 31–41; "On the Value of Archival History in the United States," *Libraries & Culture* 23 (Spring 1988): 135–151.

15. See Barbara L. Craig, "Outward Visions, Inward Glance: Archives History and Professional Identity," *Archival Issues* 17: 2 (1992): 117; and James O'Toole, "The Future of Archival History," *Provenance* 13 (1995): 1, 3. Examples of conference presentations or commissioned statements include "Other Atlantic States: Delaware, Florida, Georgia, Maryland, New Jersey, and South Carolina," in H. G. Jones, ed., *Historical Consciousness in the Early Republic: The Origins of State*

Historical Societies and Collections, 1791–1861 (Chapel Hill: North Caroliniana Society, Inc. and North Carolina Collection, 1995), pp. 102–124; and "The Failure or Future of American Archival History: A Somewhat Unorthodox View," *Libraries & Culture* 35 (Winter 2000): 141–154.

16. "The Failure or Future of American Archival History" suggests that most of the recent important writing about the history of archives and record-keeping systems was coming from outside of the field. Others, much earlier, had lamented about archivists contributing to their own field of scholarship, such as Lester J. Cappon, "Tardy Scholars Among the Archivists," *American Archivist* 21 (January 1958): 3–16.

17. *Closing An Era.*

18. Neil Postman, *Building a Bridge to the Eighteenth Century: How the Past Can Improve Our Future* (New York: Alfred A. Knopf, 1999), p. 173.

19. The only major study of a state's archival development is H. G. Jones, *For History's Sake: The Preservation and Publication of North Carolina History 1663–1903* (Chapel Hill: University of North Carolina Press, 1966). Presidential libraries are a more difficult topic. There are hundreds of articles about these libraries and many books, but these writings are either promotional arguments made by the staffs of these institutions or descriptions intended to be used by those wanting to visit their museums or to use their archival holdings. My preliminary evaluation of these institutions is "America's Pyramids: Presidents and Their Libraries," *Government Information Quarterly* 19, no. 1 (2002): 45–75.

20. For example, James M. Lindgren, *Preserving Historic New England: Preservation, Progressivism, and the Remaking of Memory* (New York: Oxford University Press, 1995); and James E. Young, *The Texture of Memory: Holocaust Memorials and Meanings* (New Haven, Conn.: Yale University Press, 1993).

21. *American Archival Analysis* included two chapters, one on research needs concerning educational approaches and the other chronicling the historical changes. *The First Generation of Electronic Records Archivists in the United States: A Study in Professionalization* (New York: Haworth Press, 1994) also considers the failure of graduate and continuing education to assist the profession in resolving electronic records management issues. *Documenting Localities: A Practical Model for American Archivists and Manuscripts Curators* (Metuchen, N.J.: Scarecrow Press and Society of American Archivists, 1996) includes a chapter describing the impact of weak graduate education supporting the archival appraisal function.

22. Editor, "Educating the American Archivist for the Twenty-First Century," *Journal of Education for Library and Information Science* 34 (Winter 1993).

23. Editor, "Archival Education and Student Research: Essays from the University of Pittsburgh," *Provenance* 12: 1 and 2 (1994): 1–150.

24. For example, "Educating Archivists: Speculations on the Past, Present, and Future," *Journal of the American Society for Information Science* 39 (September 1988): 340–343.

25. Some of this had to do with my involvement in profession-wide planning, reflected in my "Strategies for Archival Action in the 1980s and Beyond: Implementing the SAA Goals and Priorities Task Force Report," *Provenance* 3 (Fall 1985): 22–37, and my interests in professional boundaries, as reflected in "Archivists and Public Historians in the United States," *Public Historian* 8 (Summer 1986): 25–41. These interests led to a stronger concern for the nature and substance

of an archival professionalism and at least one writing that has been frequently cited over the past decade—"Professionalism and Archivists in the United States," *American Archivist* 49 (Summer 1986): 229–247, an essay I commented on at a later point in "Professionalism and Archivists Revisited: A Review Essay," *Midwestern Archivist* 15: 2 (1990): 5–15.

26. "The History of Primary Sources in Graduate Education: An Archival Perspective," *Special Collections* 4: 2 (1990): 39–78; "The Masters of Archival Studies and American Education Standards: An Argument for the Continued Development of Graduate Archival Education in the United States," *Archivaria* 36 (Autumn 1993): 221–231.

27. "Continuing Education and Special Collections Professionals: The Need for Rethinking," *Rare Books & Manuscripts Librarianship* 10: 2 (1995): 78–96.

28. With Edie Rasmussen, "Reinventing the Information Professions and the Argument for Specialization in LIS Education: Case Studies in Archives and Information Technology," *Journal of Education for Library and Information Science*, 38 (Fall 1997): 255–267.

29. "Employing Records Professionals in the Information Age: An Analysis of Entry-Level Archives Job Advertisements, 1976–1997, in the United States," *Information Management Journal* 34 (January 2000): 18–33.

30. "A Sense of the Future: A Child's View of Archives," in *Archivists: The Image and Future of the Profession; 1995 Conference Proceedings*, eds. Michael Piggott and Colleen McEwen (Canberra: Australian Society of Archivists Inc., 1996), pp. 189–209.

31. "The Concept of Public Memory and Its Impact on Archival Public Programming," *Archivaria* 36 (Autumn 1993): 122–135.

32. "International Perspectives on the Image of Archivists and Archives: Coverage by *The New York Times*, 1992–93," *International Information & Library Review* 25 (1993): 195–231.

33. "Archives and Archivists in the Twenty-First Century: What Will We Become?" *Archival Issues* 20: 2 (1995): 97–113.

34. For additional views on such limited perspectives, see my unpublished essay on archival certification on my personal homepage, *http://www.sis2.pitt.edu/rjc*. Because of such views, much of what I teach about concerns instituting change *within* the records profession, as well as advocating for greater societal awareness of records and their importance. See my "Advocacy in the Graduate Archives Curriculum: A North American Perspective," *Janus* 1 (1997): 30–41 for a discussion of this teaching emphasis.

35. Vernon R. Smith, "Pedagogy and Professionalism: An Evaluation of Trends and Choices Confronting Educators in the Archival Community," *The Public Historian* 16 (Summer 1994): 23–43. I believe that the profession is at a crossroads in many of its professional endeavors, especially graduate education. To see an example of my thinking on this, refer to my "The Society of American Archivists and Graduate Education: Meeting at the Crossroads," *American Archivist* 63 (Fall/Winter 2000): 368–379.

36. With Elizabeth Yakel, David Wallace, Jeannette Bastian, and Jennifer Bastian, "Archival Education in North American Library and Information Science Schools: A Status Report," *Library Quarterly* 71 (April 2001): 141–194. A shorter

version was published in the *Journal of Education for Library and Information Science* 42 (Summer 2001): 228–240.

37. With Lynn W. Cox, "Selecting Information of Enduring Value for Preservation: Contending with the Hydra-Headed Monster," in *Rethinking the Library in the Information Age: Issues in Library Research: Proposals for the 1990s* (Washington, D.C.: U.S. Government Printing Office, 1988), pp. 115–130; "Selecting Historical Records for Microfilming: Some Suggested Procedures for Repositories," *Library & Archival Security* 9: 2 (1989): 21–41.

38. "A Documentation Strategy Case Study: Western New York," *American Archivist* 52 (Spring 1989): 192–200.

39. "The Documentation Strategy and Archival Appraisal Principles: A Different Perspective," *Archivaria* 38 (Fall 1994): 11–36; "Records Management Scheduling and Archival Appraisal," *Records and Information Management Report* 14 (April 1998): 1–16.

40. For my contribution to this conference, see "The Archival Documentation Strategy and Its Implications for the Appraisal of Architectural Records," *American Archivist* 59 (Spring 1996): 144–154.

41. "The Archival Documentation Strategy: A Brief Intellectual History, 1984–1994 and Practical Description," *Janus* 2 (1995): 76–93; "The End of Collecting: Towards a New Purpose and Definition of Archives," in Terry Cook and Joan Schwartz, eds., *Archival Science*, forthcoming; "Meta-Scheduling: Rethinking Archival Appraisal and Records Management Scheduling," in *Bridging Records, Information, and Knowledge: ARMA Proceedings* (Prairie Village, Kans.: ARMA, 1999), 59–66; and "The Archivist and Collecting," *Encyclopedia of Library and Information Science*, vol. 70, supp. 33 (New York: Marcel Dekker, 2002), 1–21.

42. For example, "Access in the Digital Information Age and the Archival Mission: The United States," *Journal of the Society of Archivists* 19: 1 (1988): 25–40.

43. For example, "The Concept of Public Memory."

44. My participation in this institute and the preparation of reports and evaluations of it led to an essay as part of a larger study on professionalization and electronic records. See my chapter on the institute in my *The First Generation of Electronic Records Archivists*—a work cited as a benchmark analysis of electronic records management, and, as a benchmark, also the source of some controversial discussion. A quite critical commentary on my book was provided by Thomas Elton Brown, "Myth or Reality: Is There a Generation Gap Among Electronic Records Archivists?" *Archivaria* 41 (Spring 1996): 234–243, an article I responded to in *Archivaria* 42 (Fall 1996): 4–5.

45. "The Roles of Graduate and Continuing Education in Preparing Archivists for the Information Age," *American Archivist* 56 (Summer 1993): 444–457.

46. "Blown to Bits: Electronic Records, Archivy, and the Corporation," in James M. O'Toole, ed., *The Records of American Business* (Chicago: Society of American Archivists, 1997).

47. "Re-Defining Electronic Records Management," *Records Management Quarterly* 30 (October 1996): 8–13.

48. "Computer Literacy and Records Professionals," *Records & Retrieval Report* 12 (October 1996): 1–16.

49. "Why Technology Convergence Is Not Enough for the Management of Information and Records," *Records & Retrieval Report* 13 (October 1997): 1–16.

50. "Re-Discovering the Archival Mission: The Recordkeeping Functional Requirements Project at the University of Pittsburgh; A Progress Report," *Archives and Museum Informatics* 8: 4 (1994): 279–300; "The Record in the Information Age: A Progress Report on Research," *Records & Retrieval Report* 12 (January 1996): 1–16; "More Than Diplomatic: Functional Requirements for Evidence in Recordkeeping," *Records Management Journal* 7 (April 1997): 31–57; with Wendy Duff, " Warrant and the Definition of Electronic Records: Questions Arising from the Pittsburgh Project," *Archives and Museum Informatics* 11 (1997): 223–231.

51. "The Record: Is It Evolving?" *Records & Retrieval Report* 10 (March 1994): 1–16; "Archives as a Multi-faceted Term in the Information Professions," *Records & Retrieval Report* 11 (March 1995): 1–15; "The Record in the Manuscript Collection," *Archives and Manuscripts* 24 (May 1996): 46–61; and "The Importance of Records in the Information Age," *Records Management Quarterly* 32 (January 1998): 36–46, 48–49, 52.

52. Linda J. Henry, "Schellenberg in Cyberspace," *American Archivist* 61 (Fall 1998): 309–327 (see especially p. 313, fn 7). This article was highly critical of the new paradigm for a number of reasons. I responded, in part to the charge that there is such a cohort controlling electronic records management issues, with my "Searching for Authority: Archivists and Electronic Records in the New World At the Fin-de-Sie¢cle," *First Monday* (January 2000), available at *http://www.firstmonday.dk/issues/issue5_1/cox/index.html*.

53. The essay was published as "Buscant l'autoritat: arxivers i documents electronics al Nou Mon de fi de segle," *Lligall: Revista Catalana d'Arxivistica* 14 (1999): 133–148. An expanded English version was published as "Searching for Authority."

54. In one sense, my 1992 book on *Managing Institutional Archives* fits into this kind of writing as it was an effort to advocate for the establishment of institutional archives.

55. "Messrs. Washington, Jefferson, and Gates: Quarrelling about the Preservation of the Documentary Heritage of the United States," *First Monday* (August 1997), available at *http://www.firstmonday.dk/issues/issue2_8/cox/index.html*.

56. "Drawing Sea Serpents: The Publishing Wars on Personal Computing and the Information Age," *First Monday* (May 1998), available at *http://www.firstmonday.dk/issues/issue3_5/cox/index.html*.

57. "Declarations, Independence, and Text in the Information Age," *First Monday* 4 (June 7, 1999), available at *http://www.firstmonday.dk/issues/issue4_6/rjcox/index.html*.

58. "Archival Anchorites: Building Public Memory in the Era of the Culture Wars," *Multicultural Review* 7 (June 1998): 52–60.

59. With Jane Greenberg and Cynthia Porter, "Access Denied: The Discarding of Library History," *American Libraries* 29 (April 1998): 57–61.

60. "Testing the Spirit of the Information Age," *Journal of Information Ethics* 10 (Fall 2001): 51–66.

61. See, for example, Luciana Duranti, "The Archival Body of Knowledge: Archival Theory, Method, and Practice, and Graduate and Continuing Education," *Journal of Education for Library and Information Science* 34 (Winter 1993): 8–24.

62. For example, as editor of the *American Archivist,* I prepared an analysis of

the current state of research in order to identify research that could be undertaken by both masters and doctoral students; see "An Analysis of Archival Research." Drawing from my teaching of a course on archival appraisal, I have written several key essays on this topic, including "The Documentation Strategy and Archival Appraisal Principles." Drawing from a course on understanding information, I wrote "Do We Understand Information in the Information Age?" *Records & Information Management Report* 14 (March 1998): 1–12; and "Drawing Sea Serpents"; "Employing Records Professionals in the Information Age" was written to help provide students additional information on first employment trends in the archives and records management discipline.

63. The best example of this is some of my writing emanating from a multiyear research project on record-keeping functional requirements for use in electronic systems, such as "The Record: Is It Evolving?"; "Archives as a Multi-faceted Term"; and "The Long-Term Maintenance of Records," *Records &Retrieval Report* 12 (April 1996): 1–16.

64. Neil Postman, *Amusing Ourselves to Death: Public Discourse in the Age of Show Business* (New York: Penguin Books, 1986), p. 136.

65. In Geoffrey Nunberg, ed., *The Future of the Book* (Berkeley: University of California Press, 1996), p. 67.

66. Teaching and the production of scholarship can be seen in a work such as my volume on documenting localities. My original work on this developed from my work at the New York State Archives in 1986–1988, especially with the western region of that state. Drawing on this work, and continuing discussions with colleagues like Tim Ericson and Helen Samuels, I taught or co-taught workshops on this topic at the 1988 Society of American Archivists, April 1989 New England Archivists, and May 1989 Mid-Atlantic Region Archives Conference meetings; and for other groups such as the Library Council of Metropolitan Milwaukee, District of Columbia Historical Records Advisory Board, and various Society of American Archivists workshops. Drawing on the teaching of my regular appraisal course, I developed and am teaching an "advanced" workshop on archival appraisal for the Society of American Archivists.

67. I have published a fuller description of my views on students and research in the archives field, "Dancing: Archival Education and Student Research," introducing a special issue of papers completed by students in my archives courses.

68. "Local Government Records Programs," in *Documenting America: Assessing the Condition of Historical Records in the States*, Lisa B. Weber, ed. (Albany, N.Y.: National Association of State Archives and Records Administrators and the National Historical Publications and Records Commission, 1984), pp. 19–36.

69. Principal author, *Assessing Alabama's Archives*.

70. Principal author, *Strengthening New York's Historical Records Programs: A Self-Study Guide* (Albany: New York State Archives and Records Administration, 1988).

71. This development can be seen in the following essays: Richard C. Berner, "Archival Education and Training in the United States, 1937 to Present," *Journal of Education for Librarianship* 22 (Summer/Fall 1981): 3–9; Terry Eastwood, "Nurturing Archival Education in the University," *American Archivist* 51 (Summer 1988): 228–251; Jacqueline Goggin, " 'That We Shall Truly Deserve the Title of Profession': The Training and Education of Archivists, 1930–1960," *American Ar-*

chivist 47 (Summer 1984): 243–254; and Robert Sidney Martin, "The Development of Professional Education for Librarians and Archivists in the United States: A Comparative Essay," *American Archivist* 57 (Summer 1994): 544–558.

72. See, for example, my "The History of Primary Sources in Graduate Education: An Archival Perspective," *Special Collections* 4: 2 (1990): 39–78; "The Masters of Archival Studies and American Education Standards: An Argument for the Continued Development of Graduate Archival Education in the United States," *Archivaria* 36 (Autumn 1993): 221–231; and "The Roles of Graduate and Continuing Education."

73. See, for example, my "Researching Archival Reference as an Information Function," *RQ* 31 (Spring 1992): 387–397; and "Archivists and the Use of Archival Records: Or, A View from the World of Documentary Editing," *Provenance* 9 (1991 [1992]): 89–110 (a critique of a research study).

74. For example, my "Continuing Education and Special Collections Professionals: The Need for Rethinking," *Rare Books & Manuscripts Librarianship* 10: 2 (1995): 78–96.

75. For example, my "Advocacy in the Graduate Archives Curriculum."

76. "A Sense of the Future: A Child's View of Archives," p. 204.

Index

About the Author

RICHARD J. COX is Professor, School of Information Sciences, University of Pittsburgh.